Drawing Near

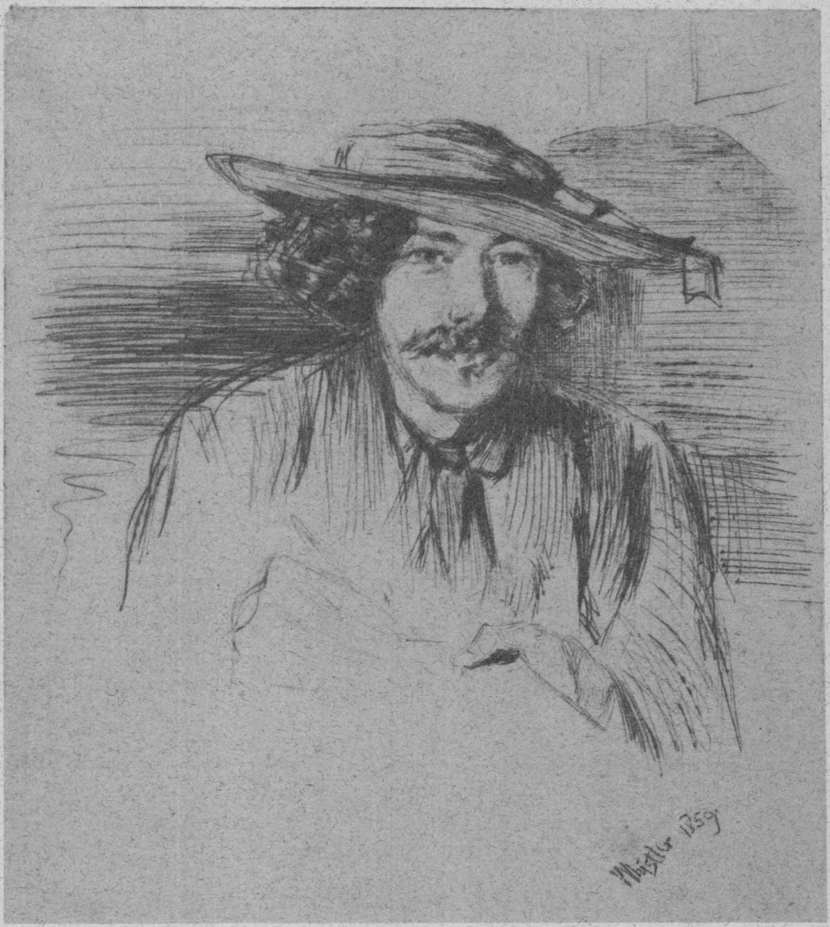
Whistler 1859

Drawing Near

Whistler Etchings from the Zelman Collection

by

Ruth E. Fine

with an annotated bibliography by Eric Denker

Los Angeles County Museum of Art

EXHIBITION ITINERARY:

Los Angeles County Museum of Art
June 20–September 27, 1984

University Art Museum, University of California, Berkeley
October 31–December 30, 1984

Elvehjem Museum of Art, University of Wisconsin, Madison
March 9–April 30, 1985

Dallas Museum of Art
May 23–July 21, 1985

University of Maryland Art Gallery, College Park
August 29–October 27, 1985

LIBRARY OF CONGRESS CATALOGING IN PUBLICATION DATA

Fine, Ruth, 1941–
Drawing near.

Includes index.
1. Whistler, James McNeill, 1834-1903–Exhibitions.
2. Zelman, Julius L.–Art collections–Exhibitions.
3. Zelman, Anita–Art collections–Exhibitions.
4. Etching–Private collections–California–Los Angeles –Exhibitions. I. Whistler, James McNeill, 1834–1903. II. Los Angeles County Museum of Art. III. Title.
NE2012.W45A4 1984 769.92'4 84-2908
ISBN 0-87587-119-4

Cover: ***Portrait of Whistler,** 1859*
(cat. no. 10)

Published by the
Los Angeles County Museum of Art
5905 Wilshire Boulevard
Los Angeles, California 90036

Printed in the U.S.A.

Edited by Mitch Tuchman
Designed in Los Angeles by Jeffrey Mueller

Text set in Bembo Typefaces by
Mondo Typo, Santa Monica, California

Printed in an edition of 5,500 copies
on Starwhite Vicksburg Vellum/Natural
by The Castle Press

CONTENTS

The art of etching, in decline in Europe since the invention of lithography at the end of the eighteenth century, experienced a revival by the middle of the nineteenth century. Societies for the publication of etchings were founded by artists in both England and France. By 1862 Charles Baudelaire published his famous essay *"L'eau-forte est à la mode,"* and among the etchers he singled out for praise was the young American expatriate James Abbott McNeill Whistler, whose prints he described as "creating the profound and complex poetry of a vast city [London]."

Ultimately, Whistler's work was as important for the nineteenth and early twentieth centuries as Rembrandt's was for the seventeenth. His deftness of line, his innovative manipulation of tone, his spontaneous response to his environment, and his uncanny ability for establishing intimacy with his subjects, be they friends or strangers, made him the figure to emulate, though his exquisite refinement remained elusive.

The Los Angeles County Museum of Art is pleased to present this exhibition of Whistler's work in etching and drypoint drawn entirely from the collection of Julius L. and Anita Zelman. (Mr. Zelman is the current chairman of the Graphic Arts Council at the Museum.) In little more than a decade and a half, the Zelmans have assembled the major representation of Whistler's etchings in private hands in the United States. Their collection is as distinguished in its breadth as it is in the excellent quality of the impressions they have selected. The Museum is fortunate indeed that the Zelmans intend that the eventual home of a significant portion of the collection will be the Los Angeles County Museum of Art in the city in which the collection was formed.

Ruth E. Fine, curator in the Department of Graphic Arts at the National Gallery of Art in Washington, D.C., because of an enduring interest in Whistler, became acquainted with the Zelmans in the mid-1970s, visiting their Los Angeles home intermittently to view additions to the collection. Her knowledge of Whistler's life and work is generously reflected in this exhibition and in the writing of its catalogue.

Earl A. Powell III
DIRECTOR

This exhibition was drawn entirely from the splendid collection of J. A. M. Whistler's etchings formed by Julius L. Zelman, a Los Angeles real estate developer, and his wife, Anita, a freelance writer. The Zelmans started collecting Whistler etchings about fifteen years ago, although their interest in the artist's work by that time had been developing for more than two decades.

Between college (University of California, Los Angeles, majoring in cartography) and graduate school (University of California, Berkeley, majoring in engineering), Mr. Zelman worked in Washington, D.C., for the United States Coast and Geodetic Survey, where, by coincidence, Whistler had learned the process of etching and made his first prints in the medium a century earlier. Zelman encountered Whistler's art during this period at Washington's Freer Gallery of Art, which possesses one of the great Whistler collections of the world. Like many a novice, he made his first actual purchases in the form of reproductions, which he framed and hung on the wall where he could study and enjoy them. This was in the early 1940s.

Not until 1969 did the Zelmans, who met at Berkeley, actually begin to buy originals. That year, just after they had seen a catalogue of Whistler etchings issued by Associated American Artists Gallery, they were in New York, visited the gallery, and made their first acquisition, *Black Lion Wharf.* They went on to make the rounds of other galleries that might handle Whistlers and made a second purchase, an impression of *The "Adam and Eve," Old Chelsea.* (Recently a finer impression of this print has been acquired in good print connoisseur fashion.)

Having begun to think seriously of Whistler, the Zelmans read increasingly about the artist and formed a library of Whistler reference books and Whistleriana. On their travels they included time for stops at print sellers in various cities; dealers, knowing of their interest, brought special impressions to their attention. On occasion they were tempted to buy something by another artist: a Sloan or a Bellows in the American field or a Rembrandt or Meryon from among Whistler's predecessors. In the end, however, while they would have liked these too, their final decision was: Why not another Whistler instead? According to the Zelmans, what they were most drawn to in Whistler's etchings was his ability to "get as much as he did with a single line, his superb draftsmanship in black and white," as well as his attitude as an artist, "always showing an empathy for his subjects, despite the fact that they often lived in a world quite different from his own."

In forming their collection, they aimed for completeness, generally buying additional Whistler images rather than state variations of subjects already in the collection. To date they have acquired about one-third of the artist's very extensive body of etchings.

Enormous appreciation is due Anita and Julius Zelman for their friendship and hospitality and for their great generosity in sharing their Whistler collection, not only in the course of preparing this exhibition but for several years prior to its planning. It has been a pleasure to watch their superb collection grow.

I would like to thank Margaret F. MacDonald, who, again over years, has shared her vast knowledge of Whistler. Most recently she spent several days suggesting sources and reviewing various materials at the University of Glasgow. I must also thank her husband, Norman MacDonald, and their daughters, Kathy and Helen, for their kind hospitality during several stays in Glasgow. Robert H. Getscher, also doing research there, was exceedingly generous, marking voluminous press cutting albums in the university library at points he thought I would find useful. This essentially allowed four weeks of work to be accomplished in the two that were available to me. I am extremely grateful to Nigel

Thorp for confirming and correcting quotations from the Whistler manuscripts in the Glasgow University Library.

Eric Denker compiled and annotated the bibliography and was very helpful in tracking down numerous leads. Robert A. Grove also was of great assistance in many ways. Katharine A. Lochnan generously shared her work on dating Whistler's early etchings, and M. Lee Wiehl made available the galleys for her exhibition catalogue documenting Whistler's American admirers (see bibliography). Larry Day listened and commented as ideas were developing.

For assistance at various institutional collections I would like to thank: Christopher Allan, Martin Amt, David P. Curry, Sinclair Hitchings, Martin Hopkinson, the late Harold Joachim, Craig S. Korr, Dorothy Marlborough, Robert Rainwater, Sue W. Reed, Kristin Spangenberg, Esther Sparks, Tobin Sparling, Marilyn Symmes, Nigel Thorp, and David Weston; also the library and photo services at the National Gallery of Art and the photo services at the Freer Gallery of Art and the Los Angeles County Museum of Art. In addition I would like to thank John Wilmerding and Andrew Robison for their interest in the Whistler exhibition.

At the Los Angeles County Museum of Art, Earl A. Powell III, Myrna Smoot, Letitia Burns O'Connor, Andrea P. A. Belloli, Phil Freshman, Jeffrey Mueller, Ebria Feinblatt, and Bruce Davis have made this project a pleasurable one. I am particularly grateful to Mitch Tuchman for his keen editorial contribution to the catalogue.

R.E.F.

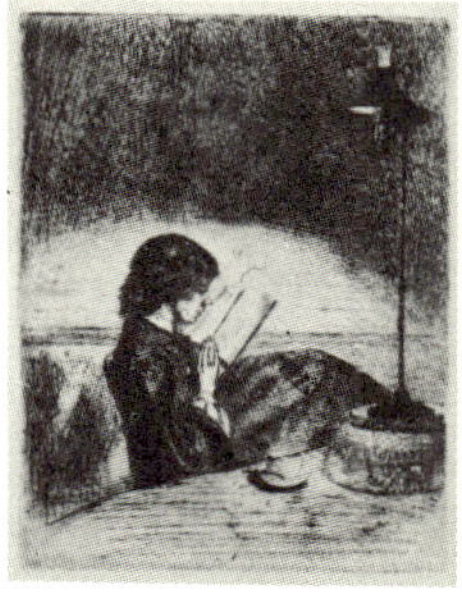

I.
Reading by Lamplight, *K. 32*
6 3/16 x 4 9/16 in. (15.8 x 11.6 cm.)
Freer Gallery of Art

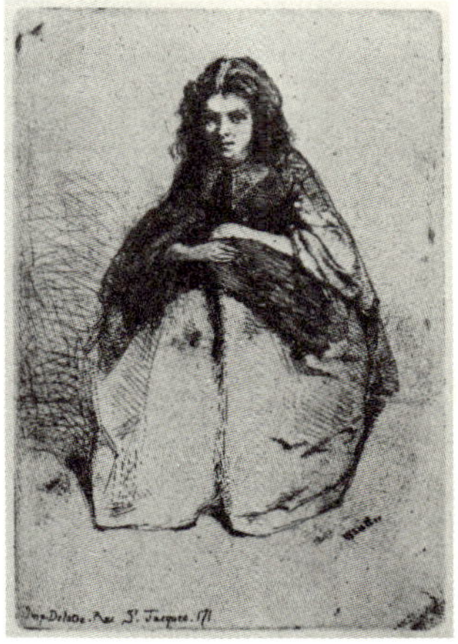

II.
Fumette, *K. 13*
6 3/8 x 4 1/4 in. (16.2 x 10.8 cm.)
Julius L. and Anita Zelman

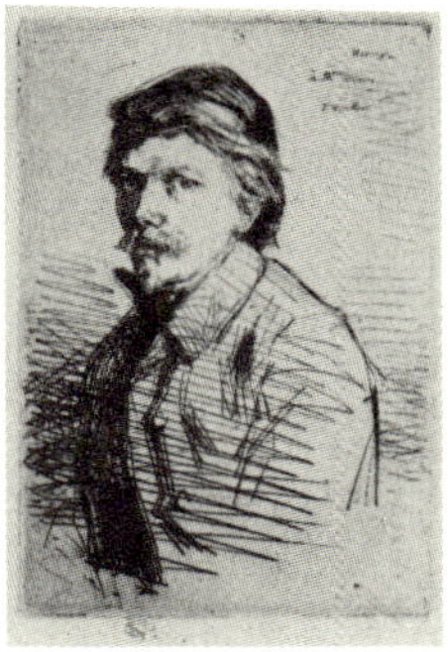

III.
August[e] Delâtre, *K. 26*
3 3/16 x 2 1/8 in. (8.2 x 5.4 cm.)
National Gallery of Art,
Rosenwald Collection

1834 Born, son of Major George Washington Whistler and his second wife, Anna Matilda McNeill, Lowell, Massachusetts.

1837 Family moves to Stonington, Connecticut.

1840 Family moves to Springfield, Massachusetts.

1843 Family travels to St. Petersburg, Russia, joining father, who had gone earlier to work on Russian railroad system.

1845 Begins drawing classes at Imperial Academy of Fine Arts in St. Petersburg, where the following year he wins first place in his class for drawing heads from life.

1847 Suffers attack of rheumatic fever; with mother and siblings travels to England for several months; half-sister Deborah (fig. I), marries surgeon and etcher Francis Seymour Haden.

1848 Second bout with rheumatic fever; leaves St. Petersburg for England.

1849 Father dies; family returns to United States, settling in Pomfret, Connecticut.

1851 Enters West Point, where he studies drawing with Robert W. Weir, father of painter J. Alden Weir.

1852 Publication of song sheet "United States Military Academy Song of the Graduates" with a drawing by Whistler reproduced lithographically as a cover illustration.

1854 Expelled from West Point as a result of a deficiency in chemistry; works briefly in Baltimore at Winans's locomotive plant (a lithograph survives from this period); joins drawing division of United States Coast and Geodetic Survey, Washington, D.C., and learns the rudiments of etching.

1855 Resigns upon request from Coast Survey; after a stop in London to visit the Hadens, travels to Paris to study art, spending much of the following three years there, with travel throughout the Continent and to England; enrolls in École Impériale et Spéciale de Dessin.

1856 Enrolls in Charles Gleyre's atelier.

1857 With Henri Martin travels to Manchester to see "Art Treasures Exhibition," which includes several paintings by, or attributed to, Velázquez, Goya, and Zurbarán.

1858 Mistress and model during this period, Fumette (fig. II); with Ernest Delannoy makes walking and sketching tour of northern France, Luxembourg, and the Rhineland; *Douze eaux-fortes d'après nature/*Twelve Etchings from Nature (generally called the French Set) printed by Auguste Delâtre (fig. III), published in France and, later in the year, in England from the address of Seymour Haden; meets Courbet; with Henri Fantin-Latour and Alphonse Legros forms Société des Trois; moves to London, although continuing to spend considerable time on the Continent.

1859 Paris Salon accepts two etchings; takes rooms in Wapping and produces several etchings later issued as A Series of Sixteen Etchings of Scenes on the Thames and Other Subjects (generally called the Thames Set).

1860 Mistress during this period, Joanna ("Jo") Hiffernan, poses for several etchings, drawings, and paintings.

1861 Meets Manet and Degas; paints in Brittany while recovering from third bout of rheumatic fever.

1862 *Passages from Modern English Poets,* published by Day and Son, Ltd., includes two Whistler etchings; becomes member of newly formed Société des Aquafortistes.

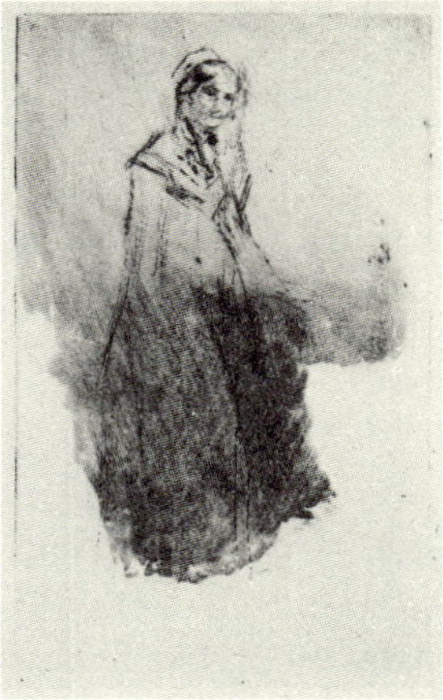

IV.
Whistler's Mother, *K. 97*
9 7/8 x 6 in. (25.2 x 15.2 cm.)
Freer Gallery of Art

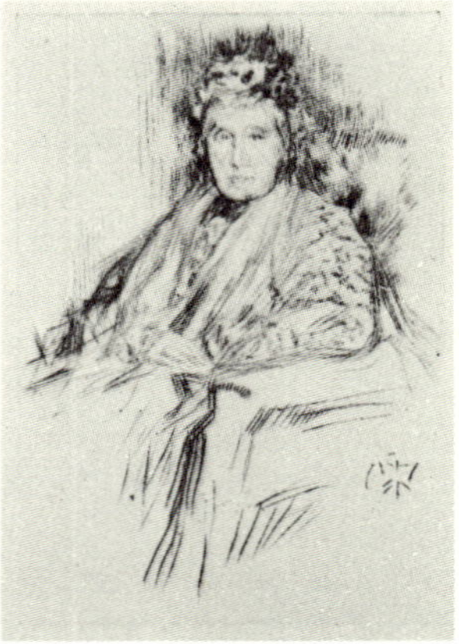

V.
F. R. Leyland's Mother, *K. 103*
9 x 6 in. (22.9 x 15.2 cm.)
Freer Gallery of Art

1863 Makes first trip to Amsterdam with Legros, who earlier in the year moved to London; moves to 7 Lindsey Row, Chelsea, overlooking the Thames, where he is neighbor of Dante Gabriel Rossetti; decorates house in the Oriental mode with fans, screens, and Blue and White porcelain; meets architect E. W. Godwin; mother (fig. IV) comes to share home.

1865 Meets Albert Moore, who before long replaces Legros in Société des Trois; travels to Cologne, then to Trouville, where he paints with Courbet, Monet, and Daubigny.

1866 Mysterious trip of almost a year's duration to Chile, purportedly to participate in Chilean war of independence; relationship with Joanna Hiffernan apparently ends.

1867 Exhibits first work with a musical title, the painting *Symphony in White, No. 3* (Young et al., no. 61); battles with Haden and Legros, ending both friendships; moves to second house in Chelsea, 2 Lindsey Row, also decorated in the Oriental mode.

1869 First visit to Speke Hall, Liverpool home of his patron Frederick R. Leyland (many visits follow, and many Whistler portraits of members of Leyland family [e.g., fig. V] are executed before relationship is ruptured in 1876).

1871 Messrs. Ellis and Green publish A Series of Sixteen Etchings of Scenes on the Thames and Other Subjects.

1872 Exhibits first paintings titled Nocturne, Dudley Gallery, London.

1874 First solo exhibition, Flemish Gallery, Pall Mall, London.

1875 Mother moves from London to Hastings.

1876 Executes Peacock Room at Leyland's London home, 49 Prince's Gate, but various misunderstandings regarding design and cost lead to disruption of this association; becomes involved with Maude Franklin, third important mistress/model.

1877 Grosvenor Gallery opens in London as alternative exhibition space to Royal Academy: in discussing Whistler's pieces in *Fors Clavigera,* John Ruskin equates *Nocturne in Black and Gold: The Falling Rocket* (Young et al., 170) to "flinging a pot of paint in the public's face," causing Whistler to sue for libel; commissions Godwin to design White House in Tite Street, Chelsea.

1878 Begins working in lithography, completing seventeen stones before leaving for Venice; publication of *Catalogue of Blue and White Nanking Porcelain, forming the Collection of Sir Henry Thompson* with nineteen of twenty-six illustrations after drawings by Whistler; collaborates with Godwin on several projects, including interior exhibited at Paris Exposition Universelle and Whistler's White House, into which he moves mid-year; *Whistler* v. *Ruskin* tried, with Whistler winning legally but bankrupted by court costs; publishes *Whistler v. Ruskin: Art and Art Critics.*

1879 Several individual etchings published by Fine Art Society; White House, its contents, and many of Whistler's paintings sold at auction to cover debts (a second auction of effects held in 1880); leaves for Venice, where he stays fourteen months, producing approximately fifty etchings, ninety pastels, and several paintings.

1880 Exhibition of Venice: Twelve Etchings (generally called the First Venice Set) at Fine Art Society.

1881 Exhibition of fifty-three Venice pastels at Fine Art Society; mother dies.

1882 Meets Walter Sickert, who leaves Slade School of Art to become Whistler's student and assist with printing of Venice etchings.

1883 Exhibition of Venice and other recent etchings at Fine Art Society; visits Paris.

1884 Trip to St. Ives with Sickert and Mortimer Menpes; spends time at Dordrecht, where he makes several etchings; elected member, Society of British Artists.

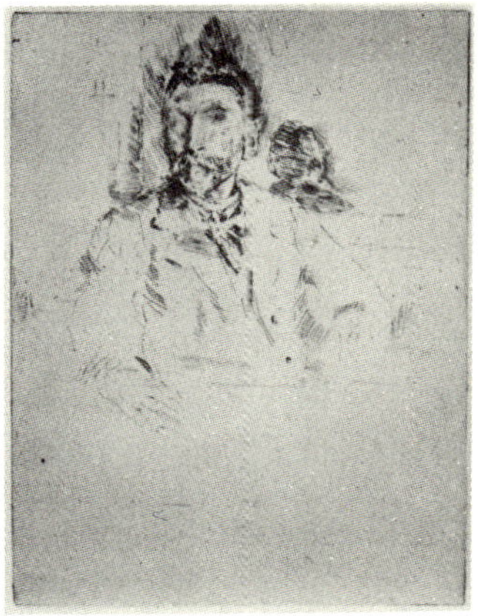

VI.
Portrait of Mallarmé, *not in K.*
8 $^{15}/_{16}$ x 6 $^{3}/_{4}$ in. (22.8 x 17.2 cm.)
Hunterian Art Gallery, University of Glasgow, Birnie Philip Bequest

1885 "Ten O'Clock" lecture (discussion of distinction between art and nature, attacking Ruskin's aesthetics) first presented in London and repeated several times before publication; travels to Belgium and Holland with William Merritt Chase and spends time in Dieppe with Sickert.

1886 Set of Twenty-six Etchings (generally called the Second Venice Set, although it included five English subjects) published by Messrs. Dowdeswell and Dowdeswells in London; elected president, Society of British Artists.

1887 Works in lithography again; Notes, a set of six lithographs of the late 1870s, published by Boussod, Valadon & Cie, London; twelve etchings, done in one day at Naval Review, Spithead, presented to Queen Victoria; Society of British Artists receives royal charter; visits Belgium with brother and sister-in-law, Dr. and Mrs. William Whistler.

1888 Resigns as president, Royal Society of British Artists; meets Stéphane Mallarmé (fig. VI), who translates "Ten O'Clock" lecture into French; marries Godwin's widow, Beatrix ("Trixie"): honeymoon trip to Boulogne, Paris, Chartres, Tours, and Loches, during which he makes several etchings; shows in first exhibition of New English Art Club.

1889 Spends time in Amsterdam, making etchings and a few paintings.

1890 *The Gentle Art of Making Enemies,* selection of Whistler's correspondence, published, first, in unauthorized version by Sheridan Ford in Antwerp and, then, under Whistler's supervision by William Heinemann in London.

1892 Establishes Paris as residence and maintains quarters there until 1901; elected officer, Legion d'honneur.

1893 Joseph Pennell helps Whistler print etchings in Paris.

1894 Returns to London to seek medical help for Beatrix, living for a time at Savoy Hotel.

1895 Spends time at Lyme Regis, Dorset, working on etchings, lithographs, and paintings; exhibition of lithographs at Fine Art Society; several lithographs included in centenary exhibition of lithography, Paris.

1896 Beatrix dies; Whistler adopts sister-in-law Rosalind Birnie Philip as ward, makes her his executrix; shifts for several years between London and Paris.

1897 Visits Dieppe with Pennell and E. G. Kennedy; Elizabeth and Joseph Pennell begin their biographical notes on Whistler.

1898 Elected president, newly formed International Society of Sculptors, Painters, and Gravers, a position held until his death; visiting artist at Académie Carmen, Paris.

1899 Publishes *Eden versus Whistler: The Baronet and the Butterfly,* his account of lawsuit brought against him in 1895 by Sir William Eden over Whistler's portrait of Lady Eden; spends time with Beatrix's mother and sister, the Birnie Philips, near Dieppe; visits Dordrecht and London.

1900 Awarded Grand Prix for etchings and another for paintings at Paris Exposition Universelle; spends part of the summer with the Birnie Philips in Ireland; because of failing health, travels to Algiers, Tangiers, and Corsica.

1901 Visits Dieppe; lives in Tite Street with the Birnie Philips; winters in Bath.

1902 Lives at 72 Cheyne Walk with the Birnie Philips; travels in Holland with Charles L. Freer, whom he met in 1890.

1903 Granted honorary doctor of laws degree from University of Glasgow but is too ill to attend award ceremonies; dies in London.

Preliminaries

Whistler's art is divided in its content and intentions. At one extreme are the portraits, which record the artist as an insider, secure and at ease with his friends and surroundings. At the other extreme are the passages, windows, and doorways, peopled with anonymous figures: an outsider's glimpses at the ease of others. Distance and closeness, clarity and ambiguity, concentration and dissipation, and the desire to understand how a visual language could define his relationship with the world formed the substance of Whistler's art. His etchings in particular–by their very nature as step-by-step records of process and because they spanned his career–provide us with a cohesive history of the artist's discoveries.

During his own lifetime and in the decades since, Whistler's work in etching and drypoint has been almost universally praised.[1] In half a century, 1854–1901 (with specific periods of concentration), he produced about 450 works in these media.[2] It is well to remember, however, that these represent only a fraction of his total production. In addition to etchings and drypoints, Whistler made some 180 lithographs and more than 550 paintings. His drawings, watercolors, and pastels number close to 1,500, including many tiny sketches with which he often decorated his letters and miscellaneous writings (which are in themselves of interest for their demonstration of his sense of irony and his quick satirical wit).[3] Generally Whistler worked in one or two of these media at a time, his efforts in one clearly enhancing his progress in another.[4] Always of major concern was facture: the relationship of the how and the what, in some measure important for all artists, was a constant preoccupation for Whistler.

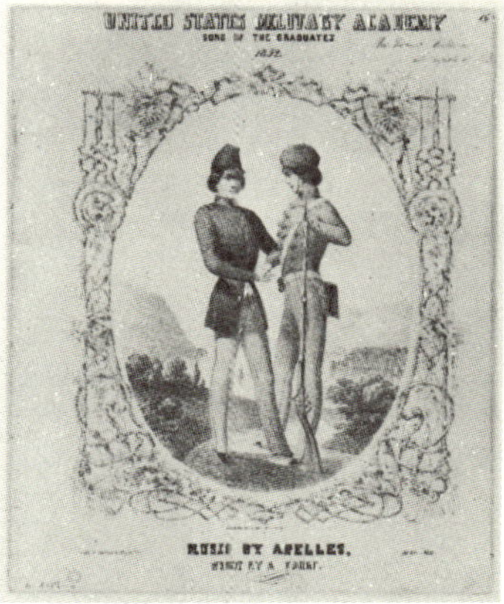

VII.
Song of the Graduates,
Lithograph, songsheet
13 x 10 1/2 in. (33 x 26.7 cm.)
National Gallery of Art,
Rosenwald Collection

Whistler was attracted from childhood to a life in art. As a boy he studied drawing at the Imperial Academy of Science in St. Petersburg. A sketchbook from this period (Hunterian Art Gallery, University of Glasgow) shows that at about age ten Whistler did not display an original vision or extraordinary talent; he did, however, have a modicum of skill and an enormous enthusiasm for drawing. In fact, by 1849, writing from England at the age of fourteen or fifteen, his career aspirations were clear: "I hope dear father you will not object to my choice, vis: a painter, for I wish to be one so very much. . . ."[5] His work as a draftsman brought Whistler recognition during his otherwise unsuccessful career at West Point (see fig. VII). A great many drawings survive from this military experience and from the period in Baltimore immediately following.[6] Copies of other artists' work and caricatures as well as direct sketches of the passing scene are among them. Much of this juvenilia was worked in pen and ink, a natural forerunner to Whistler's early skilled responses to etching and drypoint.

1. As early as 1859, two etchings were accepted for the Salon, while the painting *At The Piano* (Young et al., 24) was rejected.

2. The complete etchings are recorded in Kennedy.

3. The most recent and readily available catalogue of Whistler lithographs is Mervyn Levy, *Whistler Lithographs: A Catalogue Raisonné* (London: Jupiter Books, 1975). A revision of Thomas R. Way's 1896 catalogue is in progress by Nesta R. Spink and David Kiehl. The paintings are recorded in Young et al. Margaret F. MacDonald is nearing completion of a catalogue raisonné of the drawings. Many of Whistler's writings are published in Whistler.

4. For example, during the decade in which Whistler concentrated on lithography (1886–96), when he made drawings of subjects related to the lithographs, in particular, the figure pieces, chalks and pastels generally were used. This medium would have been more sympathetic than watercolors or pen and ink, for example, to the forms and images explored in the lithographs.

5. Donnelly and Thorp, p. 7.

6. See Nancy Dorfman Pressley, "Whistler in America: An Album of Early Drawings," *Metropolitan Museum Journal* 5 (1972): 125–48.

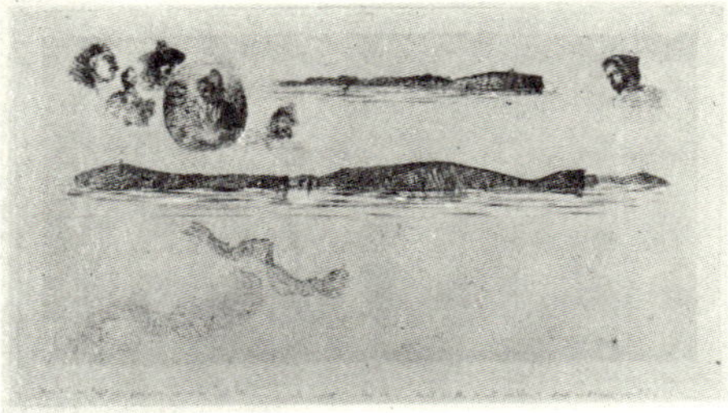

VIII.
***Sketches on the Coast Survey Plate,** K. 1*
5 1/4 x 9 3/4 in. (13.3 x 24.8 cm.)
National Gallery of Art,
Rosenwald Collection

Whistler apparently learned to etch during the few months of his employ with the United States Coast and Geodetic Survey in Washington, D.C. Two works from this period are known. His immediate skill is apparent in the carefully delineated official part of *Sketches on the Coast Survey Plate* (fig. VIII). His restlessness with the restrictions of this assignment, however, is equally apparent in the more freely drawn heads sketched above. The impulse toward freedom prevailed, and Whistler left Washington for Paris in late 1855, never to return to the United States.[7]

Whistler was a gregarious sort, whose personality and life are extensively, if not always accurately, documented. He traveled widely (as the subjects of his etchings show) and was touched by most of the important ideas and artistic currents of his time. During his early years abroad, his friendships and influences fell under a wide net, centered in Bohemian circles like those he had read about before crossing the Atlantic. He was very close to Henri Fantin-Latour, Alphonse Legros, and Seymour Haden.

Simply stated, within the traditional system of preparation for an artistic career–attendance at Charles Gleyre's Paris atelier; making copies of paintings at the Louvre–Whistler reacted against both Romanticism (Delacroix's influence) and Classicism (Ingres's influence) in favor of the Realist mode (Courbet's influence). He came to greatly admire Velázquez and Rembrandt, an admiration that made itself felt throughout his career: Velázquez's influence can be seen in Whistler's elegant and dramatic, full-length, standing portraits, low keyed and worked in close tonalities, like *The Little Velvet Dress* (fig. IX); Rembrandt's is apparent in his broad, open views, like *Zaandam* (fig. X) with its horizon punctuated by windmills and cottages.

In the early 1860s Whistler was a neighbor of Dante Gabriel Rossetti, and he temporarily was responsive to the Pre-Raphaelite circle, as can be seen in *Weary* (fig. XI), showing his mistress Jo in a languid pose. But the Pre-Raphaelites' concern with narrative content was, at bottom, an alien one to Whistler, and no strong residual influence from them is

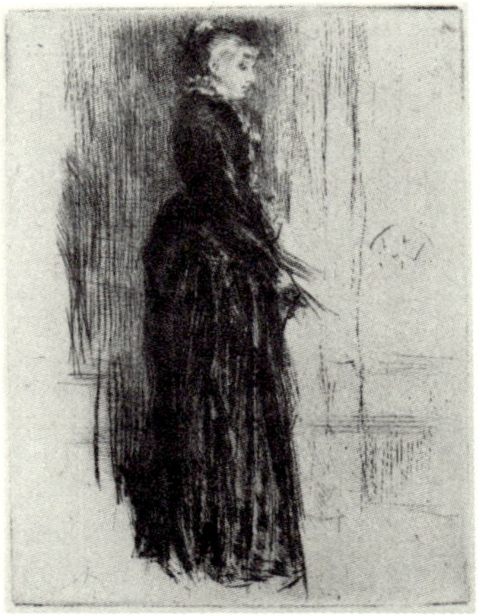

IX.
***The Little Velvet Dress,** K. 106*
6 3/8 x 4 5/8 in. (16.2 x 11.8 cm.)
Julius L. and Anita Zelman

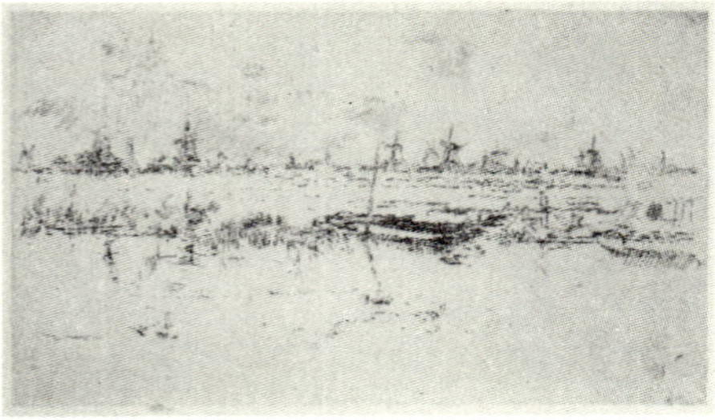

X.
***Zaandam,** K. 416*
5 1/8 x 8 5/8 in. (13 x 21.9 cm.)
National Gallery of Art,
Rosenwald Collection

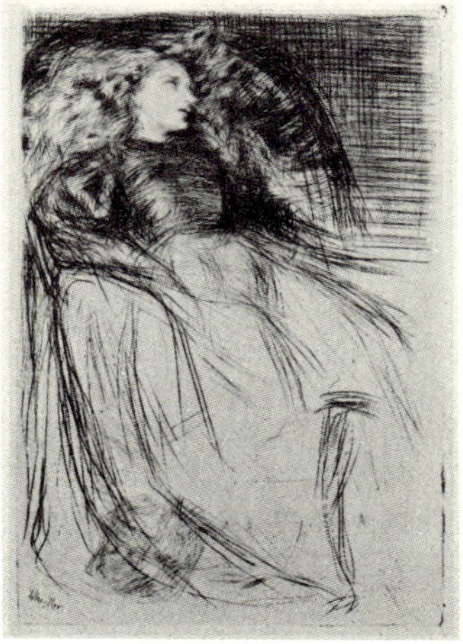

XI.
***Weary,** K. 92*
7 3/4 x 5 3/16 in. (19.7 x 13.2 cm.)
Julius L. and Anita Zelman

7. Donnelly and Thorp (p. 30) record that Thomas Winans (whose sister Julia was married to Whistler's half-brother George) lent Whistler $450 for his journey to Paris and continued to support him through further loans and early purchases of his work.

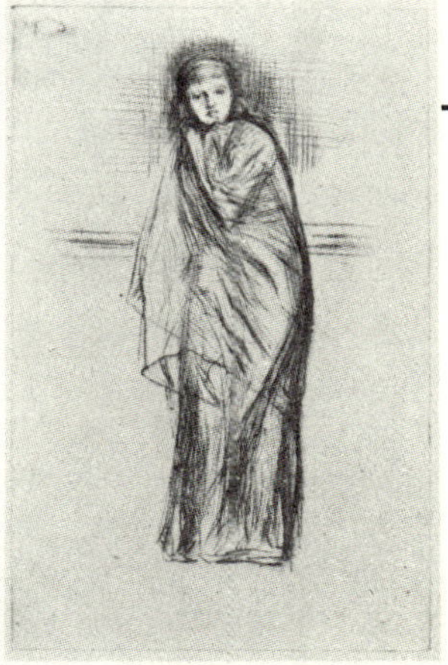

XII.
The Model Resting, *K. 100*
8 1/4 x 5 1/4 in. (21 x 13.3 cm.)
Julius L. and Anita Zelman

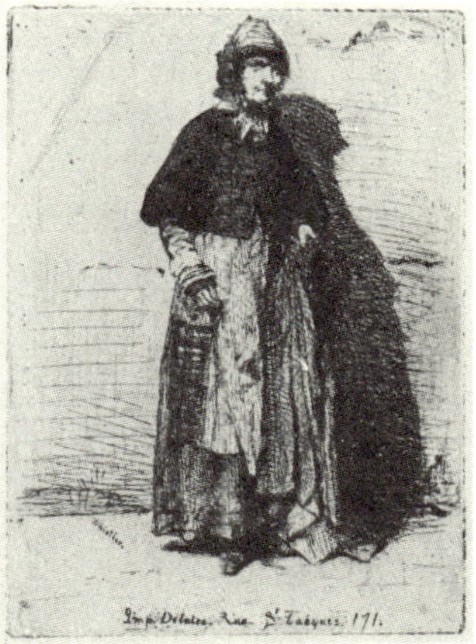

XIII.
La Mère Gérard, *K. 11*
4 7/8 x 3 1/2 in. (12.4 x 8.9 cm.)
Julius L. and Anita Zelman

felt in his later work. More important, in 1865 Whistler met Albert Moore, whose work he respected[8] and with whom he shared an admiration for Hellenistic terracotta figurines from Tanagra.[9] This interest played a role in a change in the style of Whistler's figuration, which moved toward a classical idealization of form, often enhanced by flowing draperies. Seen here in *The Model Resting* (fig. XII), this particular aspect of the artist's work is more frequently apparent in his paintings, drawings, and lithographs than in his etchings.

Crucial to all of Whistler's art, however, was his immersion around 1860 in *Japonisme:* Japanese prints and Blue and White porcelain became a passion, which continued through the rest of his life and influenced his work in countless ways.[10] In his etchings this was manifested as an increasing tendency to subordinate detail to a notion of sublime harmony and balance: a "felt" organization rather than one based on mathematical theory. Compression of space and careful distribution of objects (figures, trees, etc.) also became characteristic, whatever the subject.

Portraits, facades and doorways, close views and vistas were Whistler's subjects regardless of the medium he was using. With the etchings in particular, one finds remarkably close analogies between early and late works. *La Mère Gérard* and *La Vieille aux Loques* (figs. XIII and XIV), both from 1858, placed next to *The Wine Merchant, Ajaccio* and *The Sleeping Child, Ajaccio* (figs. XV and XVI), both from 1901, show how fully committed Whistler remained until the end of his life to the images he had adopted for himself in his youth. His depth and manner of expression changed a great deal, of course, and the evolution of that change is documented in the etchings.

8. Glasgow University Library Whistler Papers (hereafter noted as GUL Whistler), M436.

9. These terracottas were popular among Whistler's circle. Aleco Ionides, one of Whistler's friends and patrons, collected them.

10. See Gabriel P. Weisberg et al., *Japonisme: Japanese Influence on French Art, 1854–1910,* exh. cat., (Cleveland: Cleveland Museum of Art; New Brunswick: Rutgers University Art Gallery; Baltimore: Walters Art Gallery, 1975), esp. pp. 44–45.

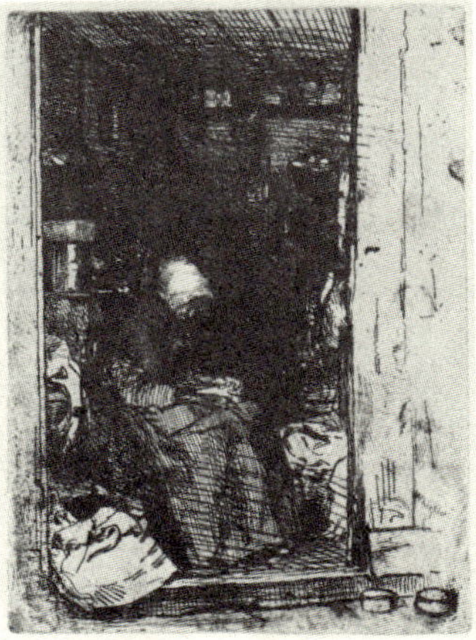

XIV.
La Vieille aux Loques, *K. 21*
8 1/8 x 5 3/4 in. (20.6 x 14.6 cm.)
Julius L. and Anita Zelman

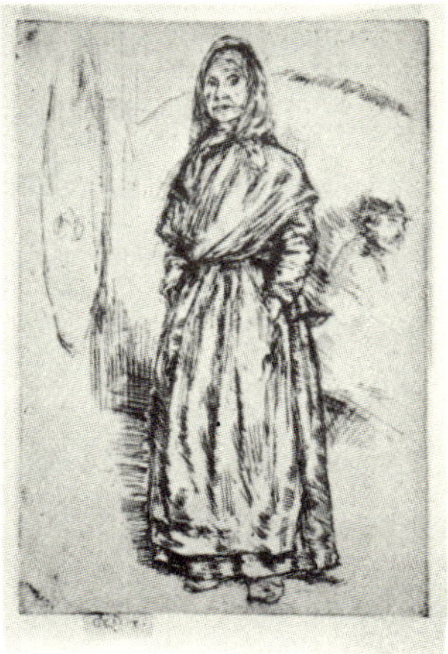

XV.
Wine Merchant, Ajaccio, *not in K.*
3 7/8 x 2 3/4 in. (9.9 x 6.7 cm.)
Hunterian Art Gallery, University of Glasgow, Birnie Philip Bequest

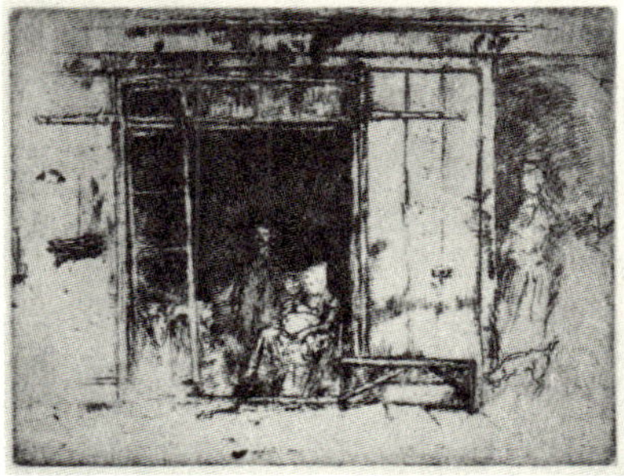

XVI.
The Sleeping Child, Ajaccio, *not in K.*
5 7/8 x 7 3/8 in. (15 x 18.8 cm.)
Hunterian Art Gallery, University of Glasgow, Birnie Philip Bequest

The French Set

Although Whistler occasionally made etchings and drypoints at other times, the majority of his important pieces, including all that were formally published, were made in four periods of concentration: 1858–61, 1870–75, 1877–80, and 1887–89. Essentially a modernist in spirit, he depicted directly, if selectively, everyday subject matter: the world around him. During his first several years abroad, that world had two centers, one in Paris and one in London, specifically, the home of Deborah (Whistler's half-sister) and Seymour Haden and their children: Annie, Francis, Arthur Seymour, and Harry.[11] During this period, Whistler's insider/outsider approach to the world (the Haden home/the milieu of the expatriate) was formed. Seymour Haden, a surgeon by profession, was an amateur etcher, and, until their friendship ended in 1867, he and Whistler encouraged each other to work in the medium. Indeed, Whistler's first published set, the 1858 London issue of Twelve Etchings from Nature (the French Set; see cat. nos. 1–5 and 8), was offered from Haden's address.

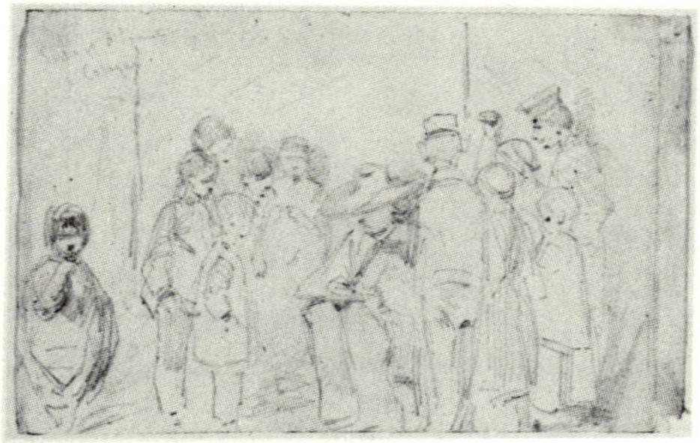

XVII.
Title to the French Set
Pencil
3 7/8 x 5 15/16 in. (9.8 x 15.1 cm.)
Freer Gallery of Art

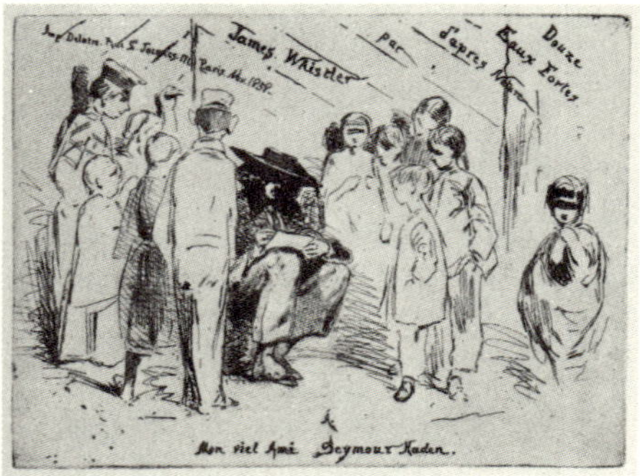

XVIII.
Title to the French Set, *K. 25*
4 3/8 x 5 3/4 in. (11.1 x 14.6 cm.)
Freer Gallery of Art

Most of the French Set subjects were selected during a walking tour Whistler made in 1858 through northern France, Luxembourg, and the Rhineland. As is generally assumed, some of these were undoubtedly drawn onto copper plates Whistler carried with him during the trip. Enough drawings on paper related directly to etchings in size, specific figuration, and with the images in reverse survive, however, to suggest that at least some in the series were based on these drawings and worked later rather than directly from the scene onto copper. Among the drawings is one for the title page illustration, reproduced here with the print worked from it (figs. XVII and XVIII). The subject is annotated as *Ernest* (Delannoy, with whom Whistler was traveling) *in Cologne,* but in the print Whistler transformed the figure into a self-portrait.

Whistler's French Set offers a very full selection of what came to be Whistlerian subjects: portraiture (e.g., cat. no. 8), the framed image (e.g., cat. no. 1), and building facades and/or street scenes (e.g., cat. no. 4). These early prints also show the artist's interest in the specific atmospheric qualities of time and place and in the play of light as it defines and describes form (e.g., cat. nos. 2, 3, and 4). Whistler was apparently totally at ease with his medium, working the etching needle with freedom, vigor, and variety. During this period, however, he did depend for printing upon Auguste Delâtre (fig. III). Delâtre was among the most important figures in the revival of artists' etching in France at mid-century. Whistler obviously studied the master at his work, because within a few years Whistler himself was adept enough to begin pulling some of his own proofs.

The French Set, with the address of Delâtre, was first issued in France, the title plate printed on white wrappers. It was then issued in London in blue wrappers with the title plate on the front and a list of contents printed by letterpress on the back. The formal edition apparently was printed chine appliqué (a process by which a thin sheet of Oriental paper is laminated to a heavier sheet during the printing process). In the French Set several colors–cream, golden yellow, blue, green, and possibly others–were appliqued onto a heavy-weight, white paper. Early proofs and later impressions on various papers exist, and precisely which are which has yet to be sorted out.[12] The cost of the set was two guineas. At least one piece from the French Set (*The Mustard Merchant* [cat. no. 1]), and possibly two (the second, an unnamed portrait) are listed as having been in the Paris Salon of 1859,[13] but little is actually known of the series' critical reception.

11. Donnelly and Thorp, p. 17.

12. A letter of 9 November (no year, but presumably 1858) from Ernest Delannoy to Whistler (GUL Whistler, D26) lists Delâtre's charges for printing, noting several categories of proofs on various papers; this letter would appear to be related to the French Set.

13. *Explication des ouvrages de peinture, sculpture, gravure, lithographie et architecture des artistes vivants . . .,* (Paris, 1859), p. 475, nos. 3673, 3674.

The Thames Set

As the French Set was being published, Whistler began work on several riverfront etchings that eventually were included in A Series of Sixteen Etchings of Scenes on the Thames and Other Subjects (the Thames Set; see cat. nos. 7, 17, 18, and 20). The etchings show "a marked propensity for shore life, river life, boat life, barge life–for everything which hints of old wharves, jetties, piers, rigging, box windows overlooking reaches of the peopled stream. . . ."[14] Subjects like *The Little Pool* (fig. XIX), a promotional piece for Whistler's etchings, were "something quite new and unexpected. English artists had rejected to observe these familiar things; busy, overloaded London had been passed by as vulgar and prosaic."[15] Whistler's Thames shipping etchings were not the only ones to receive notice, however, and his portraits and landscapes, like *Landscape with the Horse* (fig. XX), with its very peculiar, overscale figures at the right, were praised as well.[16]

In the Thames Set and other prints of the period, like *Vauxhall Bridge* (fig. XXI), Whistler used in a more freewheeling fashion the etching style he had evolved in the French Set (e.g., *The Rag Gatherers,* fig. XXII). Accumulations of small etched marks that visually make surface textures are juxtaposed with longer, more sweeping strokes that define gesture and composition; careful attention was paid to light as it established form.

Although the Thames Set plates were produced by 1861 and printed by both Delâtre and Whistler (they may well have been printed throughout the 1860s), they were not formally published until a decade later. In 1871 Messrs. Ellis and Green, King Street, Covent Garden, purchased the plates, had them steel faced,[17] and issued, as far as we know, an edition of one hundred printed by an unnamed London printer. What Whistler was paid for the plates, as well as his role in their publication, is uncertain, but he did suggest to Mr. Ellis that they "might look out the paper together. . . . I should be able to go back with you . . . to try the plate–I propose to assist myself this time at the printing and see the thing through."[18]

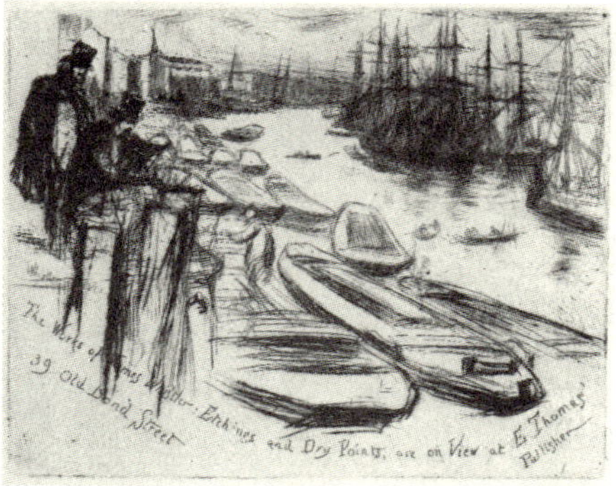

XIX.
The Little Pool, *K. 74*
4 x 4 7/8 in. (10.2 x 12.4 cm.)
Julius L. and Anita Zelman

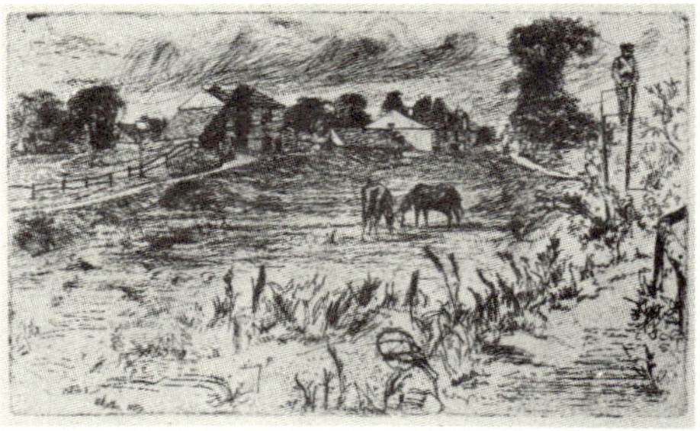

XX.
Landscape with the Horse, *K. 36*
5 x 7 7/8 in. (12.7 x 20 cm.)
Julius L. and Anita Zelman

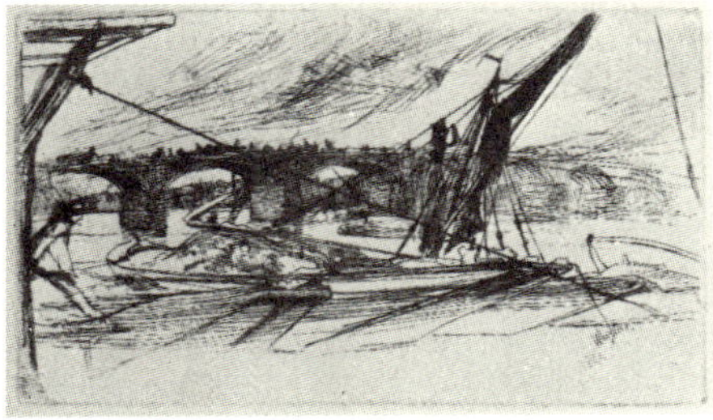

XXI.
Vauxhall Bridge, *K. 70*
2 5/8 x 4 1/2 in. (6.7 x 11.4 cm.)
Julius L. and Anita Zelman

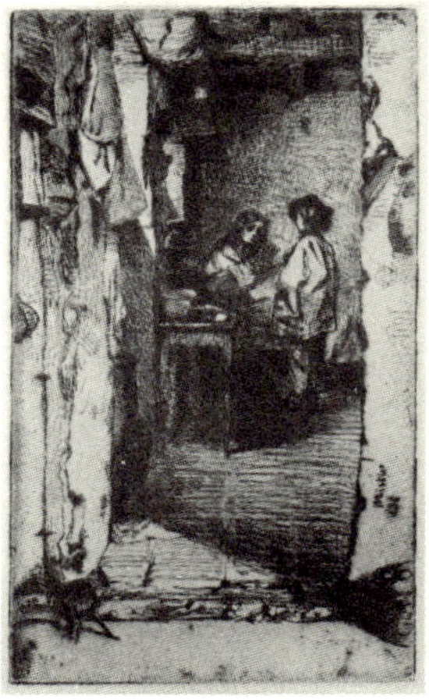

XXII.
The Rag Gatherers, *K. 23*
6 x 3 1/2 in. (15.2 x 8.9 cm.)
Julius L. and Anita Zelman

14. GUL Whistler Press Cuttings (hereafter noted as PC) 1, p. 37 (*Reader,* 4 April 1863); my thanks to Robert H. Getscher for bringing to my attention many of the press cuttings cited in this catalogue.

15. Theodore Duret, "Whistler and his Work," *Art and Letters* 1 (1888): p. 225. One notes, however, that the London Duret described frequently had been depicted for documentary, if not aesthetic, purposes.

16. GUL Whistler, PC1, p. 37 (*Reader,* 4 April 1863).

17. Steel facing on a copper plate strengthens the metal, allowing it to withstand longer editions. Unless very skillfully done, however, while protecting the plate, it somewhat obliterates the richness and delicacy of the original work.

18. GUL Whistler, E39. The wording "this time" might suggest there had been some earlier problems.

Regardless of Whistler's interest, impressions associated with the 1871 edition tend to be very cleanly wiped, lacking the subtle tonalities of earlier proofs. Whistler himself wrote in 1880 that this edition "was certainly not to be compared to Delâtre's." His account further indicated that the plates were to have been destroyed after a hundred impressions were pulled, but that they had not been and had recently been acquired by someone who had taken them to Frederick Goulding. "Goulding naturally found the etchings in their original perfect condition simply because I had had them steeled in their full bloom when I had satisfied myself by my own proofs. Goulding's impressions of these plates are very excellent. . . ."[19]

The prints, well received in the early 1860s, were enthusiastically greeted upon publication a decade later. They were celebrated as being "all the more precious because the beauties they perpetuate are dying out. . . . Whistler has immortalised Wapping, and given it the grace that is beyond the reach of anything but art. Let all lovers of good art and marvellous etching who want to know what Father Thames was like before he took to having his bed made, invest in Whistler's portfolio."[20]

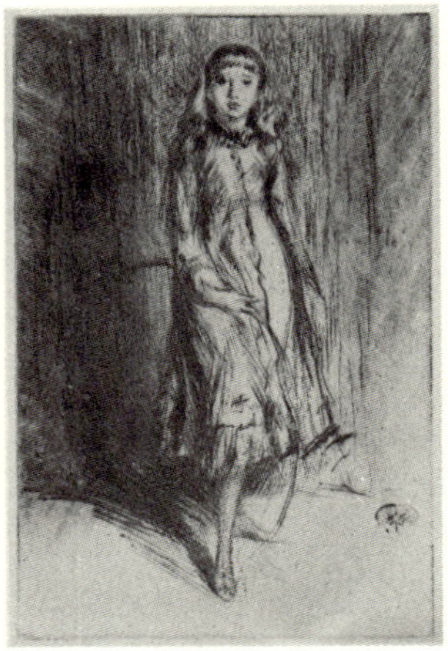

XXIII.
Florence Leyland, *K. 110*
8 3/8 x 5 3/8 in. (21.3 x 13.7 cm.)
Julius L. and Anita Zelman

The 1870s

Whistler's prints of the early 1870s, just after the Thames Set was published, are best represented by his splendid drypoint portraits of Mr. and Mrs. Frederick Leyland and their daughters.[21] The direct and spirited drawing style that characterizes these pieces, among them *Florence Leyland* (fig. xxiii), is related closely to the many lovely chalk and crayon drawings portraying the Leyland family that Whistler made during this period as well (see figs. 31a and 32a). In their freedom and breadth of execution, the drypoints present a clear break with the earlier prints. In part, this might have been dictated by the directness of the process (see "On Technique and Connoisseurship" below), although one suspects that the medium did not dictate the changes in style, but that Whistler shifted from etching to drypoint in working on copper because his aesthetic needs had changed: controlled lines, often minute, often describing surfaces rather than alluding to spaces, were not sympathetic with the broad forms with which he was engaged.

The late 1870s were a full and difficult period for Whistler. His break with the Leylands over the Peacock Room (1876)[22] was swiftly followed by his controversy with Ruskin (1877),[23] his move to the elegant White House, the Ruskin trial, which left him bankrupt (1878), his bankruptcy sale, and, finally, his commission from the Fine Art Society, a

19. GUL Whistler, PC (modern) 1849–87 (*Daily Tribune,* 12 September 1880, letter from Whistler, dated Venice, 16 August 1880); reprinted in Whistler, p. 83. Goulding apparently had the steel facing removed before printing from the plates.

20. GUL Whistler, PC (modern) 1849–87 ("A Whistler for Whistler," *Punch, or the London Charivari,* 17 June 1871, p. 245).

21. Whistler's relationship with F. R. Leyland, a Liverpool shipping magnate, yielded many fine paintings, drawings, and prints of the Leyland family as well as the Peacock Room, which is now in the Freer Gallery of Art. Unfortunately, this positive aspect has been overshadowed by the scandal of the Peacock Room episode that severed their friendship. In decorating the room in Leyland's Prince's Gate home, Whistler far exceeded his patron's commission and intentions. He then invaded Leyland's privacy by holding public views of his decorative scheme. Leyland, angered, paid the artist considerably less than Whistler considered his due, and the patron further added insult to injury by offering payment in pounds rather than guineas.

22. For an account of this phase of Whistler's life, see *The Whistler Peacock Room,* Freer Gallery of Art of the Smithsonian Institution, (Washington, D.C., 1980).

23. For Whistler's account of the episode, see Whistler, pp. 1–19.

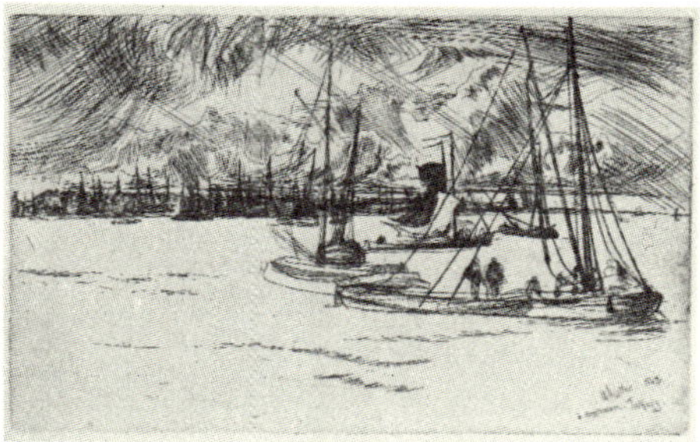

XXIV.
Amsterdam from the Tolhuis, *K. 91*
5 3/16 x 8 3/16 in. (13.2 x 20.8 cm.)
Julius L. and Anita Zelman

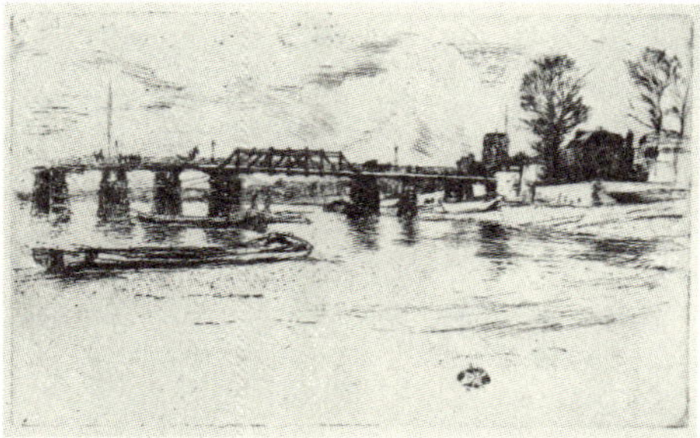

XXV.
Fulham, *K. 182*
5 3/16 x 8 in. (13.2 x 20.3 cm.)
Julius L. and Anita Zelman

London art gallery and print publisher, to do a series of etchings of Venice (1879). Amid all of this, with the prodding of Charles Augustus Howell, who was functioning as something of a business agent, he printed numerous impressions of subjects dating back to the early 1860s, among them his first etching of Amsterdam, *Amsterdam from the Tolhuis* (fig. XXIV).[24] He also produced a few splendid new picturesque views of the Thames (e.g., cat. nos. 27 and 28), several of which were immediately taken up by the Fine Art Society for publication.

A weekly newspaper, the *World,* enthusiastically reported that the artist was "again hard at work in his etching-room at the top of the house [in Lindsey Row]" and went on at some length to describe a visit there.

> It is a solemn delight to watch Mr. Whistler at work in this room, dashing away with the dry point, and pulling his proofs himself. . . . After drawing his picture at once on the plate without preliminary sketch of any kind . . . the plates, of course, are finished off with the dry point, so far as an etching should be finished, in the queer little room where we sit, watching the etcher retouch a plate here, taking a proof there, and keeping up meanwhile an unceasing flow of conversation. . . . It is gratifying to note the care with which the rapid draughtsman cleans his plate with turpentine, warms and inks it, and finally pulls the impression with his own hand.[25]

Whistler was concentrating on the quieter aspects of the Thames in these new etchings (e.g., *Fulham,* fig. XXV) rather than on the shipping activity that had interested him earlier. In their openness and serenity, they exemplify his attention to the principles of harmony and balance, which had attracted him to Japanese prints a decade before. In retrospect, the Thames prints of the late 1870s provided a link between Whistler's descriptive Thames Set and the revolutionary allusiveness of the Venice prints that soon followed.

Venice

In 1879 the Fine Art Society commissioned Whistler to go to Venice for three months and to return with a dozen etched views of the city. He had intended to produce such a series as early as 1876 and had issued a prospectus for it in October 1877, promising delivery within two months.[26] The turmoil of his life and the economic disappointment of the intervening period would have made the Society's offer especially inviting. As it turned out, however, quite apart from the great accomplishment of the art produced during this trip, the commission plagued Whistler for the rest of his life.

That Whistler endured considerable financial and physical strain during his Venice period is well documented.[27] Less clear, however, has been a real sense of just how extraordinary these hardships must have been in contrast to the elegance of Whistler's environment in the period immediately preceding his Venice trip. In some measure this can be ascertained from a description of his residence, the White House, designed by Godwin expressly for Whistler and with Whistler's collaboration: "The excellent detached

24. GUL Whistler Notebook (hereafter noted as NB) 4, pp. 1–14. During this period, Howell was also involved with the publication of Richard Josey's mezzotint reproductions of Whistler's paintings.

25. "Celebrities at Home: No. XCII. Mr. James Whistler at Cheyne-Walk," *World,* 22 May 1878, pp. 4–5.

26. GUL Whistler, NB1, p. 100 is apparently a summary list of subscribers (or, at least, a list of persons who had indicated interest in the project) in 1876 and 1877.

27. See Bacher and Getscher.

residence [had a] magnificent studio 50 ft. by 30 . . . well lighted and very lofty, with lavatory and W.C. adjoining. . . ." Its drawing room, almost eighteen by thirty feet, was also eighteen feet high, and, in addition to "three good bedrooms" for the residents, there were two more for servants "in the rear and connected by a glazed corridor." The house was further equipped with, among other things, both an American stove and a charcoal stove and a wine cellar.[28] To shift from this luxury and grandeur to one room in an art students' residence must have been unbearably difficult indeed. But shift Whistler did, and in fourteen months, not three, he produced some fifty etchings, rather than the dozen originally commissioned.

No doubt partly as a result of the extensive publicity Whistler had received during the Ruskin episode, his interpretation of the Queen of the Adriatic, as Venice was frequently called in the press, was greatly anticipated. Even before he left London, a show of the prints was scheduled for December of 1879. As the artist's return became increasingly delayed, Marcus Huish, managing director of the Fine Art Society, wrote to him worried that "the success of the Venice Set will be seriously marred if they do not very soon appear. . . ."[29] They did not appear very soon at all, however, and Whistler's response was undoubtedly not what Huish anticipated:

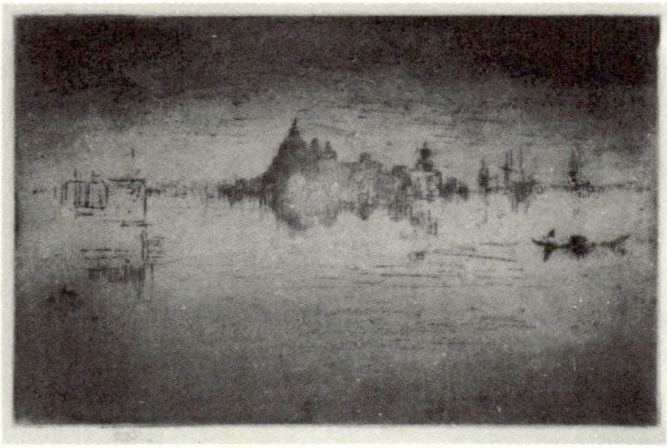

XXVI.
Nocturne: Salute, *K. 226*
6 x 8 7/8 in. (15.2 x 22.5 cm.)
Julius L. and Anita Zelman

> "The Venice" my dear Mr. Huish will be superb . . . only I can't fight against the Gods . . . by standing in the snow with a plate in my hand and an icicle at the end of my nose. . . . [However] it is even for the best . . . for had there been nothing but ordinary weather to deal with, your twelve plates would have been finished . . . before I had at all known the mine of wealth for both you and me in this place. . . . I have learned to know a Venice in Venice that the others never seem to have perceived [see fig. xxvi]. . . . The etchings themselves are far more delicate in execution, more beautiful in subject and more important in interest than any of the old set. . . . I am frozen–and have been for months–and you can't hold a needle with numbed fingers, and beautiful work cannot be finished in bodily agony–also I am starving–or shall be soon. . . . You had better send me fifty pounds at once.[30]

In addition to asking the Society for further funds, Whistler also wrote Ernest Brown, another one of its officers, to forward some old Dutch paper, some balls of etching ground, and some stopping-out varnish, complaining that "The printing business itself is very primitive and difficult here and on another pilgrimage of the kind I should certainly bring out my own press."[31]

For the next several months there was little communication between Whistler and the Society. The artist clearly was at work, and the sponsors, presumably, were fuming. The following October, however, hoping to feature Whistler's Venice etchings in a show of work by several artists, Huish wrote to plead "Cannot you send us a set of the etchings to take orders from . . . ?"[32] Whistler responded by asking for more money; but the Society, obviously of the opinion that they had invested enough for no return, informed him that they had even been "contemplating breaking into your parcel and making what we could of the contents."[33] Whatever the contents of the parcel might have been, given the auc-

28. *Particulars & Conditions of Sale of an Excellent Brick Detached Residence . . . known as "The White House," Tite Street, Chelsea . . . ,* Baker and Sons, 18 September 1879.

29. GUL Whistler, F36.

30. GUL Whistler, Letter Book (hereafter noted as LB) 3/8

31. GUL Whistler, F37.

32. GUL Whistler, F40.

33. GUL Whistler, F41.

tion of Whistler's home and personal effects the year earlier, this threat of further invasion of privacy was presumably the last straw. After further discussion of funds to be advanced and more promises to return, Whistler went from Venice to London.

In December 1880, precisely a year late, Venice: Twelve Etchings (the First Venice Set) was exhibited at the Fine Art Society's galleries. The etchings selected were the largest and the most complicated of the lot and, of the fifty, the closest to conventional Venetian views (see cat. nos. 40, 49, 54, 55, 57, 59, and 65). But Whistler was right: he had found a Venice never before perceived. It was a Venice drawn with great selectivity and printed with much elaboration. The critical response was mixed: "On the whole, we think that London fogs and the muddy old Thames supply Whistler's needle with subjects more congenial than do the Venetian palaces and lagoons";[34] or, "His present works are greatly in advance of his former productions of the kind–richer in tone, more restrained in style, and more complete. We know, indeed, of no modern examples of the art [of etching], English or Foreign, so subtle in suggestion, and at the same time displaying so absolute a mastery over the technicalities of the method. . . ."[35]

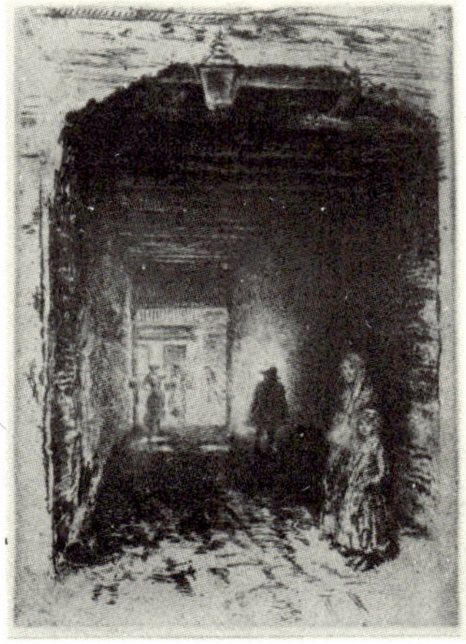

XXVII.
***The Beggars,* K. 194**
12 x 8 1/4 in. (30.5 x 21 cm.)
Julius L. and Arnita Zelman

The Venice prints were sought by collectors, and the Society was very keen to obtain the editions due them. Whistler's agreement called for editions of one hundred, twenty of which originally were to be printed by the artist. In addition to the seven hundred-pound cost of the plates, Whistler was to receive an additional two guineas (later five) per set printed. Throughout 1881 Huish and Brown wrote Whistler frequently, complaining both of the high costs (in addition to Whistler's fee, the Society was providing him with a workspace, a press, and an assistant) and of the slow pace of his printing; and they were insensitive to the growing importance to the artist that he himself perform, or at least closely supervise, the work.[36] Whistler, nevertheless, tried to convince the Society that the production rate, and the resultant aging of the plates, was an advantage. Huish was unconvinced: "It's all very nice to talk about your scheme of laying these plates down like old wine but unfortunately our purse is not long enough nor are our shareholders sufficiently lenient enough to allow of our so doing–it has yet to be proved too that etchings increase in value like wine with age."[37] Neither was the project a financial success at that point. Two hundred forty-seven prints (20.72 sets) had been sold for under seven hundred pounds, while expenses had come close to a thousand.

Gradually it must have become clear that Whistler was not going to allow a professional printer to complete his editions. He worked at them sporadically for the rest of the decade.[38] In late 1889 he wrote to Brown, "About the F.A.S. [Fine Art Society] Venetian etchings, I believe they will come out far more beautifully than ever! I am making of them wonderful new states!!"[39] (This renewed enthusiasm, however, did not get the editions fully printed. *The Beggars* [fig. XXVII] and *The Doorway* [fig. 44a] were eventually completed by Frederick Goulding, engaged by the executrix of Whistler's estate, Rosalind Birnie

34. GUL Whistler, PC6, p. 11 (*Daily News,* 7 December 1880).

35. GUL Whistler, PC6, p. 11 (*Globe,* 3 December 1880).

36. Edition printing is essentially repetitive work, and it is unlikely that Whistler really enjoyed the activity in large doses. He obviously knew, however, that his plates without steel facing, which he seems not to have considered, could not possibly hold up for editions of one hundred without considerable reworking. The most efficient way to decide the appropriate times for reworking, which ultimately is what put the Venice plates through so many states, was to oversee the printing at all stages.

37. GUL Whistler, F74.

38. GUL Whistler, F149.

39. GUL Whistler, F132.

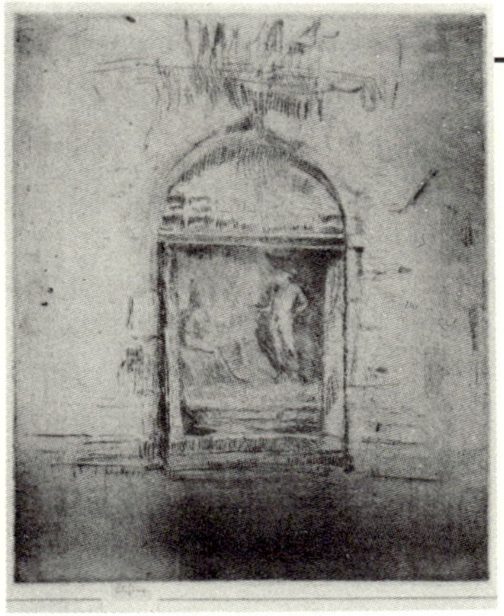

XXVIII.
Wool-Carders, *K. 221*
11 1/4 x 9 in. (28.6 x 22.9 cm.)
Julius L. and Anita Zelman

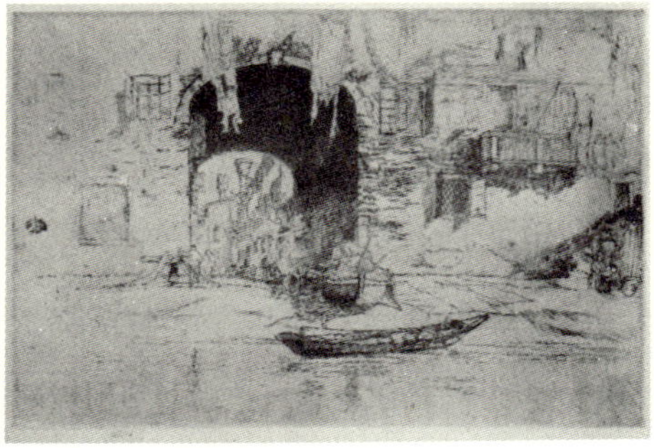

XXIX.
San Biagio, *K. 197*
8 1/4 x 12 in. (21 x 30.5 cm.)
Julius L. and Anita Zelman

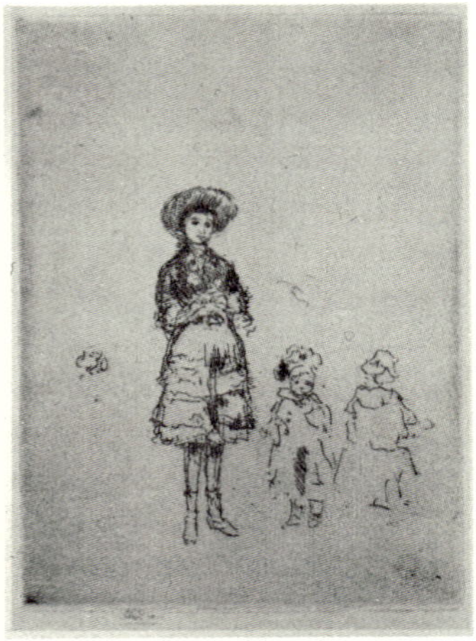

XXX.
The Little Nurse, *K. 302*
5 x 3 3/4 in. (12.7 x 9.5 cm.)
Julius L. and Anita Zelman

Philip, within months of the artist's death. Goulding also cancelled the plates and printed the necessary cancellation proofs.)[40]

In February 1883, notwithstanding that the editions of the First Venice Set remained incomplete, Whistler exhibited a larger selection of the Venice etchings at the Fine Art Society in a room of his own design, "Arrangement in White and Yellow." The arrangement, and Whistler's "cheeky catalogue,"[41] received far more attention in the press than the etchings themselves, and at times the arrangement was accused of detracting from the prints. Presumably Whistler didn't agree with this view, and when the Venice prints were shown in New York at Messrs. H. Wunderlich & Sons later that year, a similar scheme was installed in the galleries:

> The walls covered with white felt, the white frames of the etchings, the yellow base and moulding, the yellow plush seats and the little yellow and white chairs and tables and other furniture, partly brought from London to increase their value; the yellow tiled fireplace and yellow Chinese vases, the boy in white and yellow at the door, and finally the strip of yellow material stuck up under the ceiling with the artist's queer mark [the butterfly] upon it.

In the midst of all this hung Whistler's photograph with a big, round monocle in one eye.[42]

Included in these two 1883 shows were etchings from the First Venice Set, etchings never formally published, like *Wool-Carders* (fig. XXVIII), and etchings that were published as the Set of Twenty-six Etchings (Second Venice Set) three years later (1886), like *San Biagio* (fig. XXIX), by Messrs. Dowdeswell and Dowdeswells. Of the pieces in this second publication, twenty-one were scenes of Venice and five were English subjects (see cat. nos. 29, 41, 45–48, 52, 53, 56, 58, and 60–64). According to the prospectus, they were issued in editions of thirty in a portfolio especially designed by Whistler. Twelve additional impressions were to be printed of fifteen of the subjects and sold separately. The portfolios also contained a statement of Whistler's aesthetic position, the "Propositions." In them, he put down, among other things, his reasons for believing that etchings should be small and for his innovative trimming to the platemark of the paper on which they were printed.[43]

Whistler set aside his lingering obligation to the Fine Art Society (no impressions of the First Venice Set were turned over to the Society between July 29, 1885, and January 13, 1887),[44] and with that experience to learn from, the Dowdeswells' editions were completed by mid-July 1887.[45] One must remember, however, that apart from the official Dowdeswells publications, Whistler was printing these plates as early as August 1882[46] and that they had been exhibited in 1883, no doubt leading to sales. In fact, throughout the difficulties over the incomplete editions of the First Venice Set, Whistler sold many impressions of his other Venice plates through the Fine Art Society.

40. GUL Whistler, F330, 331.

41. See Whistler, pp. 91–105.

42. *N.Y. Mail & Express,* 24 October 1883, p. 61. In October 1983 Wunderlich & Company, Inc., was reestablished. Their inaugural print exhibition (with catalogue) was *James McNeill Whistler, Arrangement in White & Yellow: A Centennial Celebration.* A room of Whistler memorabilia was decorated as described here.

43. See Whistler, pp. 76–77.

44. GUL Whistler, F149.

45. GUL Whistler, NB1, pp. 33–35; also, GUL Whistler, D97, 16 July 1887, is a receipt for 1093 proofs at 2.5 guineas per dozen for a total to Whistler of £238.17.6

46. GUL Whistler, NB1, pp. 2–4 records sales in August 1882, including impressions of *The Dyer, Garden, Nocturne: Palaces,* and *Fishing-Boat* (cat. nos. 44, 46, 60, and 64) among others.

Circa 1887

About 1887, while working on the editions of the Second Venice Set, Whistler's interest in etching was given a new impetus, and in that year he rapidly produced almost a quarter of his entire body of work in the medium. Most clearly impressive of the prints are the grand Brussels subjects with their highly ornamental facades (see cat. no. 80). But most of the etchings of this time were rather swiftly drawn, tiny street views and shop scenes and vignettes of children, like *The Little Nurse* (fig. xxx). In fact, with the exception of the Amsterdam prints of 1889 and a few relatively highly worked figure studies of the 1890s (cat. nos. 76 and 77), tiny, spontaneous compositions like these dominate the remainder of Whistler's etchings. Typical is *Newspaper-Stall, Rue de Seine* (fig. xxxi) of the early 1890s.

The Amsterdam Prints

In 1888 Whistler married. His wife, Beatrix ("Trixie"), encouraged his work in lithography, and this medium dominated his graphic work from 1887 until her death in 1896. But in 1899, in his etchings in Amsterdam, Whistler's oeuvre in that medium, including his most fully worked etched *Nocturne* (figs. 87a and 87b),[47] reached its pinnacle. Back in London, printing the plates, "he admitted that his etchings of Amsterdam were, in his opinion, the best work he had ever given to the public." He went on to explain,

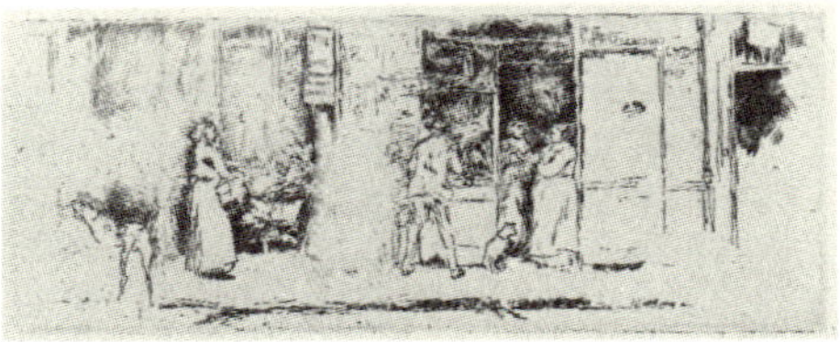

XXXI.
Newspaper-Stall, Rue de Seine, *K. 432*
3 1/4 x 7 7/8 in. (8.6 x 20 cm.)
Julius L. and Anita Zelman

> I divide myself into three periods. First, you see me at work on the Thames. Now, there you see the crude and hard detail of the beginner.[48] So far, so good. There, you see, all is sacrificed to exactitude of outline. Presently, and almost unconsciously, I begin to criticise myself, and to feel the craving of the artist for form and colour. The result was the second stage, which my enemies call inchoate, and I call Impressionism. In [the third stage, the Amsterdam etchings] I have endeavored to combine stages one and two. You have the elaboration of the first stage and the quality of the second.[49]

Exemplary is *Jews' Quarter, Amsterdam* (fig. xxxii).

From Amsterdam, while working on the plates, Whistler wrote to the Fine Art Society, offering Huish the series as follows: "The importance of these plates you can only estimate.... [They combine] a minuteness of detail with greater freedom and more beauty of execution than even the Venice Set or this last 'Renaissance' lot..." (the latter referring to the prints he made on his honeymoon in France the previous year; see cat. no. 81). Whistler's offer to the Society was for ten plates and thirty proofs of each. In addition he himself was to get five proofs, and one proof of each was to be for the British Museum. The price for the plates was two thousand guineas, including the editions printed by Whistler. The proofs were to be sold for no less than ten guineas because "the quality will be of that 'preciousness' that will class the proofs among those for which I habitually ask 12 or more."[50]

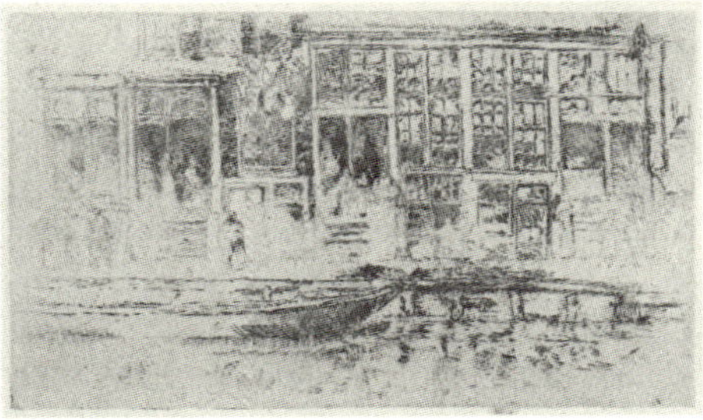

XXXII.
Jews' Quarter, Amsterdam, *K. 415*
5 1/4 x 8 11/16 in. (13.3 x 22.1 cm.)
Julius L. and Anita Zelman

47. See cat. nos. 4, 41, 59, and 60 for examples of Whistler's earlier etched Nocturnes.

48. It is interesting to note that Whistler totally ignores the French Set in his discussion. As early as 22 November (1868?), Whistler's mother, Anna, had written regarding the French Set to Mr. James Gamble, an old family friend, that Whistler "has no value for his juvenile productions [although] they may be as pleasing generally as his Thames etchings" (GUL Whistler, W534). In suggesting prints to be included in the Chicago Exposition of 1893, however, he did include some of these earliest prints.

49. GUL Whistler, PC6, p. 62 (*Pall Mall Gazette,* 4 March 1890).

50. GUL Whistler, F164.

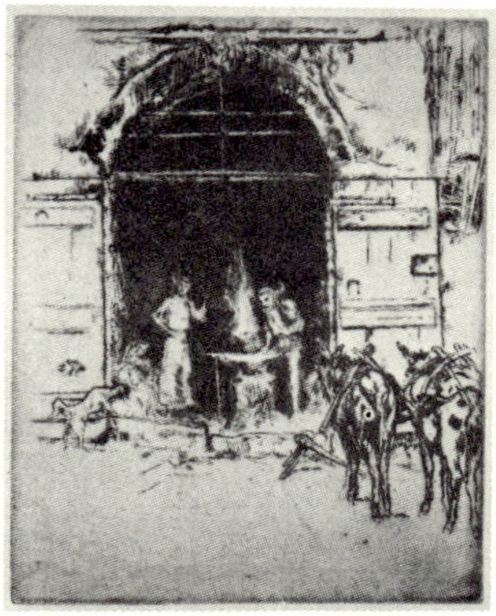

XXXIII.
The Flaming Forge, Ajaccio, *not in K.*
6 1/16 x 7 1/2 in. (15.3 x 19.1 cm.)
Hunterian Art Gallery, University of Glasgow, Birnie Philip Bequest

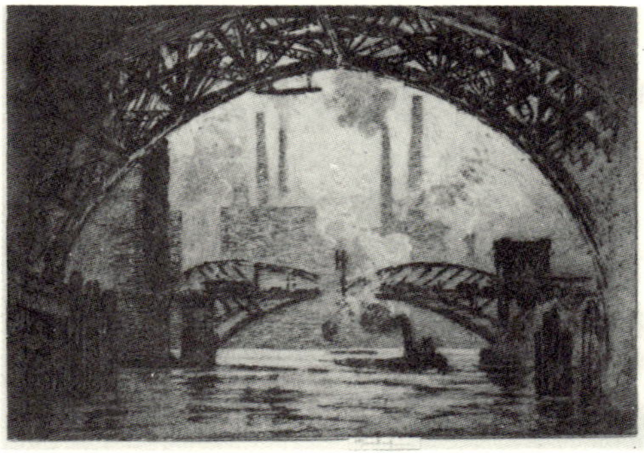

XXXIV.
Joseph Pennell (American, 1857–1926)
Under the Bridges, Chicago, *1910*
Etching and aquatint
9 1/4 x 12 1/4 in. (23.5 x 31 cm.)
National Gallery of Art, Addie Burr Clark Collection

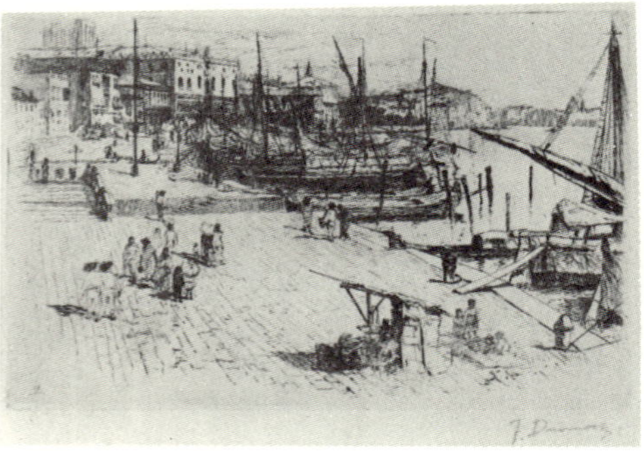

XXXV.
Frank Duveneck (American, 1848–1919)
Riva 2, *1880*
Etching
8 1/2 x 13 1/8 in. (21.6 x 33.3 cm.)
National Gallery of Art, Rosenwald Collection

Huish was glad to hear of "such a promising subject and with so much enthusiasm imparted . . . it should certainly be a success . . . ," but the price was too high to be profitable, so he asked Whistler to reconsider his proposal.[51] No publication agreement was reached, and a show of the etchings scheduled for mid-1890 was cancelled by Whistler. In December 1889, Huish lamented "that our hoped for exhibition next May is not to come off . . . but I trust that its postponement will result in increased benefit for all concerned. . . . It grieves me to think that those Dutch etchings will not illumine the world as soon as I expected.[52]

The Amsterdam prints were the last etchings Whistler conceived as a series, and they were never surpassed as the high point of his oeuvre. He continued, however, to make etchings almost until his death, the last of them dating from his 1900–1901 trip to Corsica. Among these is *The Flaming Forge, Ajaccio* (fig. XXXIII), in which a favorite theme (e.g., cat. nos. 7 and 41) in a favorite format (e.g., cat. nos. 1 and 44) is again explored. The children are there, the playful dog that activates many of the earlier prints (e.g., cat. no. 72) is there too, as is the concern with light and atmosphere, all handled with the assurance and skill that were developed over a lifetime. As Whistler's friend, the critic Theodore Duret, wrote as early as 1888, "Drawn direct from nature by a powerful artist who stamps all that he touches with his own personality, the result of work done by the tiniest of needles, printed to perfection, the etchings of Mr. Whistler form, among the productions of contemporaneous art, an exquisite, rare and unique whole."[53]

Whistler's etchings had a profound influence on the generation of artists that followed him. Among Americans Joseph Pennell, Whistler's biographer, was also his foremost disciple. Whistler's influence is clearly felt in such pieces as *Under the Bridges, Chicago* (fig. XXXIV) in its composition, its extensive use of plate tone to augment the work in etching and aquatint (a tonal process not used by Whistler), and in the fact that the paper is trimmed to the platemark with only a tab margin to carry Pennell's signature. Some etchings of the Riva (e.g., fig. XXXV) by another of Whistler's countrymen, Frank Duveneck, were actually mistaken for Whistlers in the 1881 exhibition of the Society of Painter Etchers. Among British artists, James McBey and D. Y. Cameron emulated Whistler's subjects as well as his style. The Venice pieces in particular served as models, as an etching such as Cameron's *The Palace Doorway* (fig. XXXVI) confirms.[54]

51. GUL Whistler, F165.

52. GUL Whistler, F168.

53. Duret, p. 224.

54. See Getscher and Staley for a study of Whistler's influence.

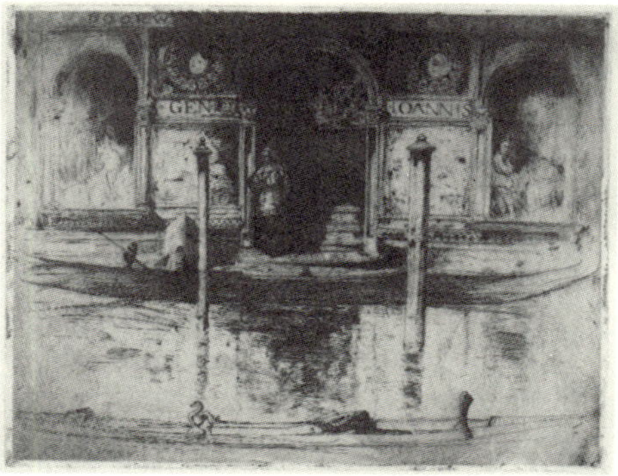

XXXVI.
D. Y. Cameron (English, 1865–1945)
The Palace Doorway, *1895*
Etching
9 1/2 x 12 in. (24 x 30.5 cm.)
National Gallery of Art, Rosenwald Collection

On Technique and Connoisseurship

Among the several methods of putting images onto copper plates for the purpose of printing them, Whistler seriously explored two: etching and drypoint.[55] To make an etching, he would coat a copper plate (of about 1 millimeter in thickness) with an acid-resist ground. He then drew through this ground, thereby exposing the areas of the plate that comprised the image. Acid (usually nitric acid diluted with water), applied to the exposed copper, etched, or "bit," the drawn lines into the metal, forming grooves capable of holding printing ink.

The quality of the etched line depended upon several factors. One was the character of the tool used to draw through the ground. Whistler used several sorts, among them large, double-ended needles and, later, needles set in wood like pencils.[56] Also critical were the strength of the acid and the length of time the plate was exposed to it. Whistler often brushed acid onto the plate with a feather. The advantage of this method over the more conventional one of immersing the plate in an acid bath was that it allowed him to vary the length of time the acid was in contact with particular areas of the plate.

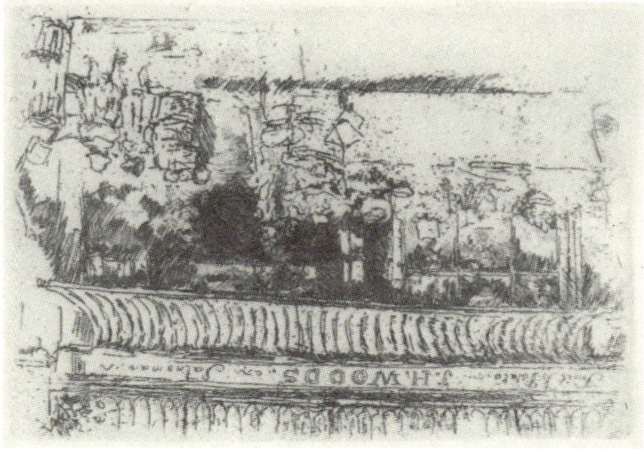

XXXVII.
Woods's Fruit-Shop, *K. 265*
3 3/4 x 5 1/4 in. (9.5 x 13.3 cm.)
National Gallery of Art,
Rosenwald Collection

Whistler also "stopped out" areas that were sufficiently bitten, using an acid-resist varnish. This made it possible for him to etch some areas lightly while continuing to bite others. On occasion, the acid would eat through the acid-resist ground, causing unexpected marks on the plate. This is called "foul bite" and is seen, for example, in the dots throughout *Woods's Fruit-Shop* (fig. XXXVII). Whistler must have chosen to leave these marks, however, as there were methods for removing them if he had found them objectionable.

For drypoints, Whistler drew his subjects onto an ungrounded plate with a tool sufficiently sharp to penetrate the metal directly. Doing so displaced the metal so that it formed a "burr" along the edges of the drawn lines of the image. This burr functioned to hold the ink, distinguishing the drypoint process from the etching process, in which the groove that was bitten into the plate by the acid held the ink. This burr gives the drypoint medium its characteristically "velvelty" quality. As seen in *Lord Wolseley* (fig. XXXVIII), the drypoint line, because of its irregular qualities, is considerably fuzzier and softer than the line one finds in an etching like *Woods's Fruit-Shop.*

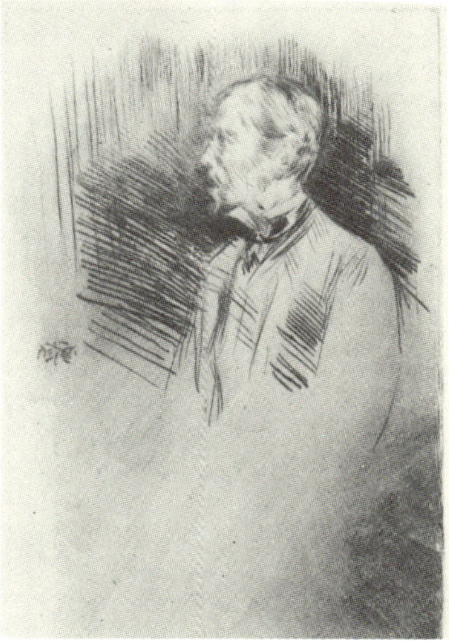

XXXVIII.
Lord Wolseley, *K. 164*
11 7/8 x 6 7/8 in. (30.2 x 17.5 cm.)
Julius L. and Anita Zelman

To print his etched copper plate, Whistler removed the acid-resist ground, forced ink into the bitten lines that comprised the image, removed the residue of ink from the surface of the plate, placed a sheet of paper (usually dampened with water to soften its fibers) on top of the plate, and rolled the plate and paper together through a press under great pressure, transferring the ink from the grooves in the plate onto the paper. The print became a mirror image of the plate. The printing of his drypoint plates followed the same procedures, the step of removing the ground being unnecessary. Because the burr that held the ink was above the surface of the plate, it would undergo especially great pressure during printing, being worn down a little with each pass through the press. Whistler's drypoint prints, therefore, were generally printed in smaller numbers than the etchings; because the drypoint wore down, the variation from early impressions to late impressions is much greater than one finds in the etchings. Whistler often combined the two techniques (e.g., cat. no. 46), touching up the etched work with the more direct means of drypoint.

55. For further technical reading related to Whistler's era, see Maxime Lalanne, *The Technique of Etching,* trans. S. R. Koehler, ed. Jay M. Fisher (New York: Dover Publications, 1981).

56. MacDonald, p. 6.

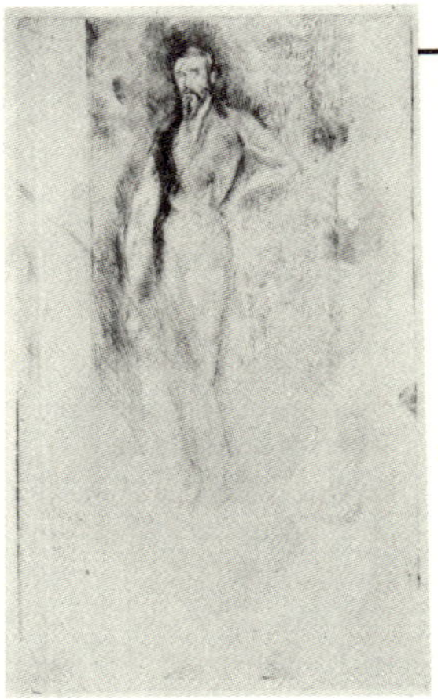

XXXIX.
F. R. Leyland, *K. 102*
11 7/8 x 6 7/8 in. (30.2 x 17.5 cm.)
National Gallery of Art,
Rosenwald Collection

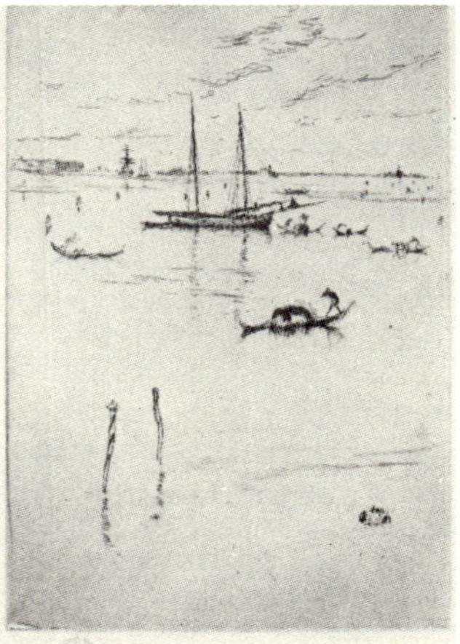

XL.
The Little Lagoon, *K. 186*
8 7/8 x 6 in. (22.6 x 15.2 cm.)
Julius L. and Anita Zelman

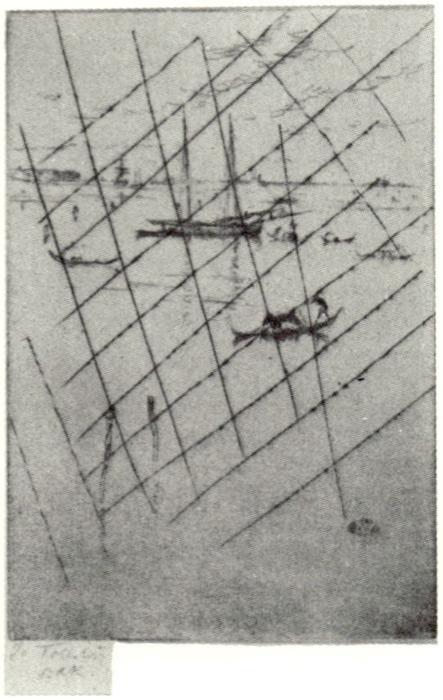

XLI.
The Little Lagoon, *K. 186*
Impression from cancelled plate
8 7/8 x 6 in. (22.6 x 15.2 cm.)
Julius L. and Anita Zelman

In developing an image, Whistler often made "proof" impressions to see the progress of his plate through various "states," each state showing a new development in the work on the plate (e.g., cat. nos. 36 and 60). Sometimes the new work took the form of additions; other times work was deleted. To remove part of an image, Whistler used special tools: the scraper was used to remove a layer of metal, thus obliterating the image; the burnisher smoothed out the areas that had been scraped, or it was used directly to rub down the metal, bringing the copper plate close to its original form (see cat. no. 45). Whistler worked directly on some of his state proofs. These "touched" proofs were a means of considering further work on the plate (see cat. no. 34).

Whistler's printing methods, particularly in his Venice etchings, were unusual. Instead of wiping the surface of the etched plates clean, leaving ink only in the bitten lines, he amplified the subtleties of the composition by carefully modulating the ink on certain areas of the plate's surface as he wiped it in preparation for printing. This method may have begun to suggest itself to him as he pulled proofs such as the portrait of F. R. Leyland (fig. XXXIX), in which he wiped the plate only to the extent necessary to study the image. The remaining surface ink was left, at first perhaps inadvertently, to enhance the line work.[57]

Regarding connoisseurship, in addition to aesthetic quality a number of matters became important to artists and collectors alike during the revival of interest in etching as a fine art medium at the end of the nineteenth century. There was considerable concern over limited editions, and organizations such as the Printsellers Association performed a monitoring function in this regard.[58] There is no evidence that Whistler actually numbered any of his prints, even when the prospectus advertised numbered impressions (see cat. no. 21). He seems instead to have considered it a matter of honor that potential buyers would know that he wasn't going to issue his work in large numbers. In discussing his lithographs (his attitude would have been the same with his etchings), he wrote to Ernest Brown at the Fine Art Society, "It is well enough known—and nobody knows it better than yourself, that my own preoccupation with my work makes it difficult enough to get things out of me—and there is no likelihood of these things overrunning the place. . . ."[59] In instances such as the Fine Art Society's Venice editions, a cancelled proof was required to mark the end of the editions (see figs. XL and XLI).

Whistler was particularly fond of fine old Dutch and Oriental papers. His editions, even with formally published sets like the Venice etchings, show no consistency in this regard: as the plates were printed over periods of several years, he was in the habit of using whatever papers he had at a given moment.

57. For extensive discussion of Whistler's printing process, see Getscher, pp. 64–73.

58. GUL Haden, 1981/54, 55.

59. GUL Whistler, F214.

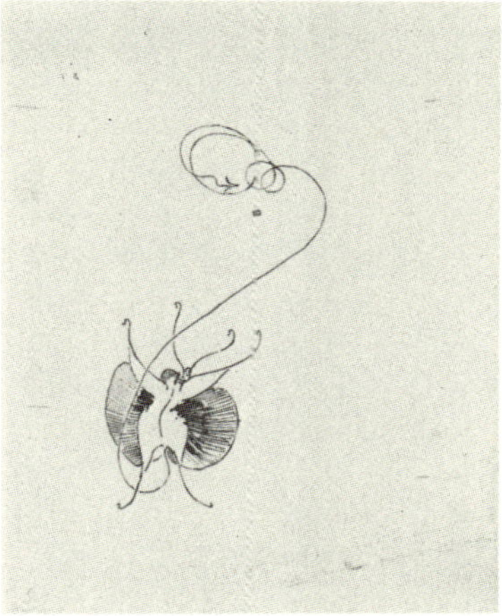

XLII.
Butterfly Design for "The Baronet and the Butterfly"
Pen and ink
7 13/16 x 6 in. (19.8 x 15.2 cm.)
Julius L. and Anita Zelman

Whistler's butterfly signature, used for both his art and his writings, apparently evolved from his initials JMW (see figs. XLII and XLIII). Changes in its details over the years make it useful in dating his prints, both in terms of execution of the plate and of time of printing (see cat. no. 51). But one must keep in mind that just as Whistler printed the same image over several years, he probably also signed impressions years after they were printed, especially as collectors occasionally asked him to sign impressions they had purchased years before.

One sees, then, that the problems of Whistler connoisseurship are complex, and attention to these matters is essential to the formation of a fine collection of Whistler's etchings. The many examples of first-state impressions, touched proofs, impressions with especially sensitive use of surface tone or velvety drypoint burr (marking only the earliest impressions from the plate), impressions on receptive, fine old papers, exceedingly rare subjects, and impressions inscribed specifically to Whistler's important friends and contemporary collectors mark the Zelman Collection as one in an impressive line of just such collections of extraordinary excellence.[60]

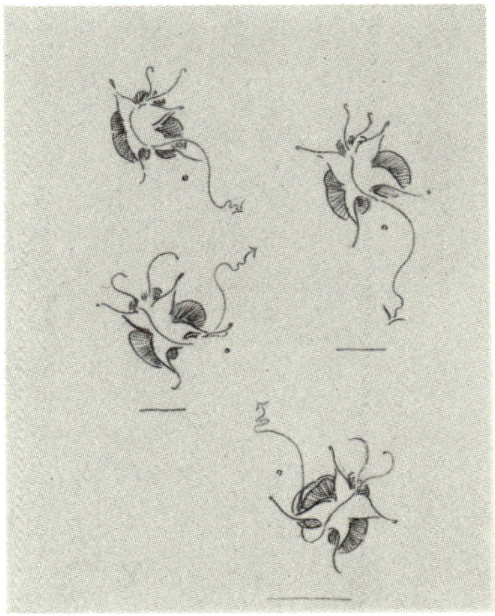

XLIII.
Butterfly Designs for "The Gentle Art of Making Enemies"
Pen and ink
11 1/4 x 8 13/16 in. (28.6 x 22.4 cm.) (sheet
Julius L. and Anita Zelman

60. For a study of American collectors of Whistler's prints, see Wiehl.

In the catalogue entries that follow, each of Whistler's four published series is referred to by its commonly used short title: *Douze eaux-fortes d'après nature*/Twelve Etchings from Nature as the French Set; Sixteen Etchings of Scenes on the Thames and Other Subjects as the Thames Set; Venice: Twelve Etchings as the First Venice Set; and Set of Twenty-six Etchings as the Second Venice Set.

The letter *K.* followed by a number refers to Edward G. Kennedy's catalogue raisonné of Whistler's etchings (see bibliography). The fraction following the K. and number indicates the state. For example, *2/3* means an impression is the second of three states.

Notes in the paper descriptions regarding miscellaneous manuscript inscriptions indicate that the sheet most likely was a flyleaf removed from an old book. Descriptions of paper weight, while necessarily approximate, are an attempt to start sorting out the problems presented by the extraordinary range of papers Whistler used.

Under provenance, Lugt numbers refer to Frits Lugt, *Les Marques de collections de dessins & d'estampes* (Amsterdam: Vereenigde Drukkerijen, 1921; with supplement, The Hague: Martinus Nijhoff, 1956). The symbol *(?)* follows provenance entries for which no evidence of former ownership is on the print.

Under literature, GUL Whistler refers to the Glasgow University Library archives. GUL Whistler may be followed by one of several letter codes. *NB* and a number refer to Notebook 1, 2, and so forth; *LB*, to a Letter Book; *PC* to Press Cuttings. Any single piece of correspondence and a number refer to a letter or other manuscript or printed document, alphabetically organized, usually by the first initial of the last name of the sender or of the organization he or she represented. When Whistler was the sender, the initial of the recipient is used.

Regarding dimension for the comparative illustrations, sheet size is used for drawings, image for lithographs, and platemark for etchings.

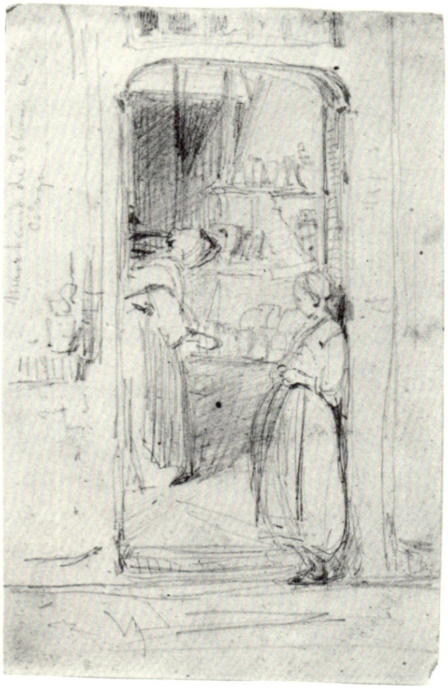

1a.
La Marchande de Moutarde
Pencil
6 x 3 7/8 in. (15.2 x 9.8 cm.)
Freer Gallery of Art

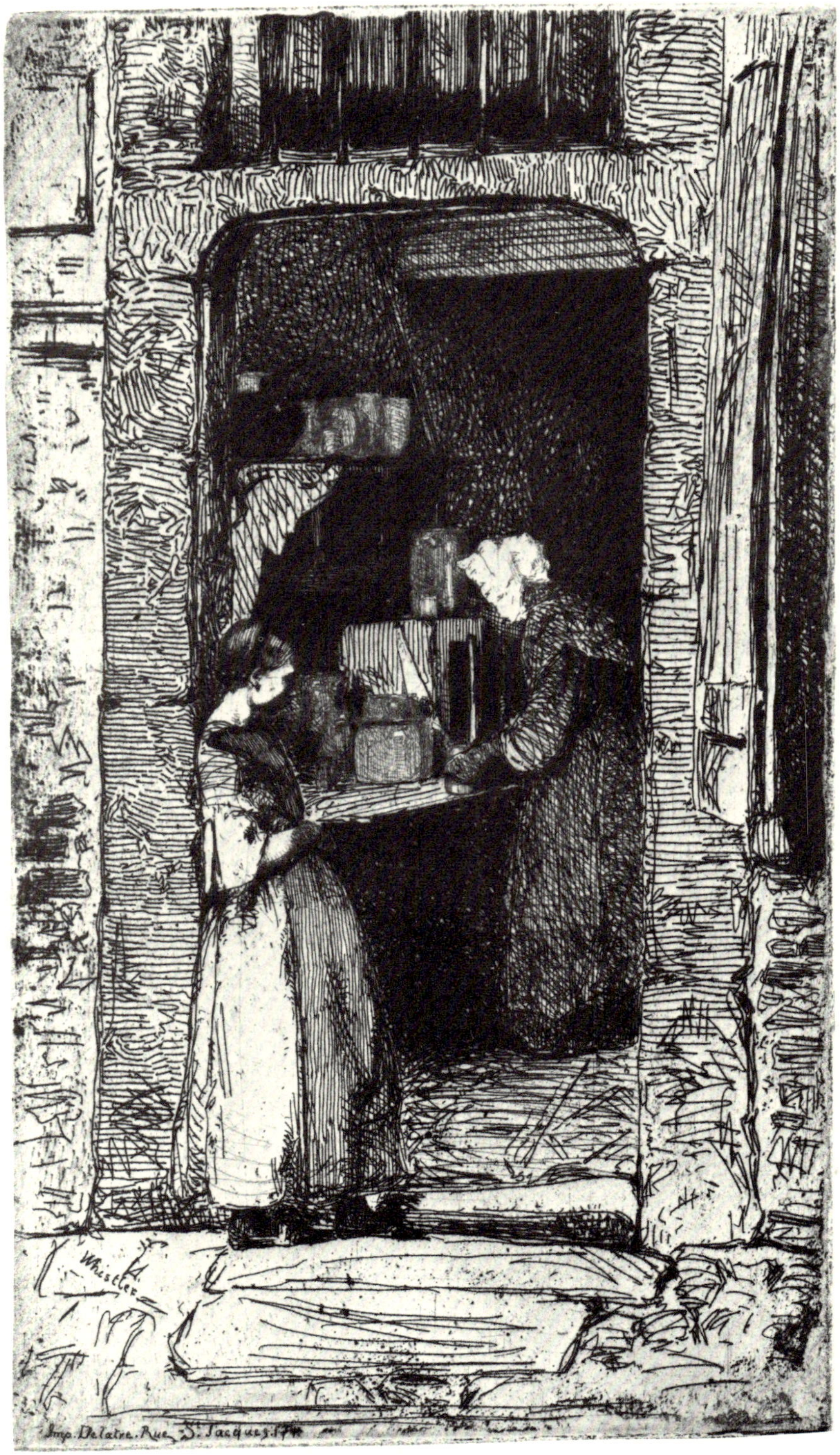

1. ***The Mustard Merchant,*** *1858*

One of the French Set

K. 22 3/5

Etching

6 3/16 x 3 7/16 in. (15.7 x 8.8 cm.)

Cool black ink on medium-weight laid paper with watermark: Brittania

Signed in plate lower left **Whistler**

Provenance: purchased from William Weston Gallery Ltd., 1970

Included in the Paris Salon of 1859, along with another etching, a portrait, this evidently was among the works that introduced Whistler's art to the public. Fifteen years later, in the first catalogue raisonné of his etchings (eighty-six plates at the time), Ralph Thomas wrote that "as a piece of work of this period in the artist's styles, this... is one of the most perfect specimens." Today too *The Mustard Merchant* is generally considered one of the artist's most charming and important early images. One of the first demonstrations of Whistler's interest in the quotidian experience as observed by an outsider, such views through doorways became a hallmark of his imagery.

This piece also offers an opportunity to study the technical means Whistler utilized for developing the surfaces of his etchings to describe volume, tone, and color, as well as surface texture itself: for instance, the woman's white hat against the dark dress, the rich shadows on the wall beneath the shelf on which the pots sit, the wooden door jamb against the brick wall. A relationship between this etching and Charles Jacque's *Récureuse* has frequently been cited (reproduced Lumsden, p. 295). Jacque's etching might well have been seen by Whistler in the printing shop of Auguste Delâtre; and Whistler appears to have been influenced by it in composition, the pose of the woman's upper torso, and the varied line work used to portray the surfaces of wall and ground.

The Mustard Merchant is based on a pencil sketch, inscribed *Marchande de Moutarde, Cologne* (fig. 1a), made during Whistler's 1858 walking tour of France and the Rhineland with Ernest Delannoy. Like most of the pencil sketches of this period, it is somewhat clumsy, offering little indication of the graceful line Whistler would later develop.

The etching is actually complete in this third state. The later two states are marked, first, by defacing and, second, by the removal of the name and address of Delâtre. These changes were made before the subject was reissued in 1886, printed by the great English printer Frederick Goulding, in an edition of two hundred impressions for the volume *English Etchings.* It is one of the best known and least rare of Whistler's early etchings.

Impressions are also known printed in brown and on various papers. The official publication impressions presumably were printed on chine appliqué.

LITERATURE: *Explication des ouvrages de peinture, sculpture, gravure, lithographie et architecture des artistes vivants...,* (Paris, 1859), p. 475, nos. 3673, 3674; E. S. Lumsden, *The Art of Etching* (1924; reprint ed., New York: Dover Publications, 1962); Mansfield, p. 14, no. 22; Naylor, p. xx, no. 12; Thomas, no. 11; Wedmore, p. 22, no. 16.

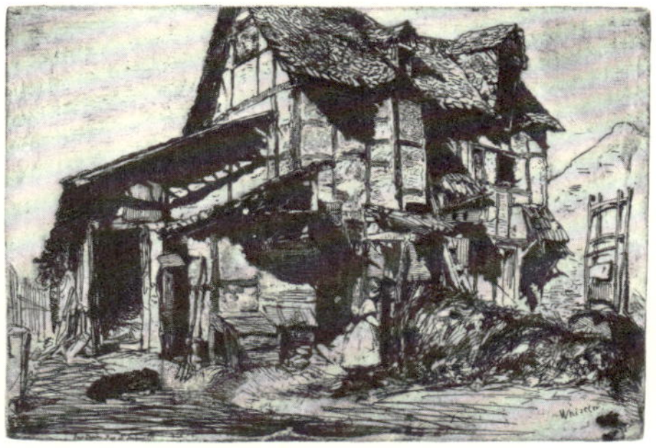

3a.
The Unsafe Tenement, *K. 17 3/4*
6 1/8 x 8 3/4 in. (15.6 x 22.2 cm.)
Julius L. and Anita Zelman

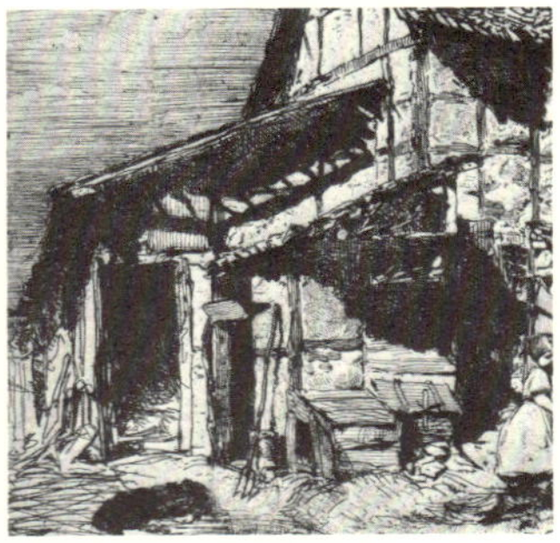

3b.
The Unsafe Tenement, *K. 17 2/4 (detail)*
Julius L. and Anita Zelman

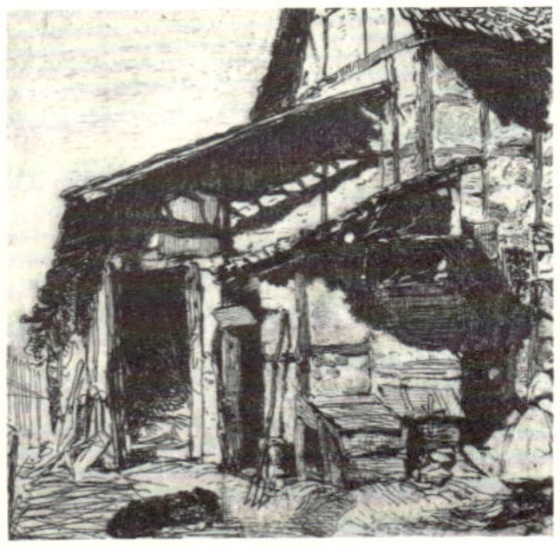

3c.
The Unsafe Tenement, *K. 17 3/4 (detail)*
Julius L. and Anita Zelman

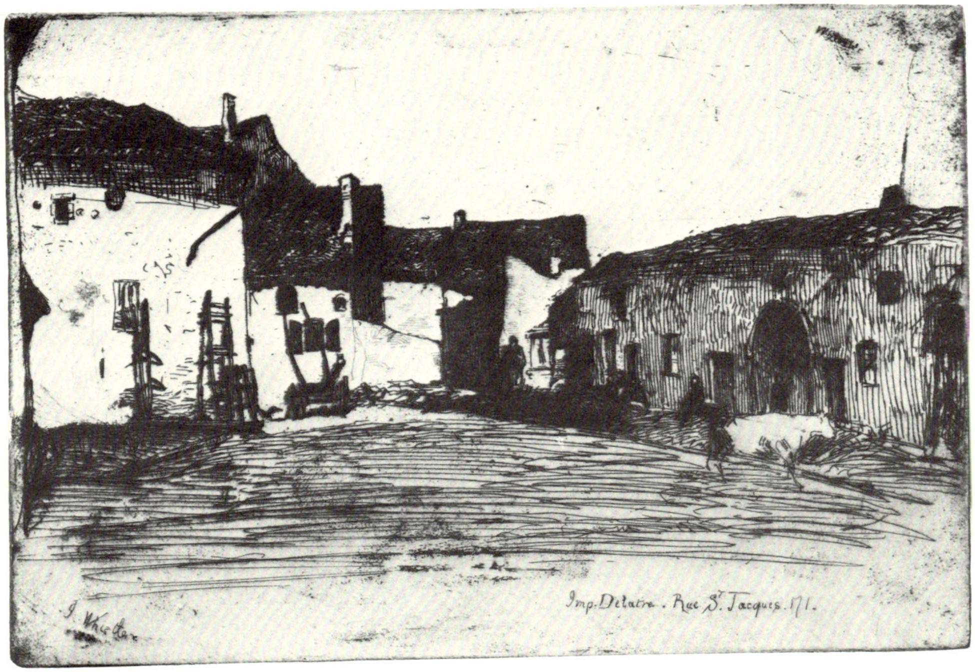

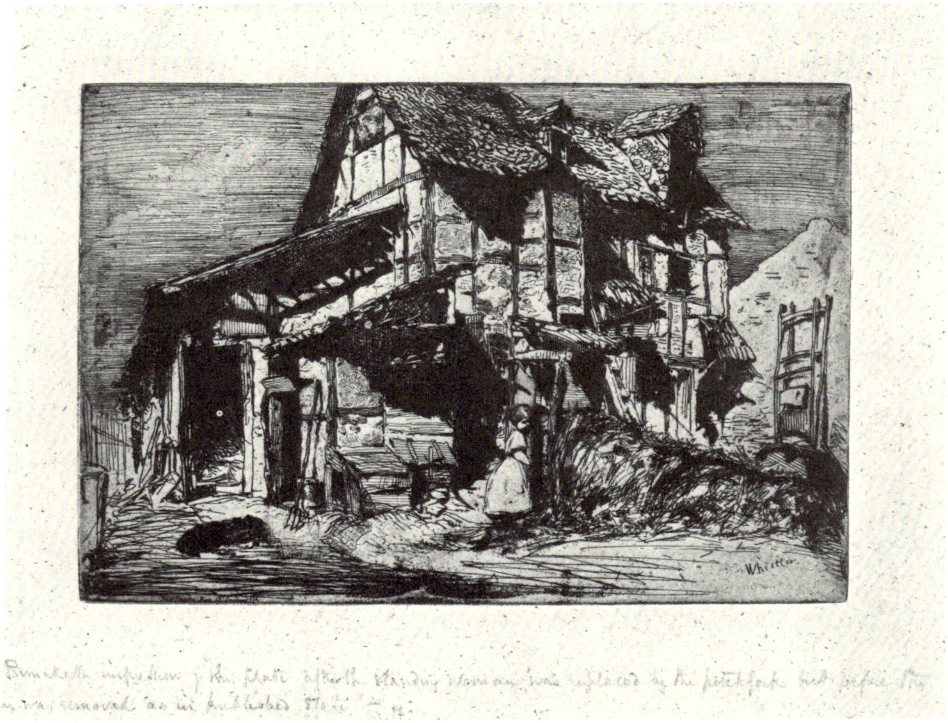

2. *Liverdun, 1858*

One of the French Set

K. 16 2/2

Etching

4 5/16 x 6 1/8 in. (10.8 x 15.5 cm.)

Warm black ink on medium-weight, antique laid paper

Signed in plate lower left **J. Whistler**

Provenance: Ralph Thomas (inscription verso); anonymous collector's mark; purchased from R. M. Light & Co., Inc., 1981

This farmyard in Liverdun, a village in Alsace-Lorraine, was another of the sites Whistler encountered on his 1858 walking tour. As with several of the early etchings in the French Set, this published state is marked by few changes from earlier states. In this case only Whistler's signature at the lower left (the signature at the upper right was present in the first state) and the name and address of the printer, Delâtre, at the lower right were added.

A sense of immediacy is characteristic of Whistler's etchings from his very earliest work in the medium; he preserved this quality throughout his etched oeuvre. In addition, the emphasis on the effects of sunlight as they dramatize the scene shows his early interest in the atmospheric phenomena that dominate the Venetian and Amsterdam etchings begun two decades later.

Impressions of *Liverdun* are known in brown ink as well as black, and those in the published set were apparently printed on chine appliqué. This sheet has a distinguished provenance, having been in the collection of Ralph Thomas, the first cataloguer of Whistler's etchings. The copper plate is in the Freer Gallery of Art.

LITERATURE: Fryberger, p. 15, no. 1; Mansfield, p. 11, no. 16; Naylor, p. xx, no. 7; Thomas, no. 2; Wedmore, p. 18, no. 4.

3. *The Unsafe Tenement, 1858*

One of the French Set

K. 17 2/4

Etching

6 3/8 x 8 13/16 in. (15.6 x 22.4 cm.)

Dark brown ink on medium-weight, antique, tan laid paper with dark flecks

Signed in plate lower right **Whistler;** *inscription by Seymour Haden in lower margin:* **Remarkable impression of the plate after the standing woman was replaced by the pitchfork but before the sky was removed as in published state. S. H.**

Provenance: Francis Seymour Haden (inscription); Henry Harper Benedict (Lugt 1298); purchased from Linda M. Papaharis (Christie's, New York, 26-27 March 1981, lot 332A)

Strong architectural elements and dark areas of shadow are countered by Whistler's selective attention to detail: light was his subject even here, where a large-scale and imposing structure dominates the image. The scratchy line that characterizes many of his earliest pieces is subsumed by a predominance of clearly articulated form.

Another scene from Whistler's trip to Alsace-Lorraine, this etching of a dilapidated farmhouse underwent two major changes. In the first state (prior to the one exhibited here) at the area to the left now occupied by a pitchfork, a woman stood sweeping. In the third state, as published, the lines that here are modulating the sky and hinting at cloud formations were nearly entirely removed, significantly altering the mood of the piece (fig. 3a). In addition to this, however, the third state was also considerably reworked throughout the area between the pitchfork and the child as well as in the shadow below the overhang at the left (figs. 3b and 3c). The changes are not of a sort characteristic of Whistler, and one wonders if Seymour Haden, who claimed that he had removed the lines in the sky for the published state of the subject, according to Kennedy, in fact, had reworked the plate even more fully. It does seem odd, however, that Whistler would have allowed Haden to work on a print he intended to publish, despite their close association at the time.

As Haden has commented in the margins, this impression of *The Unsafe Tenement* is a particularly fine one with unusually rich areas of plate tone. Impressions printed in black ink and brown on a variety of papers, Western and Oriental as well as on chine appliqué, are known.

NOTE: My thanks to Margaret F. MacDonald for discovering with me the extent to which this plate was reworked beyond the removal of the lines modulating the sky.

LITERATURE: Fryberger, p. 15, no. 2; Mansfield, p. 11, no. 17; Naylor, p. xx, no. 8; Wedmore, p. 19, no. 7; Wiehl, p. 22, no. 9.

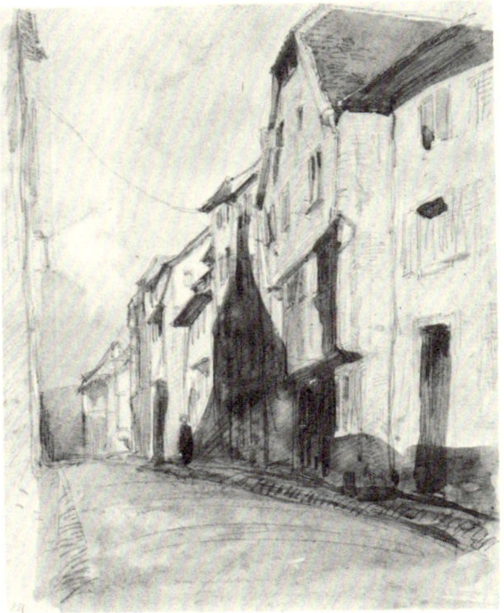

4a.
Street at Saverne
Pencil and watercolor
$11\frac{3}{4}$ x $9\frac{3}{16}$ in. (29.8 x 23.3 cm.)
Freer Gallery of Art

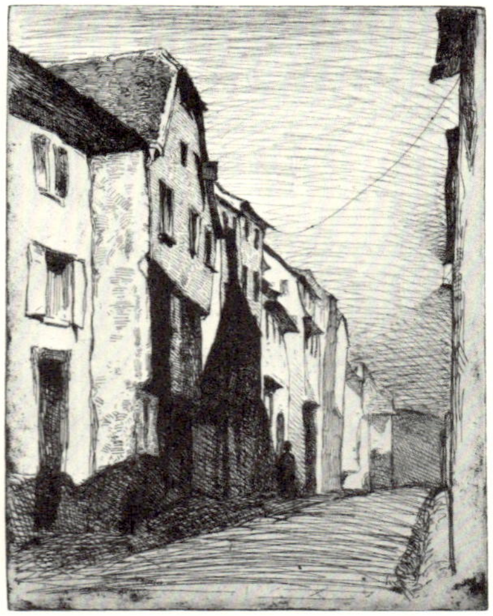

4b.
Street at Saverne, *K. 192 2/5*
$8\frac{1}{8}$ x $6\frac{3}{16}$ in. (20.6 x 15.7 cm.)
Freer Gallery of Art

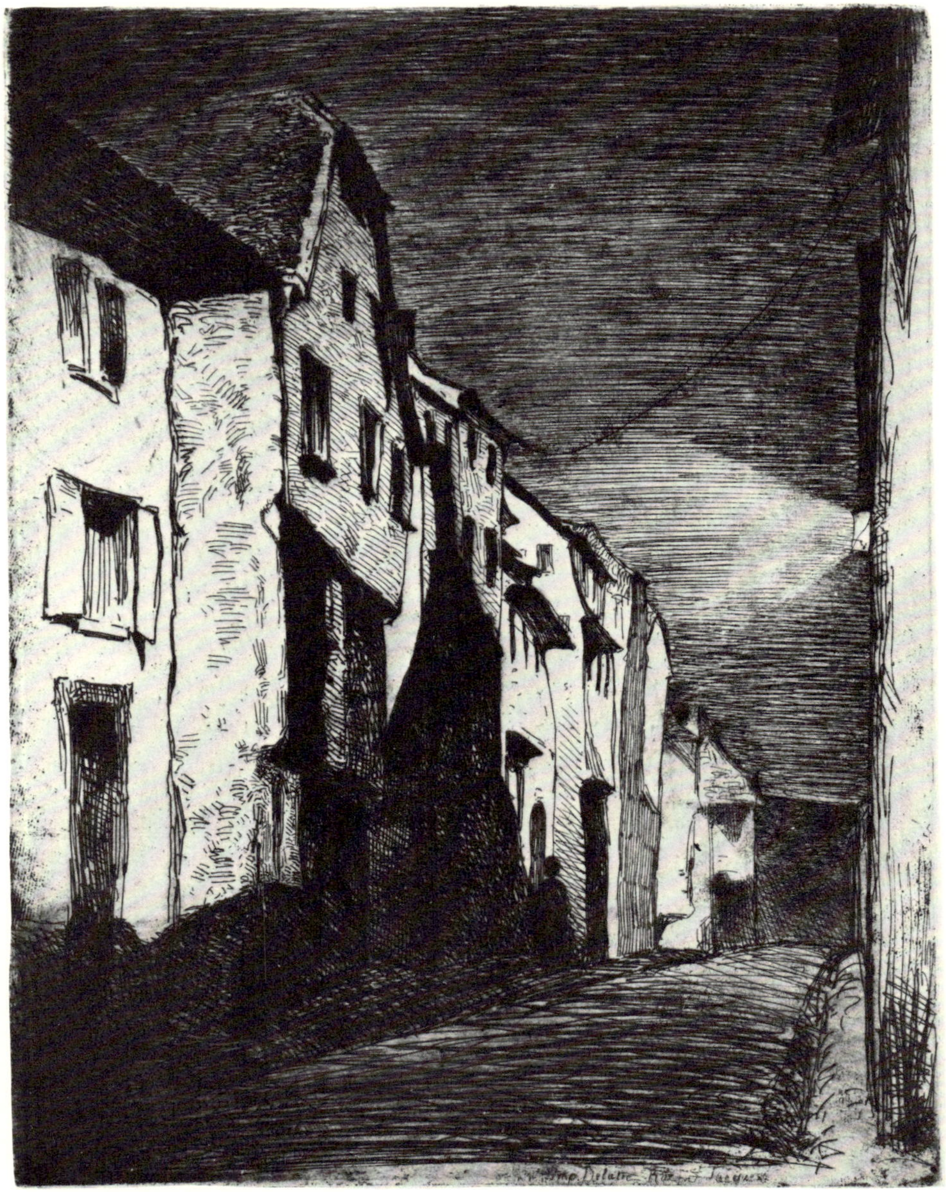

4. ***Street at Saverne,*** *1858*

One of the French Set

K. 19 4/5

Etching

8 3/16 x 6 1/4 in. (20.8 x 15.8 cm.)

Cool black ink on lightweight laid Oriental paper

Signed in plate lower left **Whistler**

Provenance: purchased from R. E. Lewis, Inc., 1970

A drawing for *Street at Saverne* (fig. 4a) in watercolor over pencil (in reverse) shows the handling of the drawn marks and strokes to be so similar to the print as to suggest that it was worked from the drawing rather than placed directly on copper at the site. The quality of light in the drawing, closer to the early states of the etching than the later states, indicates the time of day as dusk, just after the light at the left (of the drawing) would have been turned on.

Indeed, the light effects in the early states (fig. 4b) give no indication that the print will evolve into a true night piece. In them there is considerably less work in the sky, although light from the lamp, now at the right, does modulate its immediate area. As he progressed, Whistler removed many of his early lines, totally redrawing areas of the sky. He also relied on plate tone to enhance the nighttime aspect. An impression in the Boston Public Library, in the same state as that exhibited here, shows the lamp highlighted with white watercolor, giving it an exaggerated glow and emphasizing its contrast with the surrounding dark sky.

Saverne, in Alsace near Strasbourg, was on Whistler's route during his 1858 walking tour. Although not titled *Nocturne,* as Whistler's later night pieces were called, *Street at Saverne* is actually the artist's first etching of such a subject, and it is one of his most celebrated early works. It also is the first of his etchings depicting the view along a street, a theme that he frequently took up in later years (e.g., cat. nos. 24, 56, and 71).

In this impression of the published state, the areas most heavily etched are further enriched by a film of plate tone, particularly emphasizing the effects of the lantern light and moonlight on the buildings. Printed here on Oriental paper, the image is also found on a variety of Western papers and on blue- and cream-colored chine appliqué. The blue especially reinforces the nocturnal qualities of the image. The copper plate is in the Art Institute of Chicago.

LITERATURE: Fryberger, p. 16, no. 3; Getscher and Staley, p. 91, no. 55; Mansfield, p. 12, no. 19; Naylor, p. xx, no. 9; Wedmore, p. 20, no. 11; Wiehl, p. 31, no. 65.

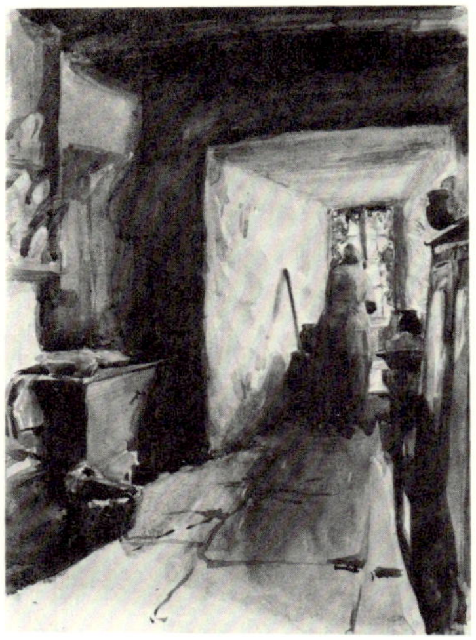

5a.
The Kitchen
Pencil and watercolor
12 x 7 3/4 in. (30.5 x 19.7 cm.)
Freer Gallery of Art

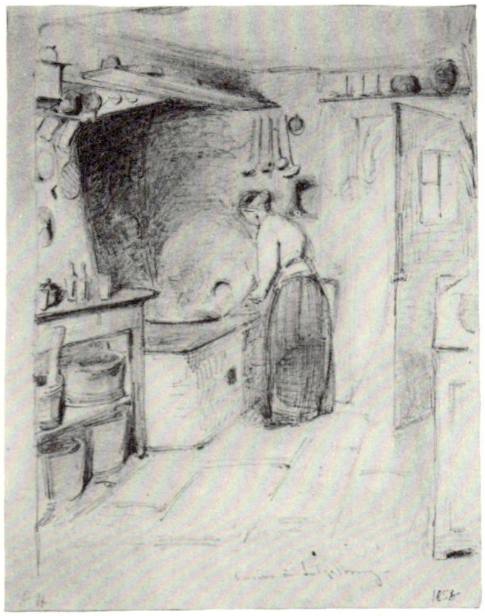

5b.
Cuisine à Lützelbourg
Pencil
8 7/16 x 6 5/16 in. (21.4 x 16.1 cm.)
Freer Gallery of Art

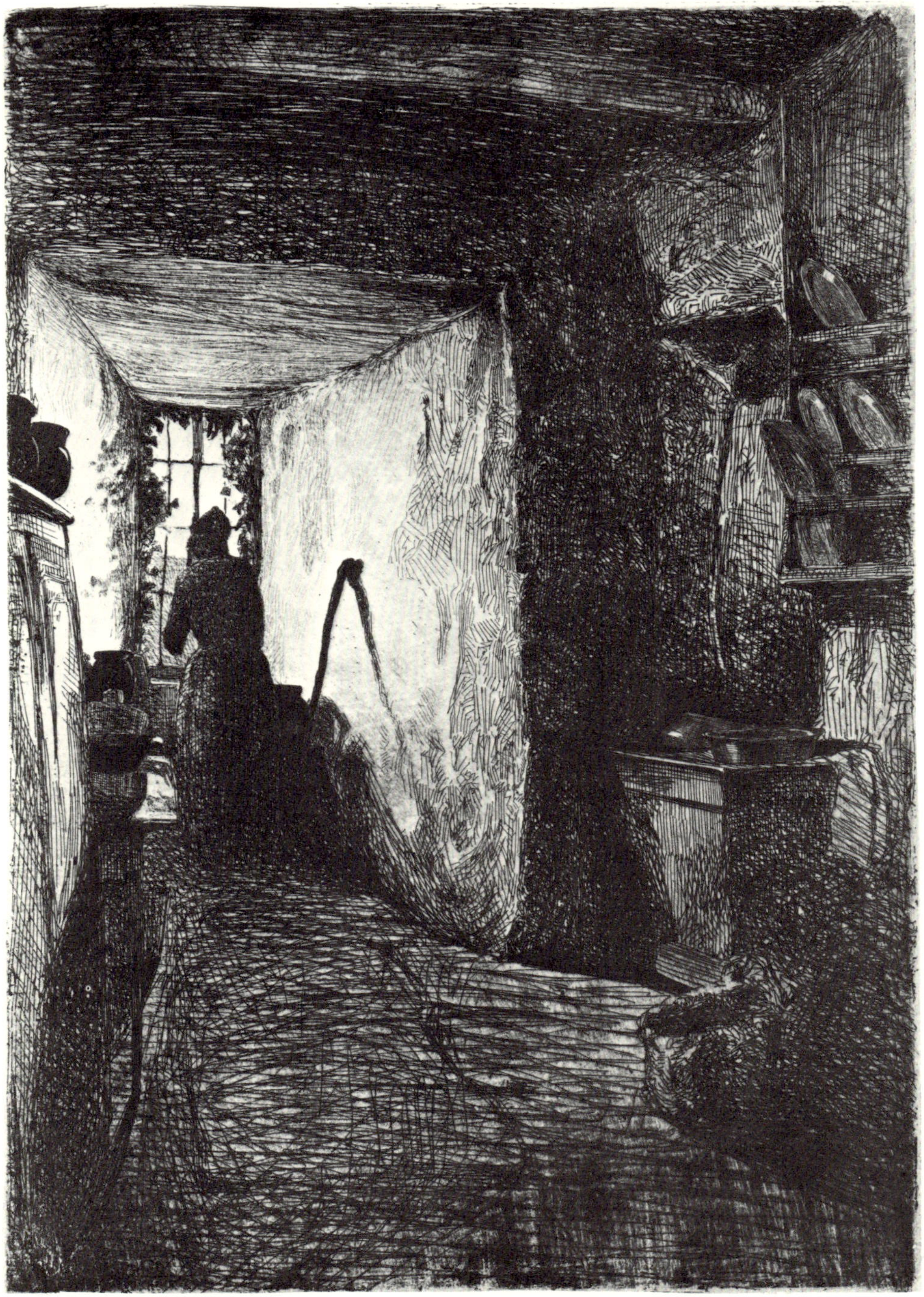

5. **The Kitchen,** *1858*

One of the French Set

K. 24 2-3/3

Etching

8 15/16 x 6 3/16 in. (22.7 x 15.7 cm.)

Dark brown ink on medium-weight, antique laid paper with watermark: CR surmounted by crown

Signed lower left on tab with butterfly and **imp**; *signed in plate lower right* **Whistler**

Provenance: purchased from Ira D. Gale, 1972

Kitchens are the subject of several of Whistler's early drawings. Among them is a rather fully realized study in watercolor over pencil (in reverse) for this etching (fig. 5a). Another pencil drawing, annotated *Cuisine à Lützelbourg* (fig. 5b), has been incorrectly listed by Mansfield and subsequent writers as the study for this etching. In fact, it is marked by many substantive differences.

The Kitchen, showing a peasant woman gazing through a window in her sparsely appointed home, was considered during Whistler's lifetime one of the most beautiful of the French Set. Thomas in 1874 praised this piece in particular for its "depth, tone, and Rembrandtish effect," calling it, in these respects, Whistler's most successful effort. Wedmore, writing some years after Thomas, compared it with a "chamber of De Hooch's." Indeed, *The Kitchen* is clear evidence of Whistler's interest in seventeenth-century Dutch art, an interest he maintained throughout his life.

Its special popular appeal no doubt encouraged Whistler to rework the copper plate for *The Kitchen* and print a new edition himself many years after its original execution; fifty impressions were thus issued by the Fine Art Society. According to both Mansfield and Kennedy, this reissue dates from 1885, but in one of Whistler's ledger books a receipt for fifty proofs of *The Kitchen,* one proof of the destroyed plate, and the cancelled plate itself is dated June 12, 1884. Assuming this receipt is not misdated, it seems more likely that the prints would have been released soon after, in 1884, not 1885.

The impression seen here is from this later period. It is undoubtedly one of the earlier ones printed, however, as it does not show various additions noted in many other impressions (e.g., work in the ceiling beam, on the floor, and beneath the dish shelves). In fact, there are at least three distinct states in this later issue, which Whistler worked in a way similar to the Venice etchings that were in process at the time *The Kitchen* was being reprinted. Influenced by his experiments in printing the Venice plates, that is, examining the effects of tonal wiping, the impressions of *The Kitchen* from the 1880s are printed in brown and greatly enhanced by rich surface tone, used in particular to emphasize the illumination in the window area. They also are marked by Whistler's butterfly tab. Earlier examples were printed in black as well as in brown. Delâtre's name and address were not removed for the 1885 edition.

LITERATURE: Fryberger, p. 16, no. 4; GUL Whistler, NB1, p. 106; Mansfield, p. 24, no. 24; Naylor, p. xx, no. 13; Thomas, no. 13; Wedmore, p. 23, no. 19.

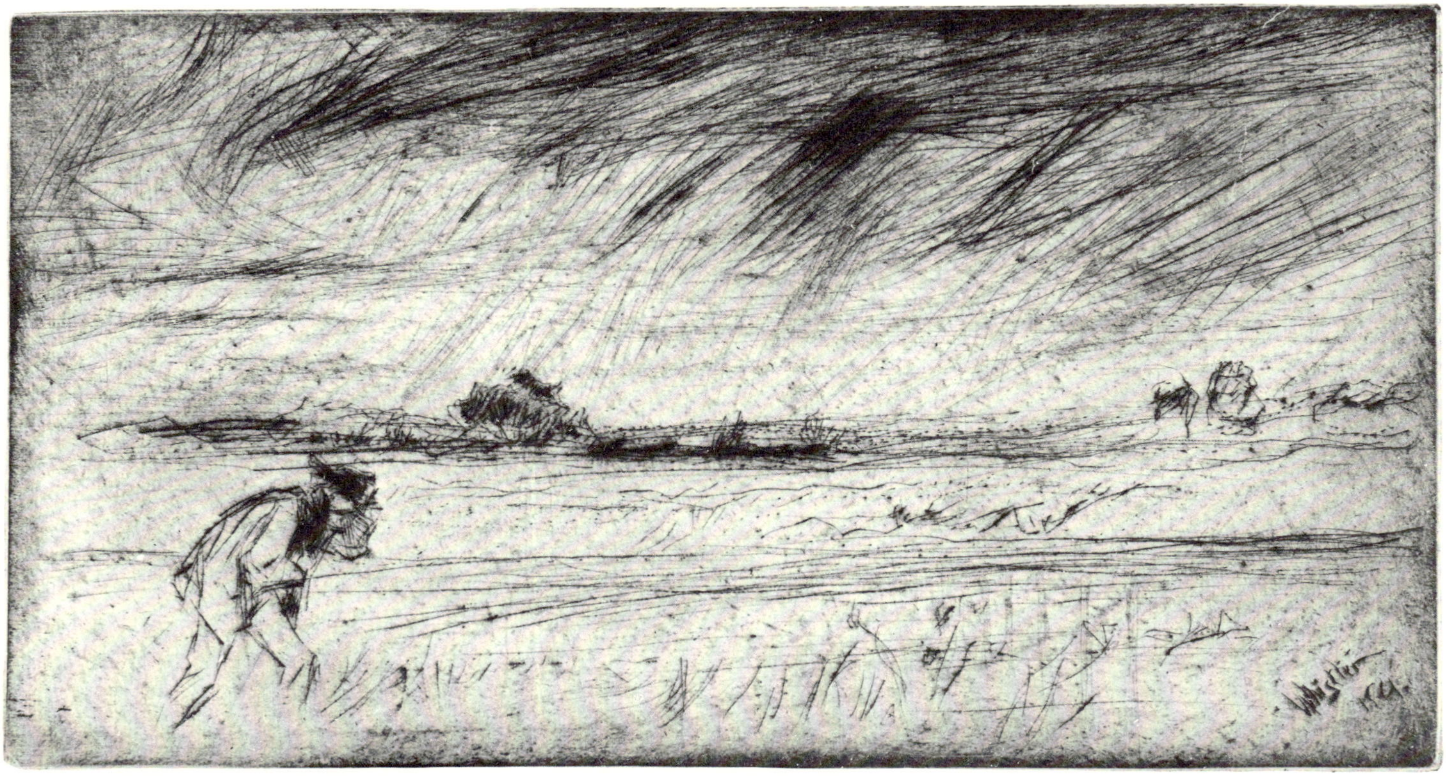

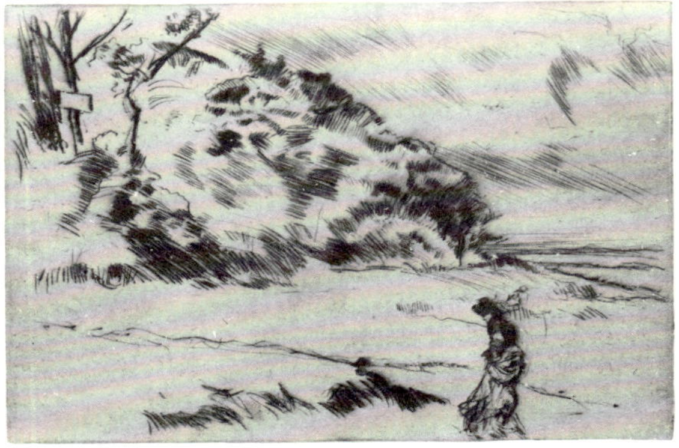

6a.
Speke Shore, *K. 144*
6 x 9 in. (15.2 x 22.9 cm.)
National Gallery of Art,
Rosenwald Collection

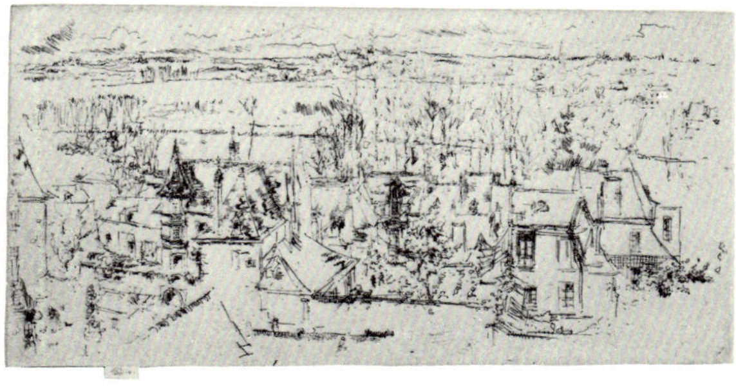

6b.
From Agnes Sorel's Walk, *K. 385*
5 1/4 x 10 1/2 in. (13.3 x 26.7 cm.)
Julius L. and Anita Zelman

6. *The Storm, 1861*

K. 81 only (after cancellation)

Drypoint

6 1/8 x 11 1/4 in. (15.6 x 28.6 cm.)

Black ink on medium-weight, antique, blue laid paper with unidentified watermark

Signed and dated in plate lower right

Whistler 1861

Provenance: anonymous collector's mark; purchased from R. M. Light & Co., Inc., 1981

The Storm is one of Whistler's early attempts at landscape, a subject that is not so unusual in his work as is generally stated. The location of this scene is unknown, but several of the 1861 drypoints were done in France, so that is one possibility. The format of the scene, a low horizontal band beneath a big sky, is quite Rembrandtesque, making *The Storm* an interesting example of Whistler's concern with another aspect of Dutch seventeenth-century art (see *The Kitchen*, cat. no. 5). The man hurrying along at the left is recorded as the artist Matthew Ridley, whose portrait Whistler later drew in drypoint (cat. no. 37). About a decade after *The Storm*, in *Speke Shore* (fig. 6a), Whistler attempted a somewhat similar landscape scheme, the modulations of the hillside replacing the activity of the stormy sky. His interest in landscape as a subject for etchings continued almost to the end of his career with examples like *From Agnes Sorel's Walk* (fig. 6b).

When Whistler's possessions were auctioned in 1880, one lot included "About 100 Copper Plates of Etchings, mostly erased." The buyer was Marcus Huish, acting for the Fine Art Society, which later published bound volumes of prints from the plates. (The various volumes have generally been dated to 1879. They contain seventy-six, fifty-seven, and forty-two of the plates respectively, including several known only in the cancelled states.) Among them was *The Storm*. Precancellation impressions are quite rare. It is highly likely that more than the four noted by Kennedy were printed, however, as they were available in the late 1870s, when Charles Augustus Howell was encouraging Whistler to print from plates made earlier. The weight one feels in the air as a storm descends is almost palpable in the densely drawn and darkly printed sky of the precancellation proofs.

Evidence of the cancellation is barely visible in two lines that cross the horizon about a third of the way from the right edge of the plate. One line is almost vertical, and the second one, to its right, is a diagonal. Known in brown ink as well as black and on both Oriental and Western papers, the postcancellation impressions, which are not common either, do show considerable wear.

LITERATURE: *Catalogue of the Decorative Porcelain, Cabinets, Paintings and other works of Art of J. A. McN. Whistler, removed from the White House, Fulham . . .* (Sotheby, Wilkinson & Hodge, London, 12-13 February 1880, lot 78); Fryberger, p. 21, no. 10; GUL Whistler, NB4, p. 9; Mansfield, p. 53, no. 83; Naylor, p. xxiv, no. 42; Wedmore, p. 45, no. 77; Wiehl, p. 30, no. 59 (regarding the albums of cancelled plates).

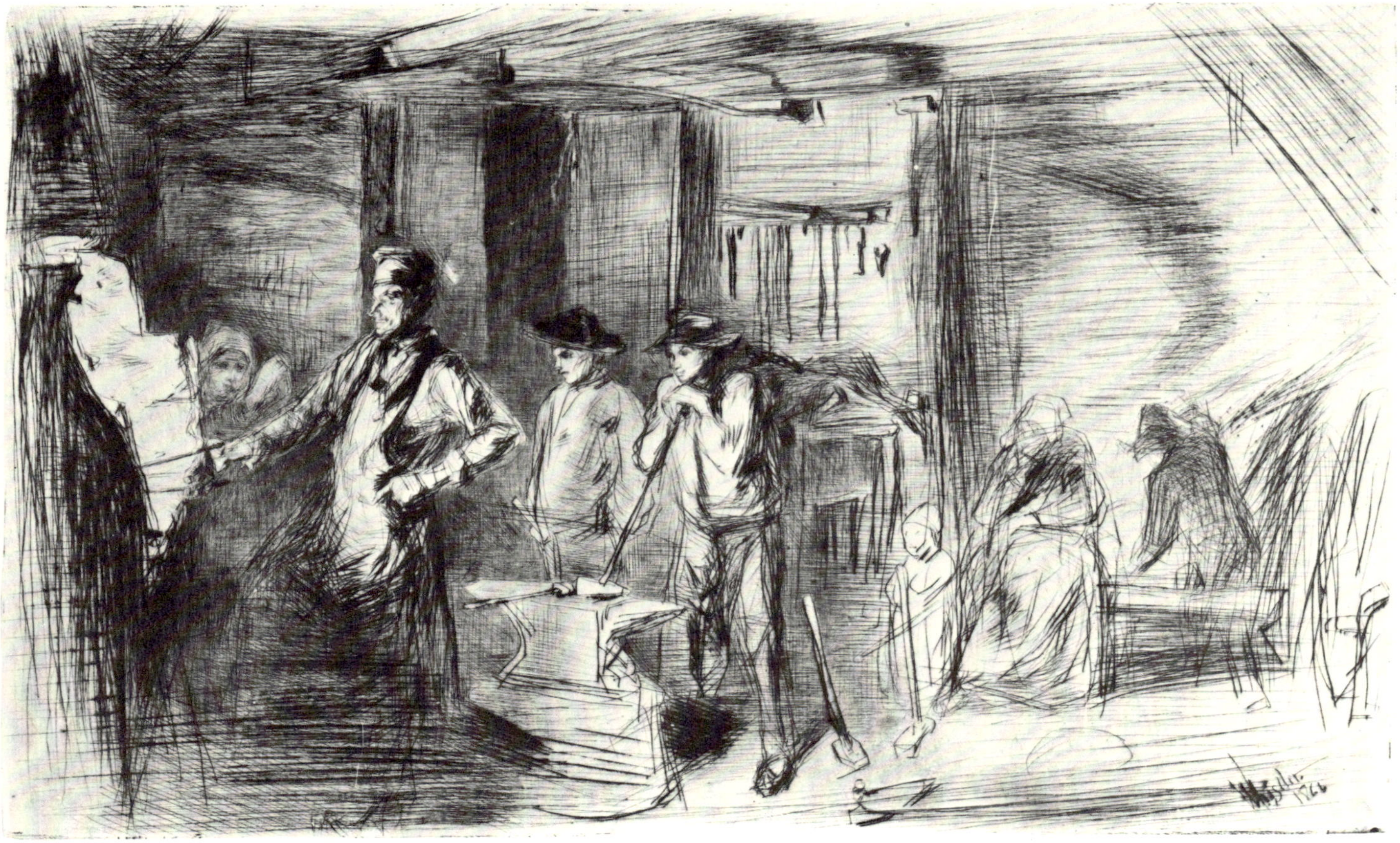

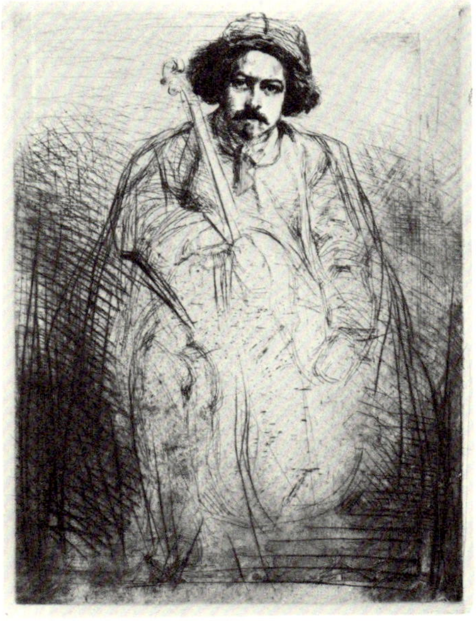

7a.
Becquet, *K. 52*
10 x 7 1/2 in. (25.4 x 19 cm.)
Julius L. and Anita Zelman

7. ***The Forge,** 1861*

One of the Thames Set

K. 68 3/4

Drypoint

7 3/4 x 12 1/2 in. (19.6 x 31.8 cm.)

Black ink on medium-weight laid

Oriental paper

Signed and dated in plate lower right

Whistler 1861

Provenance: purchased from

Kennedy Galleries, Inc., 1969

This is the sort of Whistler print that calls into play all of a connoisseur's skills. Even Thomas wrote in 1874, "The grand effect of this most magnificent drypoint can only be judged from the first proofs taken." Indeed, the drypoint wore down rapidly, and even fine impressions of the third state, such as this one, lack the brilliance of the very scarce earlier states. In them the areas of reflected light wiped clean are in vivid contrast to the velvety darkness of the spontaneous drypoint drawing. One must be cautious in studying various sheets because impressions of the fourth state, which are posthumous, according to Kennedy, look deceptively bright, the wear of the drypoint being compensated by the manipulation of surface tone.

The Forge, which was drawn at Perros-Guirec, on the coast of Brittany, and the portrait *Becquet* (fig. 7a) were the two non-Thames subjects included in the Thames Set. *The Forge* is the first of Whistler's forge/blacksmith prints, among which are a number of lithographs in addition to several etchings (e.g., cat. nos. 39 and 41). Although Whistler's autobiographical narration must always be read warily, it is worth noting that in *The Gentle Art of Making Enemies* he indicated that he had pulled proofs of all the Thames Set and that "indeed, one in the set of sixteen plates, a drypoint, called 'The Forge'... I alone printed."

Impressions of *The Forge* are most frequently printed in black ink on Oriental paper, but examples are known in brown ink and on various Western papers as well. The copper plate is in the Freer Gallery of Art.

LITERATURE: Fryberger, p. 20, no. 9; Getscher and Staley, p. 51, no. 23; Mansfield, p. 44, no. 68; Naylor, p. xxiii, no. 36; Thomas, no. 57; Wedmore, p. 41, no. 63; Whistler, p. 82; Wiehl, p. 31, no. 64.

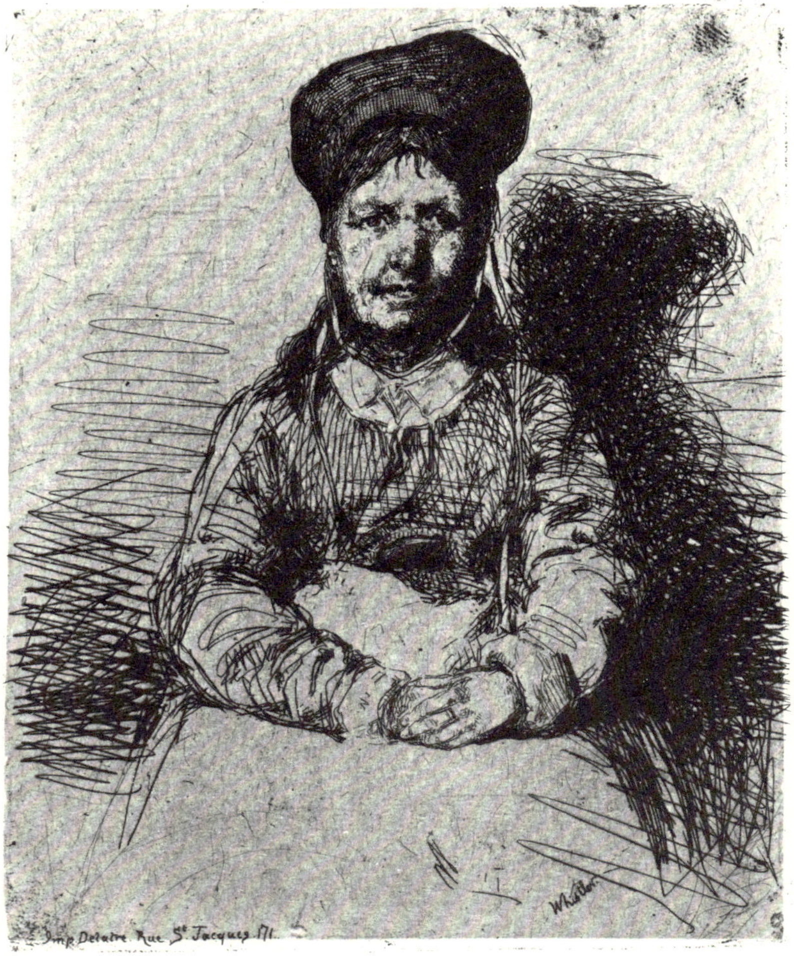
Imp. Delatre. Rue St Jacques 171.
Whistler

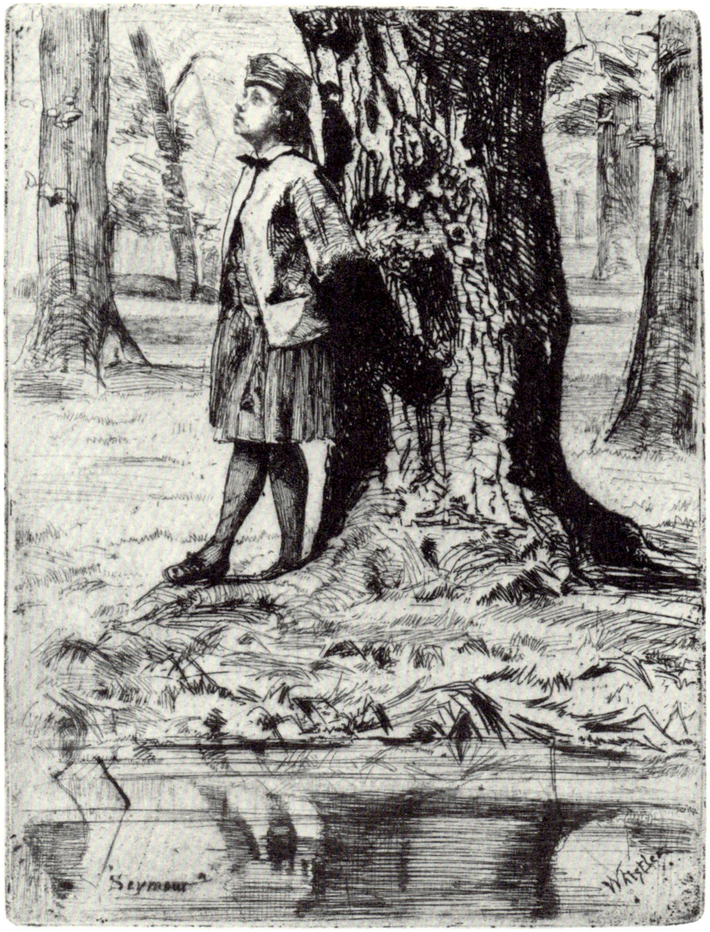
Seymour
Whistler

8. ***La Retameuse,*** *1858*

One of the French Set

K. 14 2/2

Etching

4 3/8 x 3 1/2 in. (11 x 8.8 cm.)

Warm black ink on tan chine appliqué

on heavy-weight wove paper

Signed lower right ***Whistler***

and in plate lower right ***Whistler***

Provenance: S. H. Nazeby Harrington

(Lugt 1347); purchased from

Kennedy Galleries, Inc., 1977

This middle-aged, French peasant, another subject from Whistler's 1858 walking tour, was among his earliest portraits. The intensity of her gaze suggests a strategy apparent in many later and more freely drawn encounters: direct confrontation between the artist and his subject (e.g., cat. no. 31). The image that results forcefully involves the viewer with the personality of the sitter.

Differences between this second state of the subject and the first state are few. Whistler added his name and the name and address of the printer, Delâtre. He also removed several lines in the background, although evidence of them remains in the light strokes seen above the etched lines on both sides of the woman's head. In part, early impressions can be distinguished from later ones by noting the extent to which these lines remain visible.

Printed on chine appliqué, this is an example of the French Set impressions as published. Second-state impressions printed directly onto the sheet are often seen as well. *La Retameuse* was printed in cool black ink as well as the warm black seen here.

LITERATURE: Mansfield, p. 8, no. 11; Naylor, p. xx, no. 5; Thomas, no. 3; Wedmore, p. 18, no. 5.

9. ***Seymour Standing under a Tree,*** *1859**

K. 31 2/3

Etching and drypoint

5 1/4 x 3 13/16 in. (13.3 x 9.8 cm.)

Black ink on lightweight, antique laid

paper with partial watermark:

shield with fleur-de-lis

Signed in plate lower right ***Whistler;***

inscribed in plate lower left ***Seymour***

Provenance: purchased from

Stendahl Gallery, 1971

The children of Whistler's half-sister, Deborah, and her husband, Seymour Haden, provided Whistler with subjects for almost a dozen prints during the late 1850s and early 1860s. This one depicts young Arthur Seymour, possibly in Greenwich Park, although other parklike places were the settings for several etchings of the period. *Seymour Standing under a Tree* is interesting as an example of Whistler's early landscapes as well as an example of his portraiture; his concern seems equally devoted to both aspects of the subject. The print also shows that Whistler, even in his youth, was intrigued with reflections on water. He later came to depict them with far greater elaboration and sophistication in the Venice and Amsterdam etchings (e.g., cat. nos. 54 and 85).

In the exceedingly rare first state of this subject, the inscription *Seymour* is lacking. The etching is generally printed in black ink, usually, but not always, on paper of Western origin. The copper plate is in the Freer Gallery of Art.

LITERATURE: Mansfield, p. 20, no. 32; Thomas, no. 17; Wedmore, p. 25, no. 23.

*Dates followed by an asterisk were confirmed or suggested by Katharine A. Lochnan in correspondence with the author (19 July 1983).

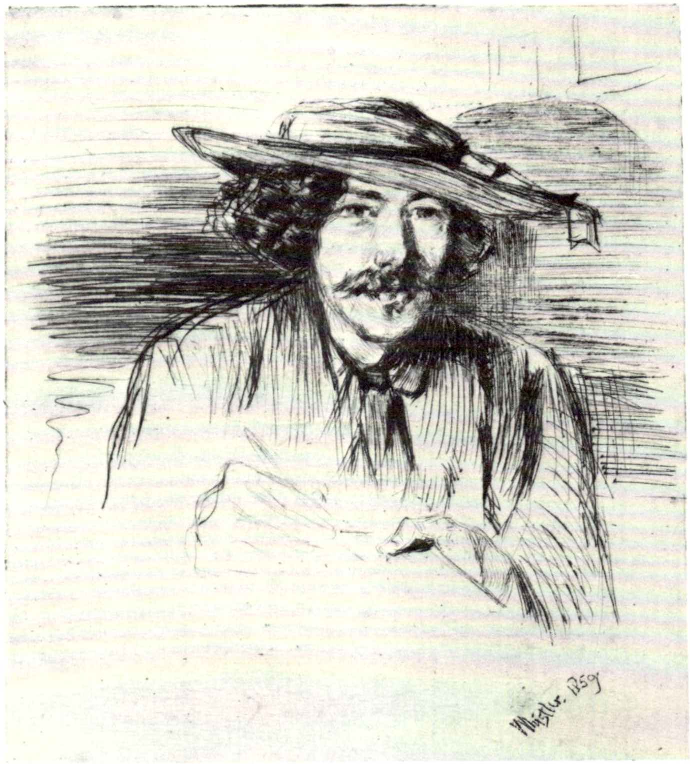

Portrait of Whistler *is shown in its entirety but trimmed above the plate mark.*

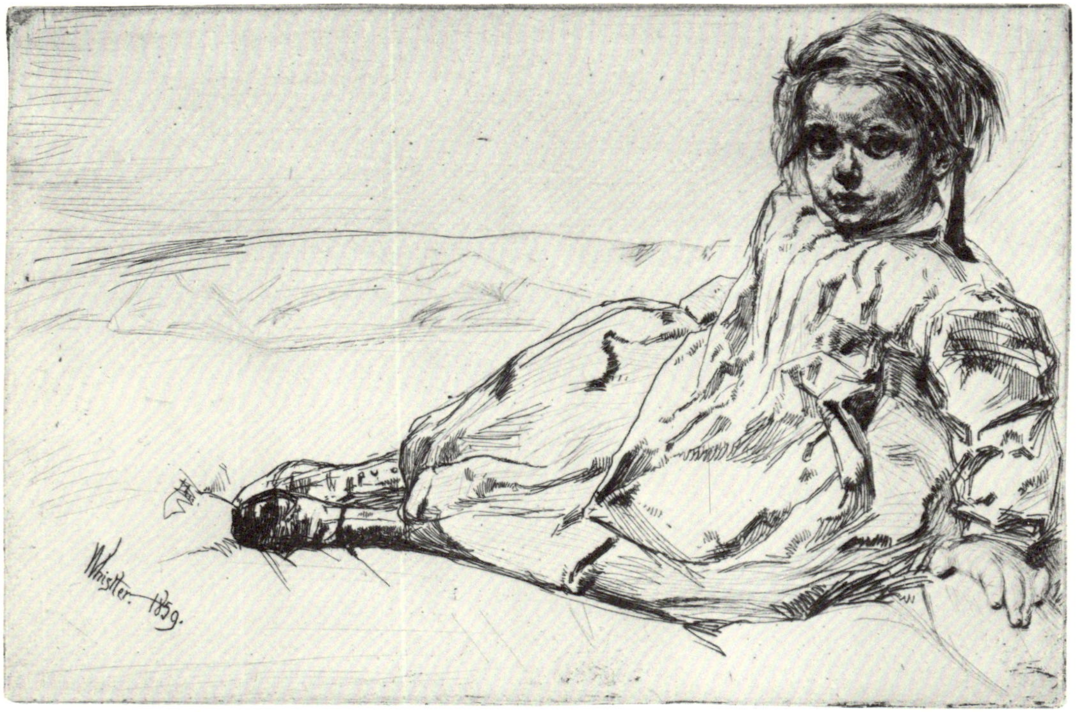

10. ***Portrait of Whistler,*** *1859*

K. 54 1/2

Etching and drypoint

8 15/16 x 6 in. (22.7 x 15.2 cm.)

Black ink on lightweight laid

Oriental paper

Signed and dated in plate lower right

Whistler 1859

Provenance: Emma Regina Martin (initials);

anonymous collector's mark;

purchased from R. M. Light & Co., Inc.,

1982

This is the second of Whistler's three self-portrait prints, the other two (K. 7 and 172) being much more difficult to find. Here, in Paris, at age twenty-five, with his student years coming to an end, Whistler concentrated on his head, particularly his gaze, all but excluding his hands and their important activity of drawing on the etching plate. Small areas of rich drypoint emphasize facial features and the complexities of the artist's curly hair. In the second, and final, state of the print, the crown and wide brim of Whistler's well-known straw boater were more heavily shaded.

First-state impressions are not especially rare. Both states are generally printed in black ink on a variety of papers. The copper plate was among those acquired by the Fine Art Society in 1880 at the auction of Whistler's possessions.

LITERATURE: MacDonald, p. 14, no. 1; Mansfield, p. 35, no 54; Naylor, p. xxii, no. 29; Thomas, no. 65; Wedmore, p. 36, no. 52.

11. ***Bibi Valentin,*** *1859*

K. 50 2/2

Etching and drypoint

6 x 8 7/8 in. (15.1 x 22.5 cm.)

Black ink on medium-weight,

antique laid paper with partial watermark:

VDL surmounted by shield with

fleur-de-lis

Signed and dated in plate lower left

Whistler 1859

Provenance: purchased from

R. E. Lewis, Inc., 1970

An inscription by Seymour Haden on an impression of *Bibi Valentin* in the Freer Gallery offers the information that Whistler's first etching was made in the home of Bibi Valentin's father, A. Valentin, an etcher and engraver who was among Whistler's Parisian friends.

Whistler's attention to the entire figure of the child has called for no sacrifice to the successful expressiveness of the head, and great care is devoted to the feet and the hand, the latter being completed in this second state. The "pinafore," Wedmore's term for the frock, is first apprehended as a massive shape on the surface, but the crucially placed shadows work to create a spatially structured figure. This kind of structuring was to be explored throughout Whistler's career, first, with much greater fluidity (e.g., cat. no. 36) and, later, with a new kind of taut precision (e.g., cat. no. 77).

This impression is a rich one, printed with *retroussage* (ink pulled from the lines during the final stages of printing to enrich the surface immediately surrounding them). This use of retroussage may be to compensate for the wear already apparent in the drypoint. *Bibi Valentin* is generally printed in black ink, often, but obviously not always, on Oriental papers.

LITERATURE: Mansfield, p. 32, no. 50; Thomas, no. 26; Wedmore, p. 27, no. 28.

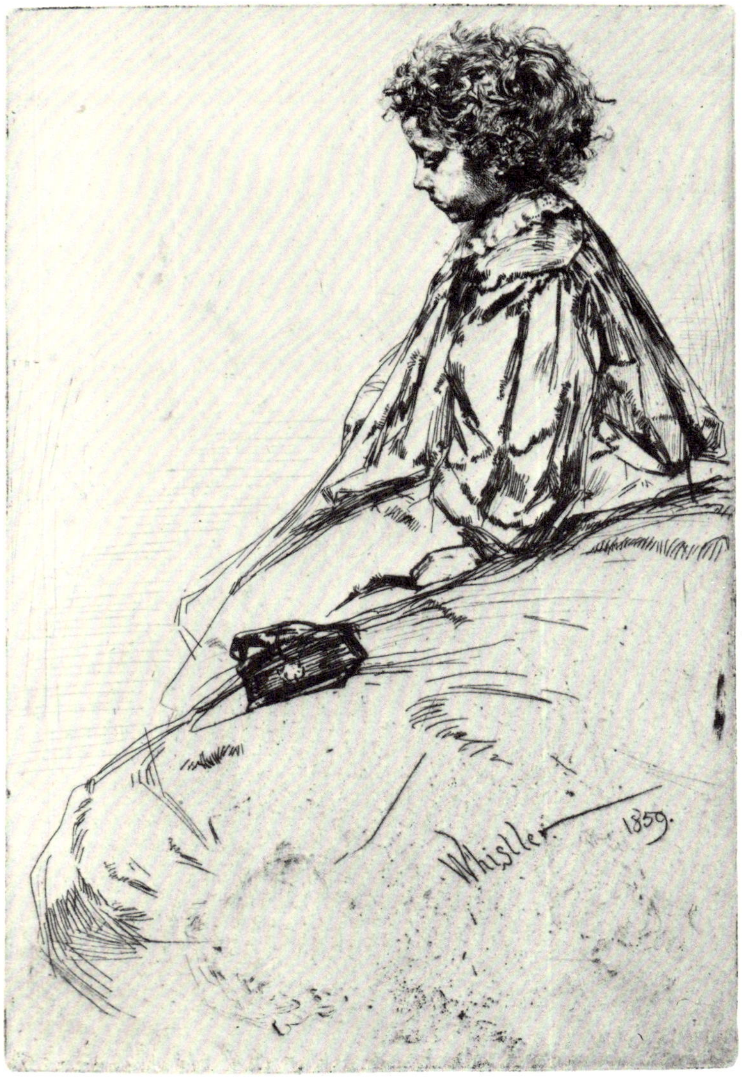
Whistler 1859.

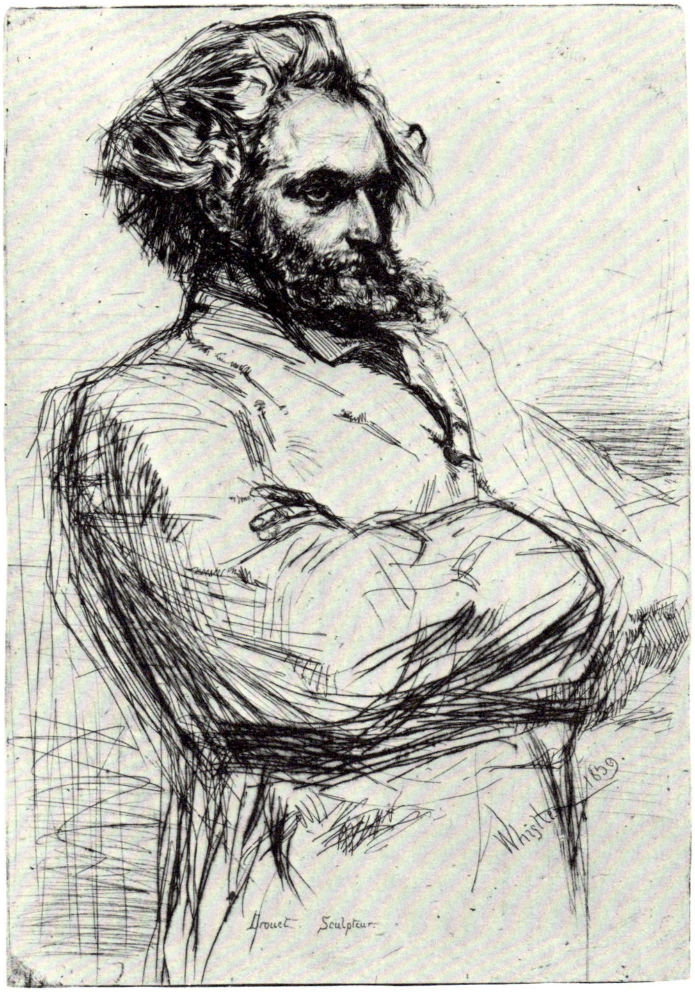
Whistler 1859
Drouet Sculpteur

12. *Bibi Lalouette, 1859*

K. 51 2/2

Etching and drypoint

8 15/16 x 5 15/16 in. (22.7 x 15.1 cm.)

Black ink on medium-weight Oriental paper

Signed and dated in plate lower right ***Whistler 1859***

Provenance: purchased from Kennedy Galleries, Inc., 1976

Bibi Lalouette's father owned a *pension* where the Société des Trois (Whistler, Henri Fantin-Latour, and Alphonse Legros) often ate meals during their student days. The profile approach to the little boy's head, somewhat unusual among Whistler's portraits, is also seen in *Jo's Bent Head* (cat. no. 15). Here, it would seem, Whistler must have adored Bibi Lalouette's curly hair (not unlike his own, see cat. no. 10) and did all that he could to emphasize it.

The remains of two heads that were removed after the first state can be seen at the bottom of the plate. It was not unusual for Whistler to turn plates upside down and reuse them like this or for drawings to be rubbed out and the sheets turned upside down and used as if new. The only other change here from the earlier state is the addition of the horizontal lines on both sides of the child.

Impressions of this subject are generally printed in black ink and are seen on a variety of Western (including a bluish sheet) and Oriental papers. An impression of the second state printed on satin is in the collection of the Art Gallery of Ontario.

LITERATURE: Mansfield, p. 33, no. 51; Naylor, p. xxii, no. 27; Thomas, no. 30; Wedmore, p. 28, no. 30.

13. *Drouet, 1859*

K. 55 2/2

Etching and drypoint

8 7/8 x 6 in. (22.5 x 15.2 cm.)

Black ink on lightweight laid Oriental paper

Signed and dated in plate lower right ***Whistler 1859****; inscribed barely visibly in plate upper right* ***Whistler maitre eau forte****; inscribed in plate lower center* ***Drouet Sculpteur***

Provenance: Sir John Day (Lugt 526); purchased from R. M. Light & Co., Inc., 1971

Critics of Whistler's first one-man show at the Flemish Gallery, Pall Mall, consistently praised the drypoints and etchings: "so highly and so justly esteemed for their truth and beauty, as well as their marvelous technical skill. Among them are some fine portrait heads, notably that of M. Drouet, the French sculptor." Charles Drouet and Whistler remained in contact for decades after the completion of this portrait. Their correspondence includes a letter of condolence at the time of Beatrix Whistler's death.

Drouet's powerful head is countered by the general forcefulness of the rest of the drawing and augmented by the essential strength and organization of the balanced composition. Rich impressions like this one are rare, and it is essential to see one like this to understand Whistler's conception. Considerable wear of the drypoint quite rapidly took its toll, especially in the shadowy area beneath the sculptor's folded arms.

Drouet was one of the cancelled plates acquired and published by the Fine Art Society in 1880. As with *The Storm* (cat. no. 6), the cancellation marks on the *Drouet* plate were rather easily effaced, and the original lines, redrawn; it is exceedingly difficult to identify impressions made after the cancellation was removed. When closely compared with a precancellation impression, such as the one exhibited here, however, one can see a slight difference at the bridge of the nose.

Generally printed in black ink, impressions are seen on a variety of papers.

LITERATURE: GUL Whistler, D165; GUL Whistler, PC1, p. 67; Mansfield, p. 35, no. 55; Wedmore, p. 37, no. 53; Wiehl, p. 30, nos. 59–61.

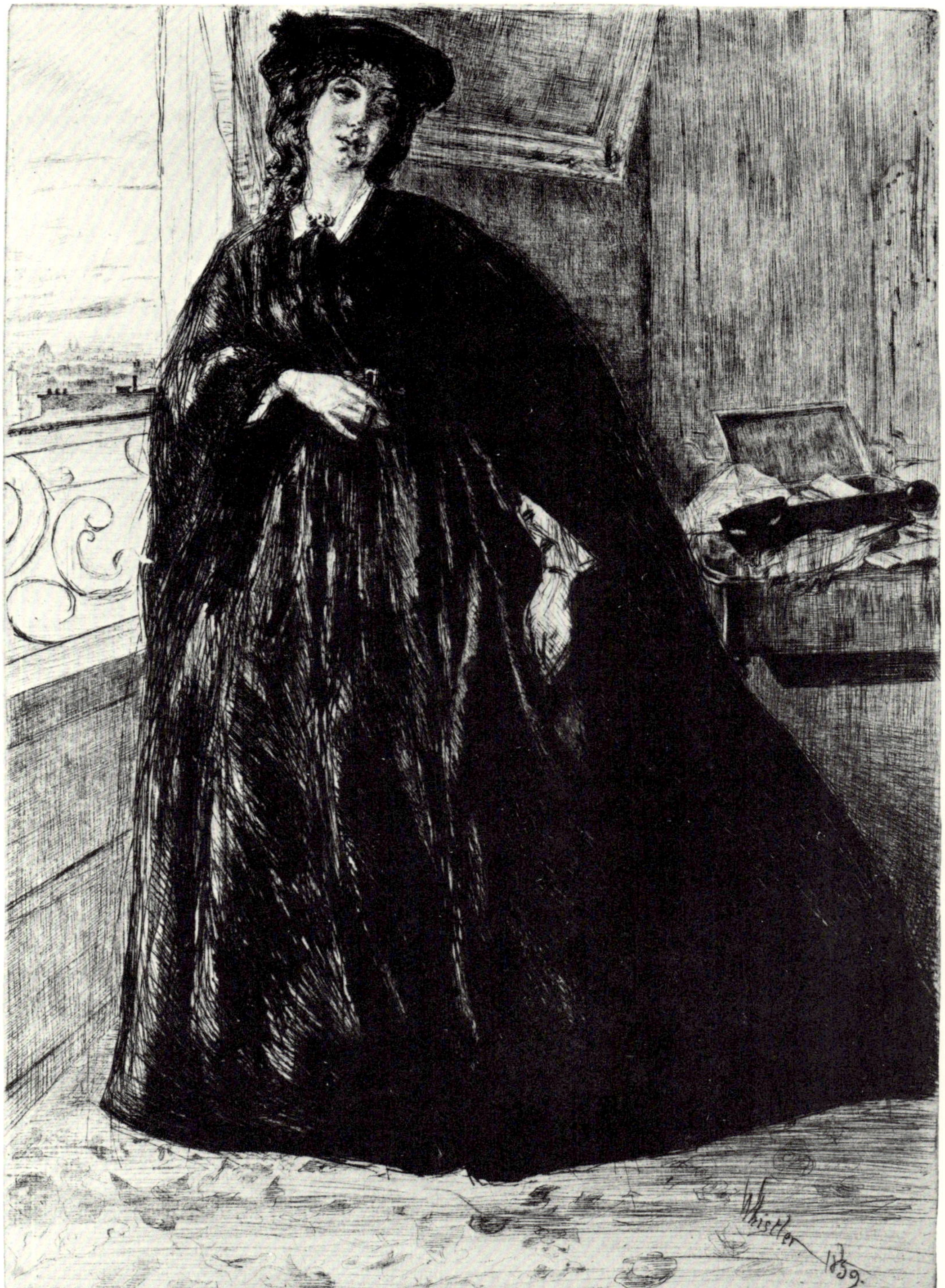
Whistler
1859.

14. *Finette, 1859*

K. 58 9/10

Etching and drypoint

11 1/4 x 7 13/16 in. (28.6 x 19.9 cm.)

Black ink on lightweight, antique laid paper

Signed lower left ***Whistler****; signed and dated in plate lower right* ***Whistler 1859***

Provenance: purchased from Kennedy Galleries, Inc., 1969

This is the most elaborately worked of Whistler's early prints, going through several more state changes than the ten listed by Kennedy. Even Thomas, whose 1874 catalogue rarely discusses states, mentions several rare early ones for *Finette* and notes also the "jealously guarded proofs of this splendid drypoint." Not until the standing portrait of Maude (cat. no. 34) more than a decade later does Whistler again involve himself with so many subtle adjustments to an image.

Finette, according to Pennell, "was a *cocotte,* very elegant, who sometimes danced the *cancan* in the dancing places." Wedmore suggested that this portrait shows her at the window of her fifth-floor Boulevard Montmartre flat. An impression in the New York Public Library is inscribed by Whistler *Lady in Blue Dress.*

In revising his etchings, Whistler often drew on his proofs, and a number of hand-touched impressions are known for *Finette,* showing changes similar to those illustrated for the later portrait of Maude. The ninth state, exhibited here, essentially represents the completed image. Whistler later made a few minor additions and burnished certain areas as if in preparation for further reworking. Instead, he cancelled the plate, and it was among those acquired by the Fine Art Society in 1880.

Though impressions exist in brown ink, most were printed in black on a variety of papers, most frequently Oriental. The copper plate is in the Hunterian Art Gallery, University of Glasgow.

LITERATURE: Getscher and Staley, p. 27, no. 5; Mansfield, p. 37, no. 58; Pennell and Pennell (1921), p. 91; Thomas, no. 56; Wedmore, p. 37, no. 54.

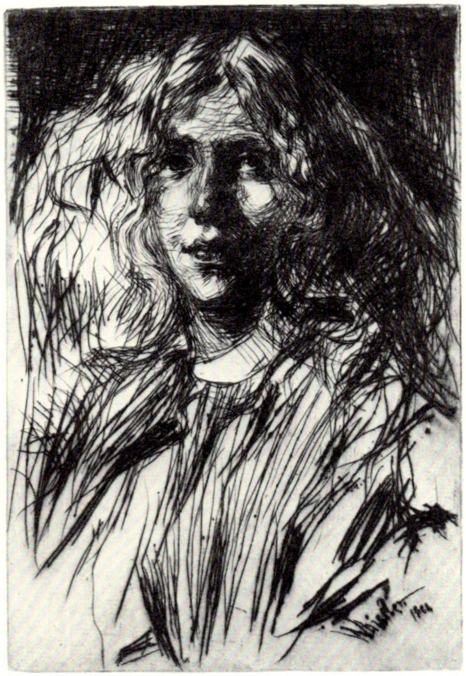

15a.
***Jo,** K. 77*
9 x 6 in. (22.9 x 15.2 cm.)
National Gallery of Art,
Rosenwald Collection

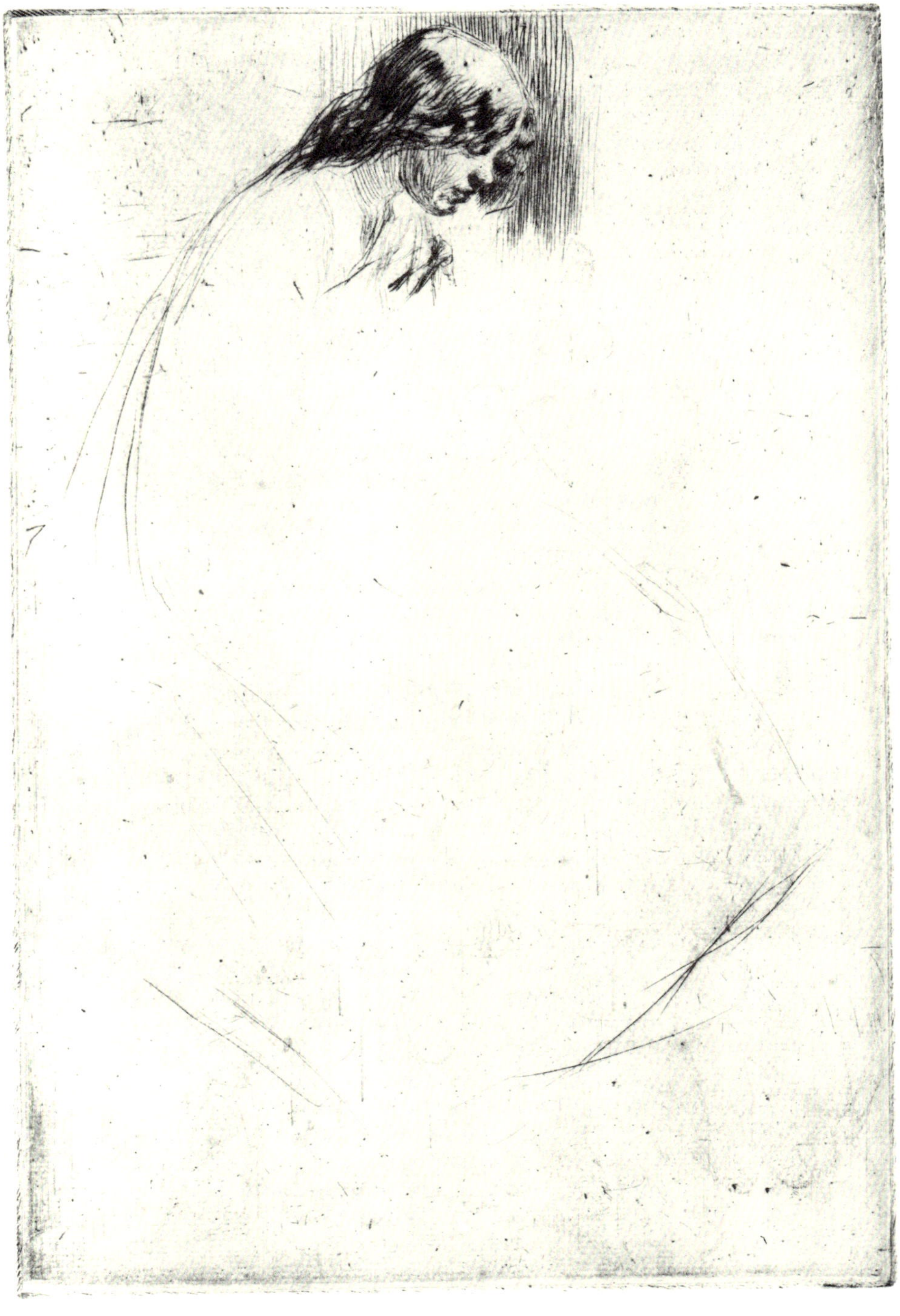

15. *Jo's Bent Head, 1861**

K. 78 2/2

Drypoint

9 x 5 15/16 in. (22.8 x 15 cm.)

Black ink on medium-weight laid paper with watermark: No 1 in a diamond

Unsigned

Provenance: purchased from R. E. Lewis, Inc. (Sotheby's, 26 May 1978, lot 300)

Jo is Joanna Hiffernan, Whistler's mistress and model throughout the early 1860s. She was the model for *Symphony in White, No. 1: The White Girl* (1862), Whistler's early painting (Young et al., 38), for *Weary* (fig. XI), the most Pre-Raphaelite of all of his etchings, and for *Jo* (fig. 15a), one of his most dynamic drypoint portrait heads. Even in so daringly spare a picture as *Jo's Bent Head,* Whistler's affection for his subject is evident. Though it is not the sort of image that one would expect to be popular with the general public, Whistler himself obviously thought highly of the plate as he continued to print it over a long period of time: impressions are thought to date from as late as the 1880s.

In the second state, a few lines lacking in the exceedingly rare first state have been added, further defining the right edge of the skirt. The use of plate tone to enhance the line work varies enormously from impression to impression. Cleanly wiped sheets like the present one may be contrasted with those that are virtually covered with a sensuous layer of surface ink (see reproduction, Getscher and Staley, p. 32).

Printed in brown ink as well as in black, the subject is generally found on Western papers. The copper plate is in the Humanities Research Center Art Collection, the University of Texas at Austin.

LITERATURE: Getscher and Staley, p. 33, no. 10; Mansfield, p. 52, no. 78; Naylor, p. xxiv, no. 41; Wiehl, p. 23, no. 17.

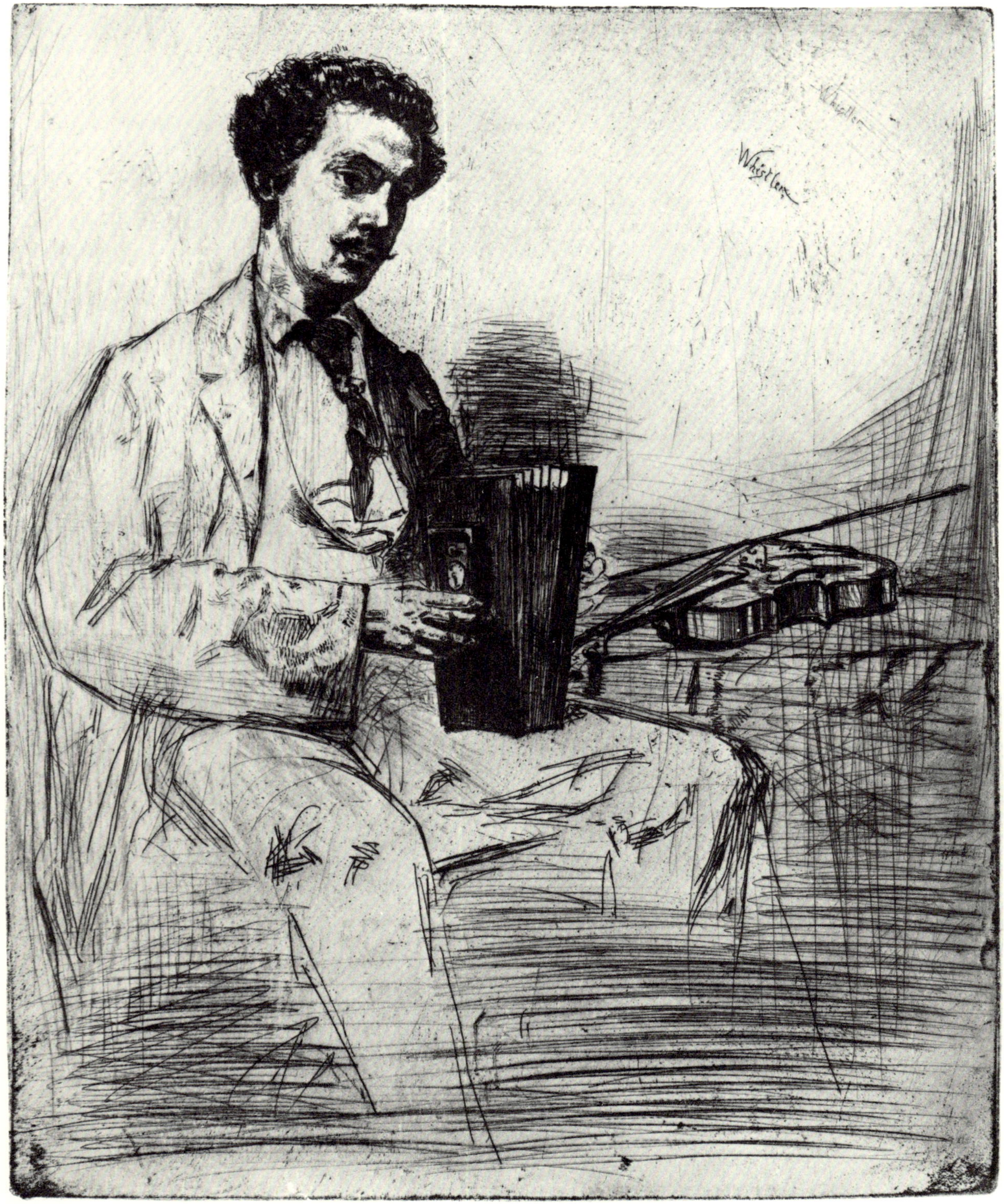
Whistler

16. *Ross Winans, 1861**

K. 88 1/2

Etching and drypoint

9 13/16 x 7 7/8 in. (24.9 x 20 cm.)

Warm black ink on medium-weight laid paper

Signed twice in plate upper right

Whistler

Provenance: Howard Mansfield (Lugt 1342); Harris G. Whittemore (Lugt 1384a); anonymous collector's stamp; purchased from R. M. Light & Co., Inc., 1981

Ross Winans's father, also named Ross Winans, owned the Baltimore locomotive works that provided equipment for the railroad Whistler's father built between Moscow and St. Petersburg during the 1840s. In 1854 Whistler's eldest brother, George, married one of the Winans and became a partner in the family business. That same year, Whistler worked for a few months as a draftsman for the locomotive firm, prior to his stint, also brief, in Washington with the U.S. Coast and Geodetic Survey.

This portrait is one of several etchings Whistler made of friends and associates in the early 1860s. (Earlier, during his months in Baltimore, he had made an amusing caricature portrait of Winans playing the violin [reproduced Pressley, fig. 36].) Whistler's real concern here was with Winans's head and face, with his musical instruments, and with the formal devices that would connect them, such as his necktie and the shadows on his left shoulder and above the accordion. The rest of the piece is rather rapidly drawn and without distinction.

This is one of several pieces in the exhibition originally in the collection of one of Whistler's cataloguers, Howard Mansfield. The Mansfield collection was formed with extensive assistance from the artist.

Impressions of *Ross Winans* are rather rare. This is an especially fine one, made before the few additions to the sleeve that constituted a second state. The portrait was printed in brown or warm black inks on a variety of papers; a first-state impression in the New York Public Library is on chine appliqué. The copper plate is in the Hunterian Art Gallery, University of Glasgow.

LITERATURE: Donnelly and Thorp, pp. 6–8, 29; Mansfield, p. 56, no. 88; Naylor, p. xxiv, no. 44; Nancy Dorfman Pressley, "Whistler in America: An Album of Early Drawings," *Metropolitan Museum Journal* 5 (1972): 147; Thomas, no. 67; Wedmore, p. 45, no. 76.

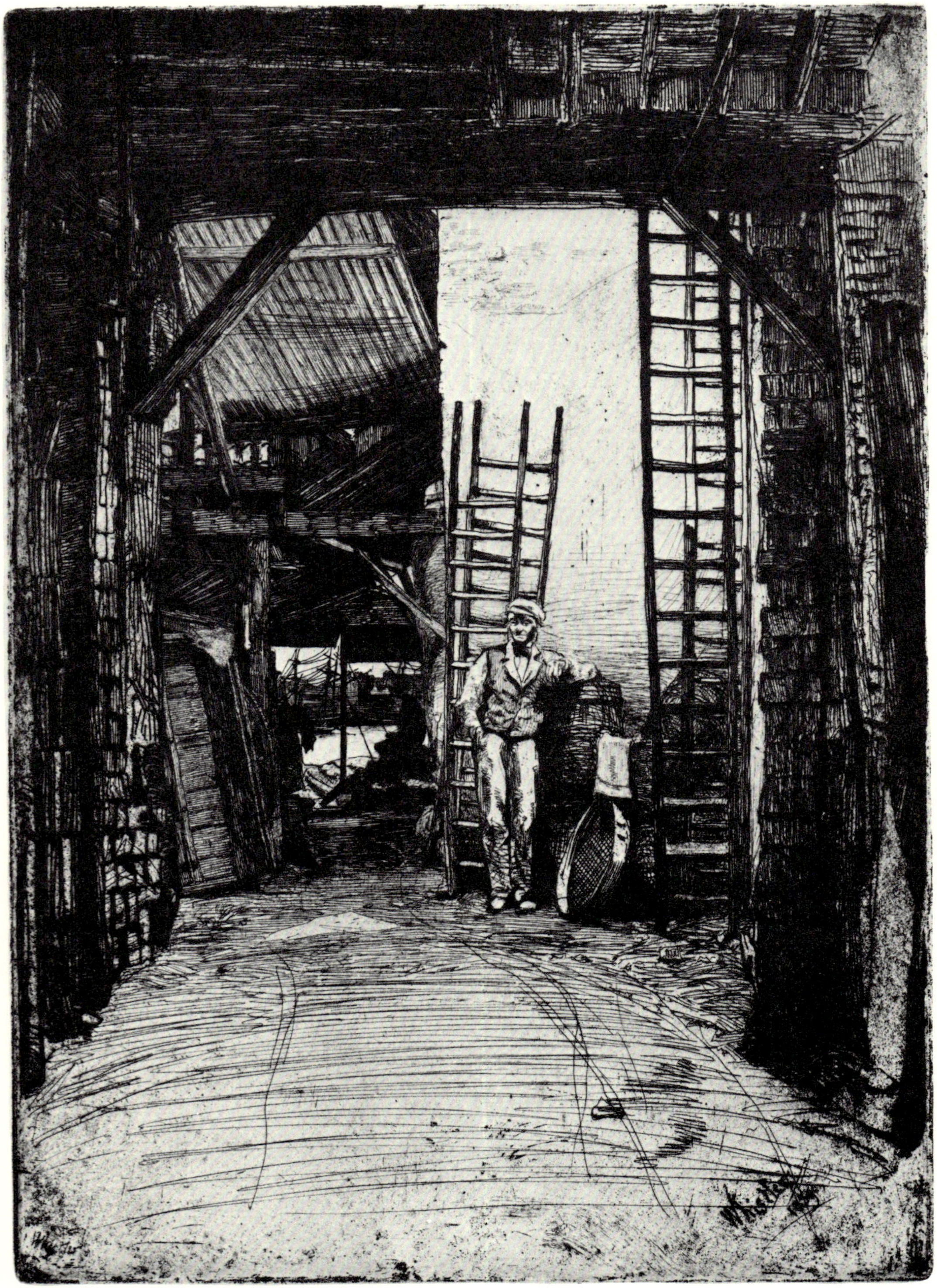

17. **The Lime-Burner,** 1859

One of the Thames Set

K. 46 1/2

Etching and drypoint

9 15/16 x 6 15/16 in. (25.2 x 17.6 cm.)

Warm black ink on medium-weight laid paper

Signed in plate lower left and lower right ***Whistler****; dated in plate lower right* ***1859***

Provenance: purchased from R. M. Light & Co., Inc., 1971

The Lime-Burner is a forceful, early example of Whistler's frame-within-a-frame imagery. The central figure is seen through a timbered entranceway, standing in a courtyard. Behind and to the left, another doorwaylike opening reveals glimpses of the shipping and factory life along the Thames, while a lean-to structure frames a dark, seated figure. The obscurity of this second figure presents a marked contrast to the portraitlike specificity of the lime-burner, who directly confronts the viewer with his gaze. Likewise, the darkness of the beams and shadows is countered by the stark white wall behind him. Like the rich and varied character of Whistler's drawing style (see cat. no. 18), the properties of light and shadow seen here and the dramatic contrasts they facilitate are important aspects in the evolution of Whistler's pictorial scheme.

Titled *W. Jones, Lime-Burner, Thames Street,* the etching was exhibited in 1860 at the Royal Academy. This impression is in the first state (which is not especially rare), before the addition of light, perpendicular lines to the right of Jones's right shoulder. If Mansfield is correct, that it was published in the second state in 1871, this would be among the earlier impressions printed by Whistler or Delâtre.

The print is known on both Western and Oriental papers. Most are printed in black, but there are exceptions in brown, including a first state in the Freer Gallery of Art which Whistler presumably liked as it is inscribed *For Mother/from J. Whistler.* The copper plate is in the Freer Gallery as well.

LITERATURE: Fryberger, p. 19, no. 6; Getscher, p. 51; Getscher and Staley, p. 47, no. 22; Mansfield, p. 29, no. 45; Naylor, p. xxii, no. 25; Thomas, no. 38; Wedmore, p. 33, no. 44; Wiehl, p. 22, no. 11.

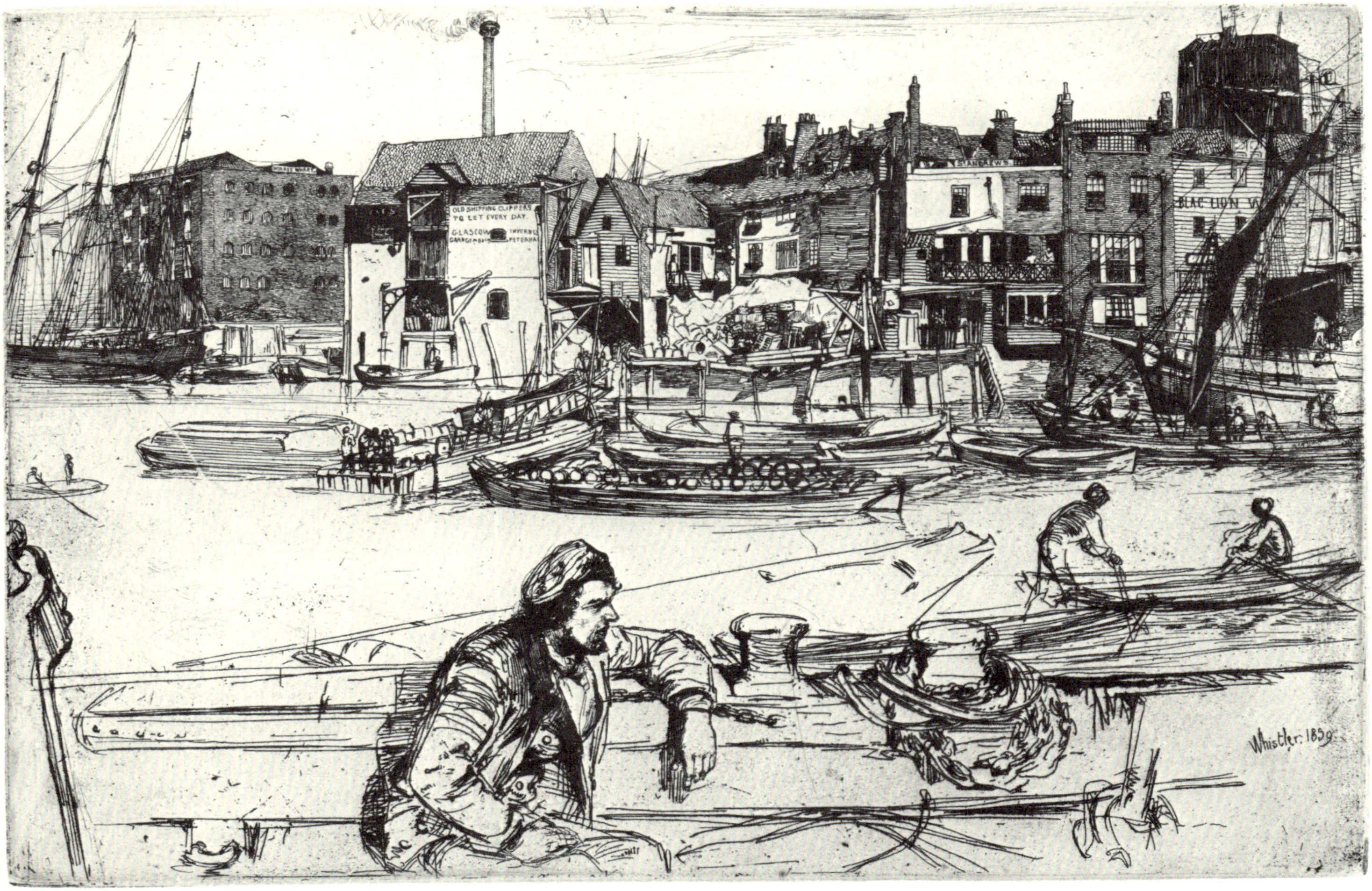
OLD SHIPPING CLIPPERS
TO LET EVERY DAY
GLASGOW
Whistler. 1859.

18. **Black Lion Wharf**, *1859*

One of the Thames Set

K. 42 3/3

Etching

5 7/8 x 8 13/16 in. (14.9 x 22.4 cm.)

Warm black ink on lightweight laid paper with watermark: F below a horn (?)

Signed and dated in plate lower right

Whistler 1859

Provenance: Otto Gerstenberg (Lugt 2785); purchased from Associated American Artists, 1969

Whistler began making etchings and paintings inspired by the industrial and commercial life along the Thames shortly after his return to London in 1859. For periods of time he lived in an inn in the Rotherhithe section of the city. According to his biographers, the Pennells, he worked for three weeks on *Black Lion Wharf* and other of the Thames Set etchings.

Black Lion Wharf is one of the best known and most admired of Whistler's picturesque views of London waterfront life. First printed in 1859 by Delâtre, it was among the plates published by Ellis and Green in 1871 (in the second state, according to Mansfield). If so, this would necessarily be a yet later impression, possibly one of those printed by Goulding after the steel facing was removed. Given its richness, this seems quite likely. Warehouses, one bearing the sign "Blac [sic] Lion Wharf," from which the piece gets its name, are intermingled with workmen's dwellings, forming a backdrop for the shipping activity that takes place in the middle distance.

The print is a splendid demonstration of some of Whistler's early concerns as an etcher: very specific rendering (seen, for example, in the variety of ways rooftops are described) is contrasted to rather casual blocking in of form (for example, in the barge in which the central figure sits in the foreground). In addition, the horizontal band of building facades that functions as the main focus of the scene foretells the artist's later preoccupation with the facade as a complete compositional structure (e.g., cat. nos. 43, 68, and 84). Exhibited at the Royal Academy in 1860, it was evidently a favorite of Whistler as it appears on the wall in his famous portrait of his mother, *Arrangement in Gray and Black* (Young et al., 101).

Most impressions seen were printed in black ink on a variety of papers, although some were printed in brown. A potentially deceptive photogravure of the subject is known. The copper plate is in the Freer Gallery of Art.

LITERATURE: Getscher, pp. 56–57; Getscher and Staley, p. 61, no. 33; MacDonald, p. 14, no. 3; Mansfield, p. 25, no. 41; Naylor, p. xxii, no. 22; Pennell and Pennell (1908) 1:92–93, 280–81; Thomas, no. 35; Wedmore, p. 33, no. 43; Wiehl, p. 32, nos. 74 (photogravure)–75.

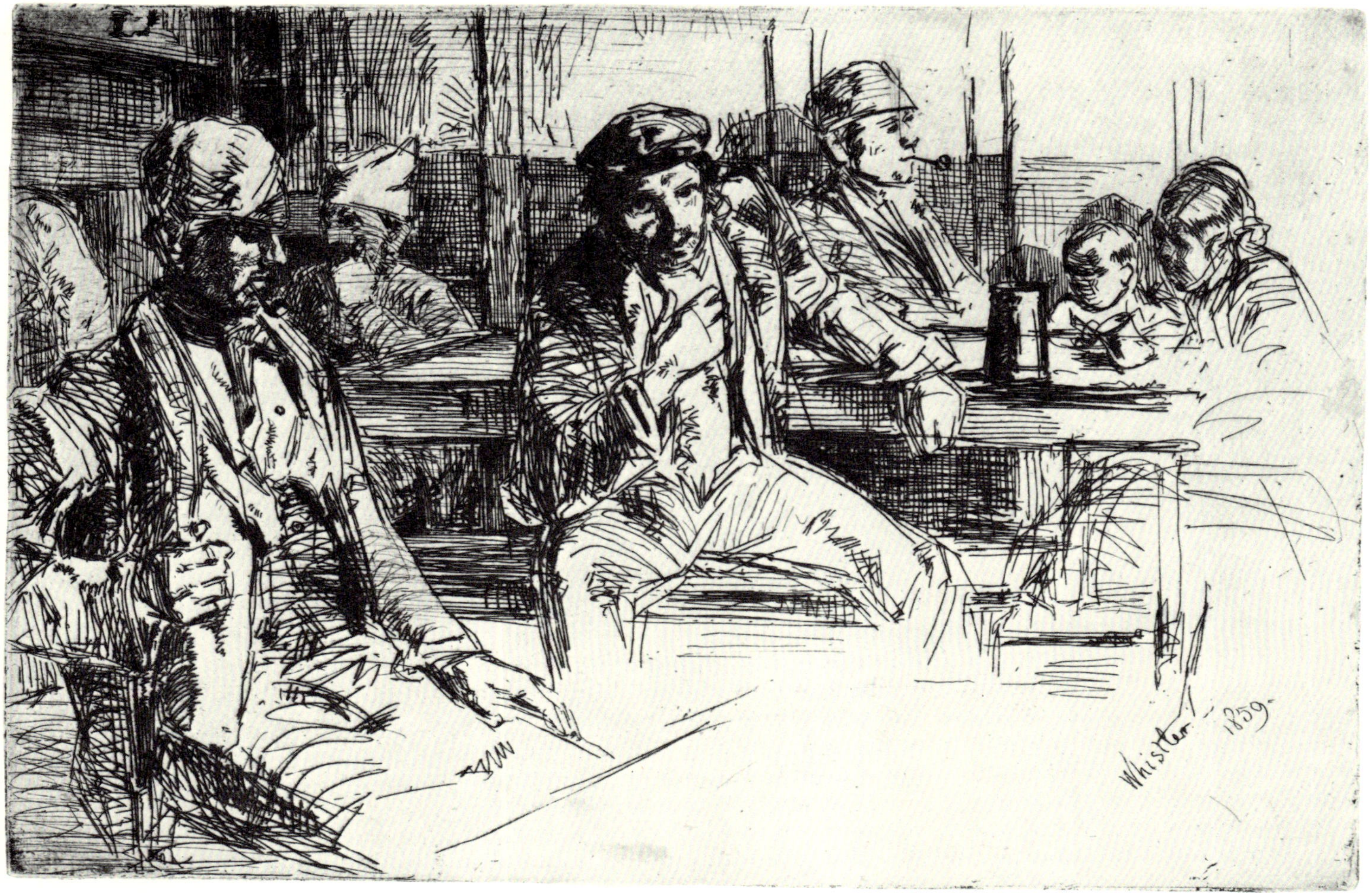

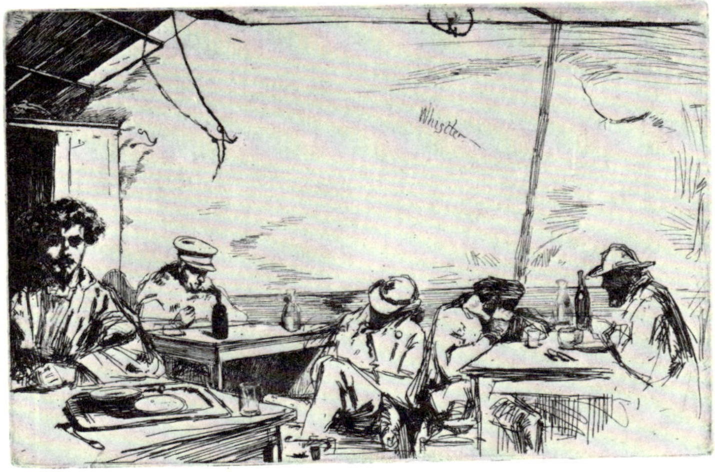

19a.
***Soupe à Trois Sou,** K. 49*
5 7/8 x 8 7/8 in. (14.9 x 22.5 cm.)
Julius L. and Anita Zelman

19. ***Longshoremen,*** *1859*

K. 45 only

Etching and drypoint

6 x 8 15/16 in. (15.1 x 22.7 cm.)

Black ink on medium-weight laid Oriental paper

Signed and dated in plate lower right

Whistler 1859

Provenance: purchased from Associated American Artists, 1970

One contemporary critic may well have been looking at *Longshoremen* or perhaps at *Soupe à Trois Sou* (fig. 19a) when he noted Whistler's "propensity for . . . that class of hard-fisted, square-shouldered, solid and stolid-faced men, on whom the odour of tar and tobacco is equally important." A scene of a tavern interior, *Longshoremen* is a fine example of Whistler's ability from the start to portray essentials of a scene with a variety of visual means. He carefully particularized the central figure and also the man smoking a pipe in the left foreground. The pipe smoker in the rear, by contrast, is rather sparsely, if lucidly, indicated, and the faces of the remaining figures are almost completely obscured by shadows. This range of linear description, given the simplicity and directness of the drawing style, shows Whistler's remarkable grasp of both his medium and his subject. The mother and child at the right are of minor importance here, but similar familial relationships feature prominently in the work of later years (e.g., cat. nos. 49 and 90).

Whistler may have been pleased with the piece in all of its details, since it is known in only one state. Nevertheless, although executed at the same time as other, related Thames waterfront subjects, *Longshoremen* was not selected for the Thames Set. Perhaps the publisher assumed that a figure subject would be less popular than the views. In any case, not having been formally published, it is rarer than many other etchings of the period.

Impressions are known in brown and in black inks on both Western and Oriental papers.

LITERATURE: GUL Whistler, PC1, p. 37 (*Reader,* 4 April 1863); Mansfield, p. 28, no. 44; Naylor, p. xxii, no. 24; Thomas, no. 45; Wedmore, p. 33, no. 43.

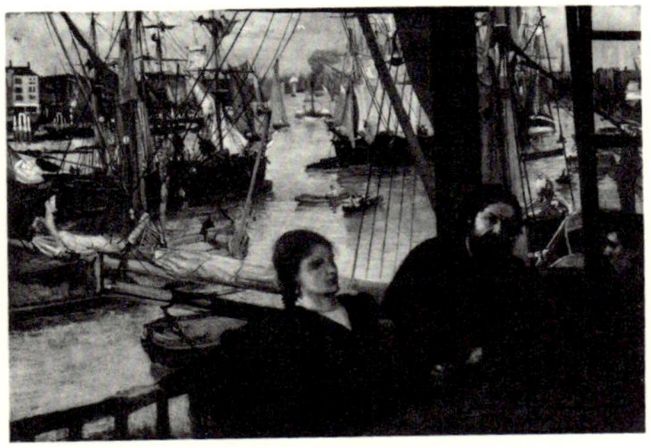

20a.
Wapping on Thames
Oil
28 ½ x 40 ½ in. (72.4 x 102.9 cm.)
National Gallery of Art,
John Hay Whitney Collection

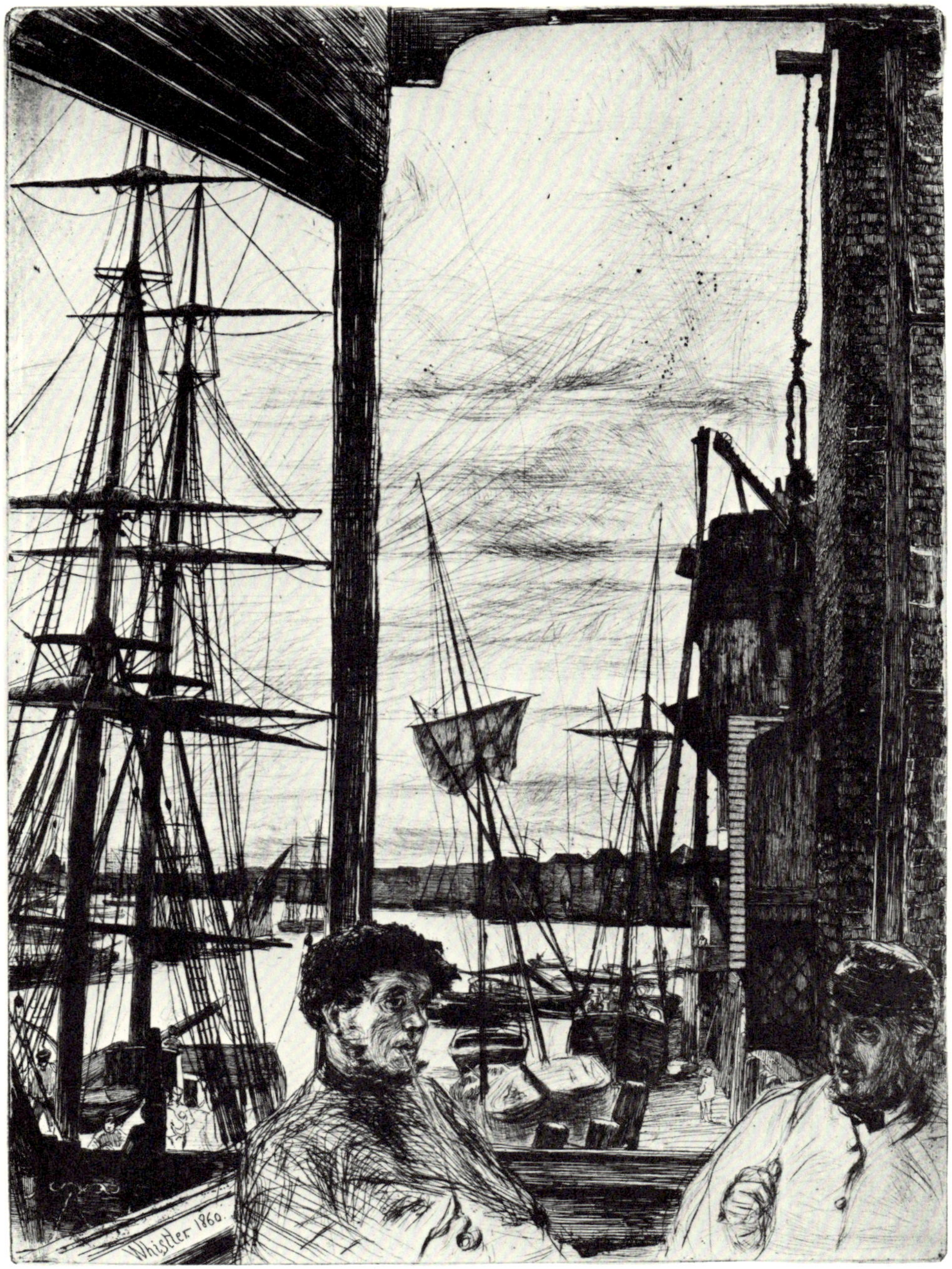

20. **Rotherhithe,** 1860

One of the Thames Set

K. 66 3/3

Etching and drypoint

10 13/16 x 7 13/16 in. (27.5 x 19.8 cm.)

Black ink on medium-weight laid paper

with watermark: De Erven Dk. Blauw

Signed and dated in plate lower left

Whistler 1860

Provenance: purchased from

R. M. Light & Co., Inc., 1970

In *Rotherhithe* Whistler tells us of his dedication to portraiture, his intrigue with the details of ships and shipping, his capacity for extravagant descriptiveness (the buildings to the right), and his love of atmospheric effects (the buildings at the rear). An encyclopedia of his etching techniques at the time, everything functions as a coherent unit.

Exhibited at the Royal Academy in 1862 as *Rotherhithe,* the etching was titled *Wapping* at the time of its 1871 publication. It is closely related to an oil painting titled *Wapping on Thames* (fig. 20a), which, begun about the same time, was not completed until 1864. The site of both images is the Angel, an inn in Cherry Gardens, Rotherhithe, looking across the Thames to Wapping.

Impressions are generally printed in black ink and are found on a variety of papers. This one, in black ink, cleanly wiped, on a modern paper with about half-inch margins, may typify the 1871 impressions. The copper plate is in the Freer Gallery of Art.

LITERATURE: Fryberger, p. 19, no. 8; Getscher and Staley, p. 57, no. 29; MacDonald, p. 15, no. 5; Naylor, p. xxiii, no. 35; Thomas, no. 41; Wedmore, p. 39, no. 60; Wiehl, p. 98, nos. 51–52.

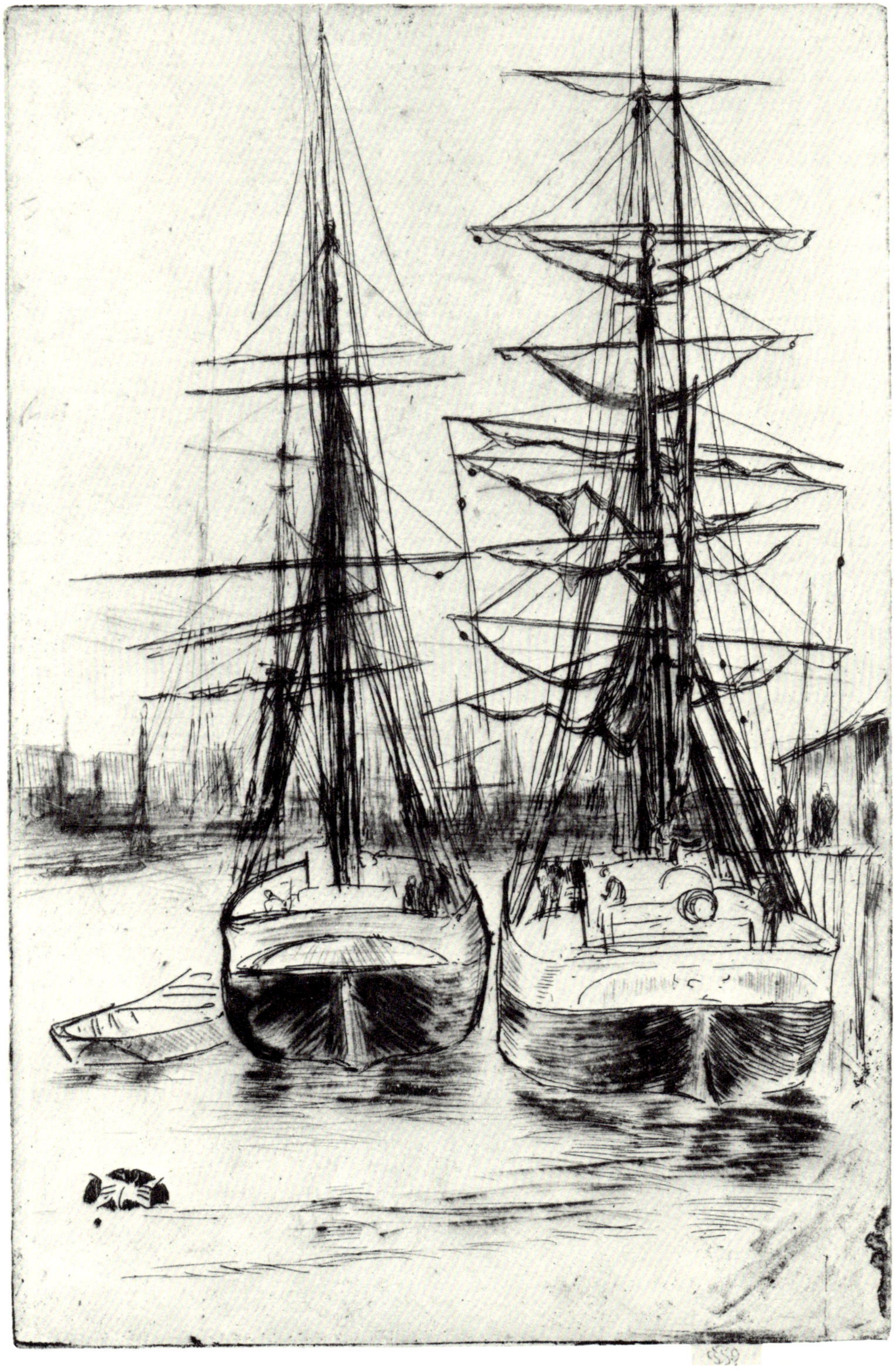

21. *Two Ships, 1875**

K. 148 2/3

Etching and drypoint

8 1/8 x 5 3/16 in. (20.8 x 13.2 cm.)

Warm black ink on lightweight Oriental paper

Signed lower right with butterfly; signed in plate lower left with butterfly

Published by Messrs. Dowdeswell and Dowdeswells, 1880

Provenance: purchased from Associated American Artists, 1970

Ships and shipping attracted Whistler on a continuing basis, and in the mid-1870s he produced several etchings that specifically focused on vessels. Wedmore identified this scene as St. Katharine's Docks and went on to say, "It had failed to please Mr. Whistler in the biting or execution, and was saved from destruction by others–whose service to mankind was in this case not considerable." Obviously Mr. Wedmore too didn't especially care for the etching.

The Dowdeswells' prospectus of 1880 for *Two Ships* (which also advertised the publication of *Tatting*, fig. 35a) indicated that the edition would be limited to thirty numbered impressions. Whether the full edition was printed is unclear, and as far as we know, none was actually numbered.

In studying the background, it seems that Whistler was trying to move away from the kind of particularizing of buildings he did, for example, in *Black Lion Wharf* (cat. no. 18). He was clearly struggling for a new way to describe distance that was based in allusion rather than description. One sees a similar struggle much later in *Little Nocturne, Amsterdam* (cat. no. 87).

LITERATURE: Fryberger, p. 31, no. 22; Mansfield, p. 90, no. 146; Wedmore, p. 56, no. 116.

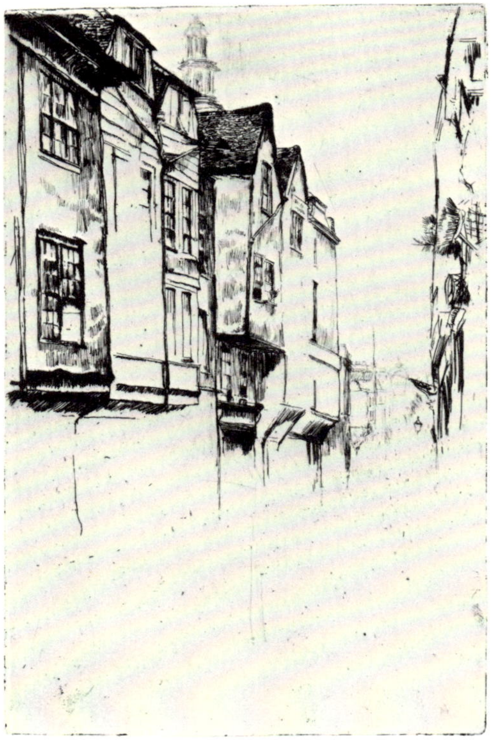

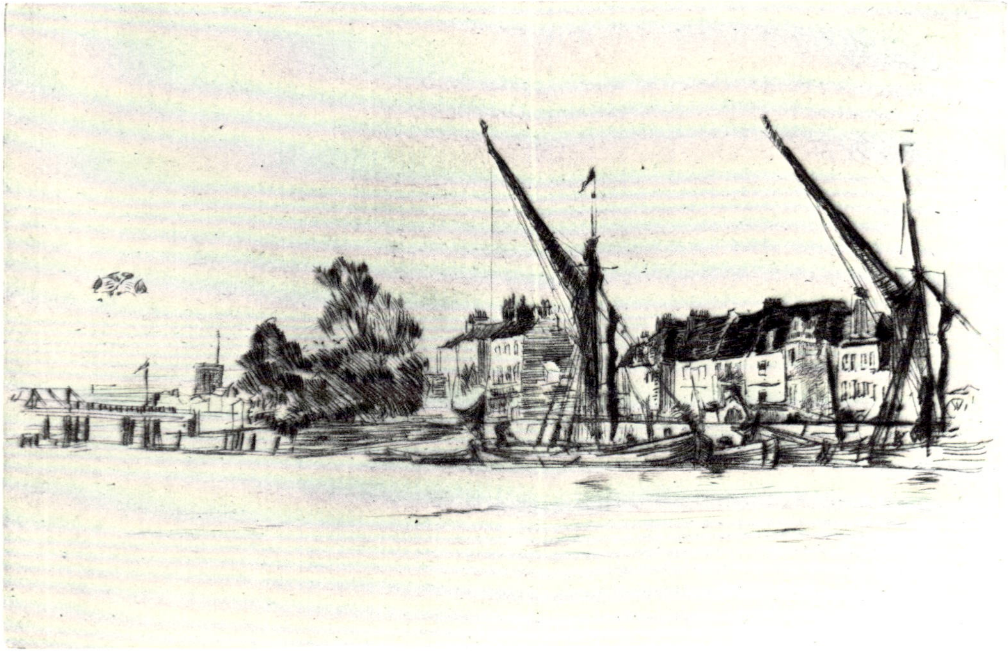

22. **Wych Street,** 1877

K. 159 2/2

Etching and drypoint

8 3/8 x 5 3/8 in. (21.2 x 13.5 cm.)

Black ink on medium-weight, antique laid paper (miscellaneous manuscript inscriptions in ink verso) with watermark: IV

Unsigned

Provenance: Howard Mansfield (Lugt 1342); Harris G. Whittemore (Lugt 1384a); anonymous collector's stamp; purchased from R. M. Light & Co., Inc., 1980

Whistler particularly enjoyed printing on beautiful old papers, and he may well have haunted used-book shops searching for flyleaves and bound volumes of blank sheets. This impression of *Wych Street* is one of several prints in the exhibition on sheets, probably flyleaves, with inscriptions on the verso (in this case in Spanish in brown ink).

There is a touched proof in the Freer Gallery of a state prior to Kennedy's state one. In it watercolor enhances the area surrounding the lantern and throughout the row of buildings at the left. This touched proof in particular shows the shadow under the overhang as much more sparsely etched than in Kennedy's first state; and the watercolor gives an indication of the work Whistler then added to this area as it developed in the impression seen here. Most of the other watercolor areas on the touched proof in the end were not added to the etching.

This impression is a particularly rich one, especially in the area of the second peak from the right; in many impressions of the state, the area is merely a thin outline. The first two impressions pulled from the plate were either printed or sold on November 15, 1887. The copper plate is now in the Hunterian Art Gallery, University of Glasgow.

LITERATURE: Getscher and Staley, p. 87, no. 54; GUL Whistler, NB4, p. 7; MacDonald, p. 19, no. 19; Mansfield, p. 97, no. 156; Naylor, p. xxvii, no. 66; Wedmore, p. 60, no. 132.

23. **Lindsey Houses,** 1877

K. 166 2/3

Drypoint

5 15/16 x 8 15/16 in. (15.1 x 22.7 cm.)

Black ink on medium-weight, antique laid paper with watermark: Arms of Amsterdam

Signed in plate center left with butterfly

Provenance: Sir John Day (Lugt 526); purchased from Kennedy Galleries, Inc., 1976

Lindsey House, Chelsea, was built about 1764. It was later divided into separate dwellings and, with additions, became Lindsey Row. Whistler lived there at two different addresses during the 1860s and 1870s. Seen here, the site is depicted backwards: Whistler as usual did not bother to draw on the plate in reverse.

Lindsey Houses is one of a number of etchings of scenes along the Thames Whistler made between completion of the Peacock Room and his trip to Venice. Perhaps it was among those to which he was referring in a letter of September 3, 1877 to Stephen Tucker: "Look here, I have got some new and lovely etchings–amateurs must take some *at once.*" Contrary to Wedmore's 1878 date for the print, several impressions are listed during 1877 in the notebooks kept by Charles Augustus Howell.

Typically, the attitude of peacefulness and silence that *Lindsey Houses* exudes presents a marked contrast to Whistler's shipping views along the Thames of the early 1860s. In the handling of form too, it is decidedly different, showing a closer formal affinity, for example, to *The Muff* (cat. no. 35) than to the earlier Thames etchings.

The state one impression in the Freer Gallery of Art is inscribed by Whistler *1st State–only proof* and signed with a butterfly. There is, however, another impression of the state at the University of Michigan Museum of Art (reproduced, Getscher and Staley, p. 69). If indeed they are the same state, the existence of a second proof of the first state reinforces the notion that Whistler's words must always be taken cautiously.

The main change between the first two states is that the bank of trees became more fully articulated. In the third state Whistler enhanced the reflections on the water and made a number of minor adjustments to the buildings and boats. The copper plate is in the Hunterian Art Gallery, University of Glasgow.

LITERATURE: Getscher and Staley, p. 69, no. 39; GUL Whistler, NB4, p. lff.; GUL Whistler, T210; Wedmore, p. 62, no. 136.

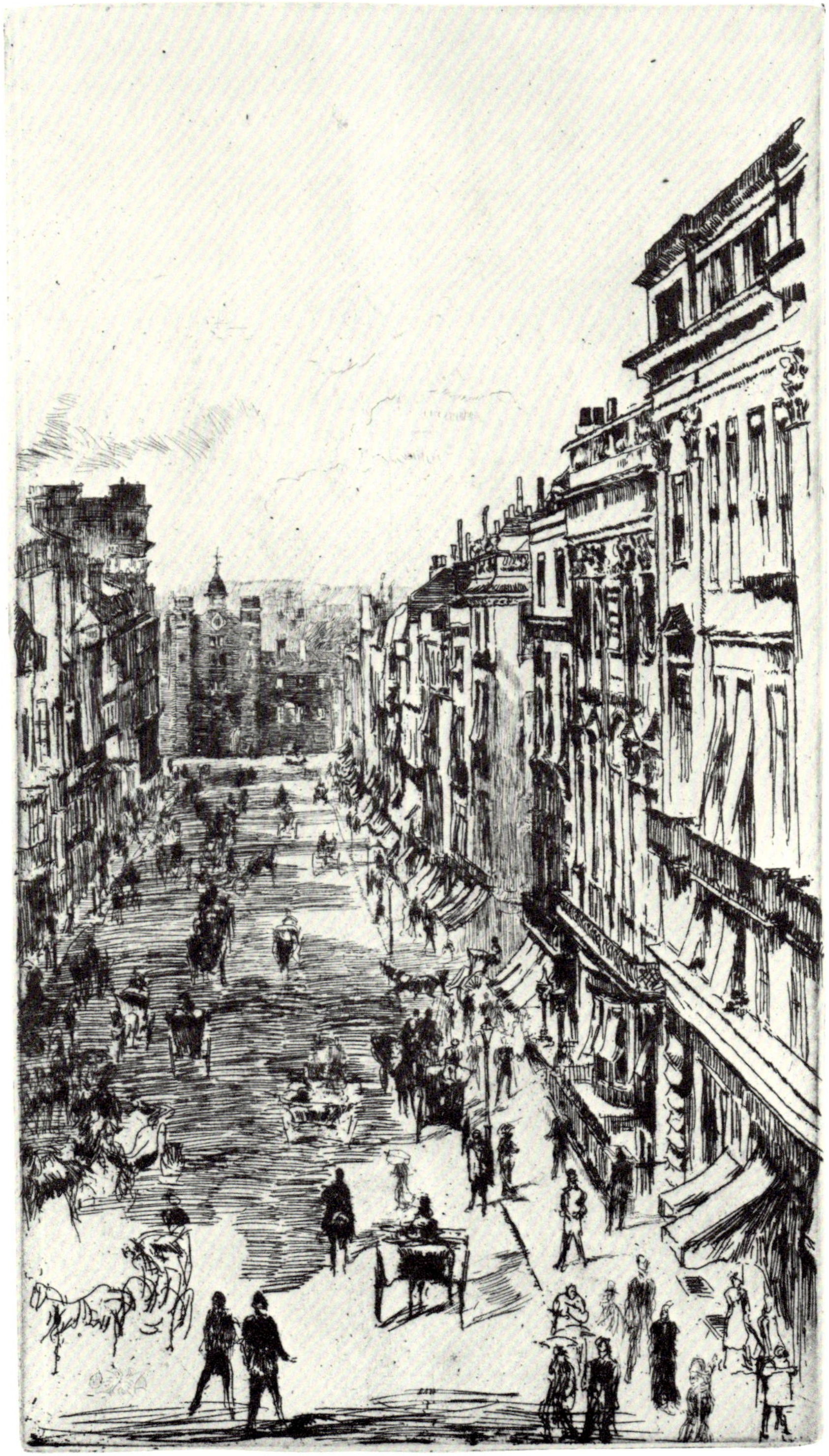

24. ***St. James's Street,*** *1878*

K. 169 4/4

Etching and drypoint

10 15/16 x 5 15/16 in. (27.8 x 15 cm.)

Warm black ink on medium-weight, antique laid paper

Signed in plate lower left with butterfly

Published by Hogarth and Son, 1879

Provenance: purchased from Kennedy Galleries, Inc., 1969

Whistler was working here in a manner that enabled him to depict a complicated scene without resorting to detailed description. The drawing style, for the most part, consists of short parallel strokes rather than the combination of longer, scratchy lines and regulated marks that accrued to form shapes, tones, and textures in such earlier works as *Black Lion Wharf* (cat. no. 18). In addition, there is a grace here and a sense of the artist's immediate apprehension and control of the entire scene. Light and atmosphere are his subjects.

St. James's Street, linking Pall Mall and Piccadilly, with a view toward St. James's Palace, is seen here in reverse. A lithographic reproduction in reverse of this, and therefore in the correct direction, was published in 1878 in *Vanity Fair,* and according to Wedmore, "Indeed, the etching was made for that purpose."

The warm black ink seen here is typical of impressions in the fourth state, after an inch-wide strip of unused copper had been removed from the left edge of the plate. Most impressions are on Western papers, and impressions of the earlier states are quite rare. The copper plate is in the National Gallery of Art, Washington, D.C., Rosenwald Collection.

LITERATURE: Fryberger, p. 31, no 23; Getscher and Staley, p. 57, no. 27; Mansfield, p. 103, no. 165; Naylor, p. xxvii, no. 70; Wedmore, p. 63, no. 140.

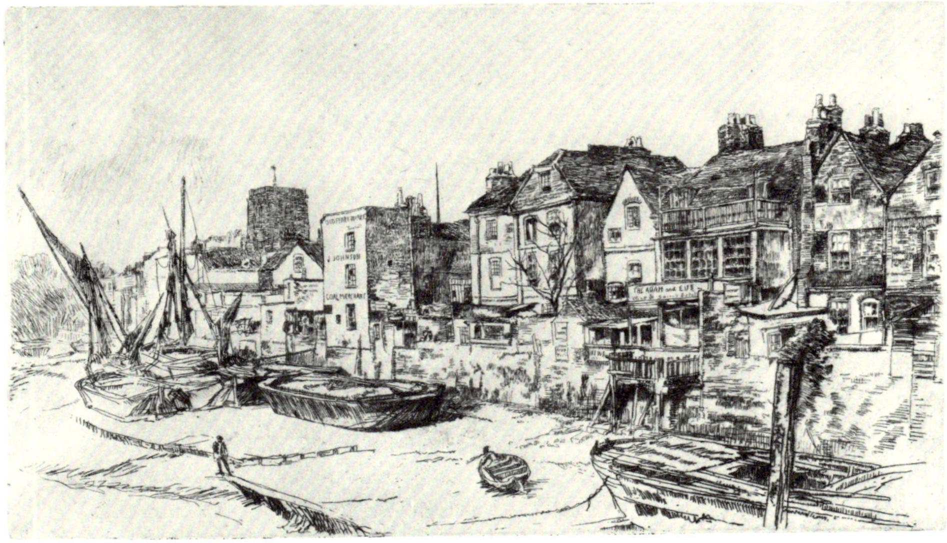
J. JOHNSON
COAL MERCHANT

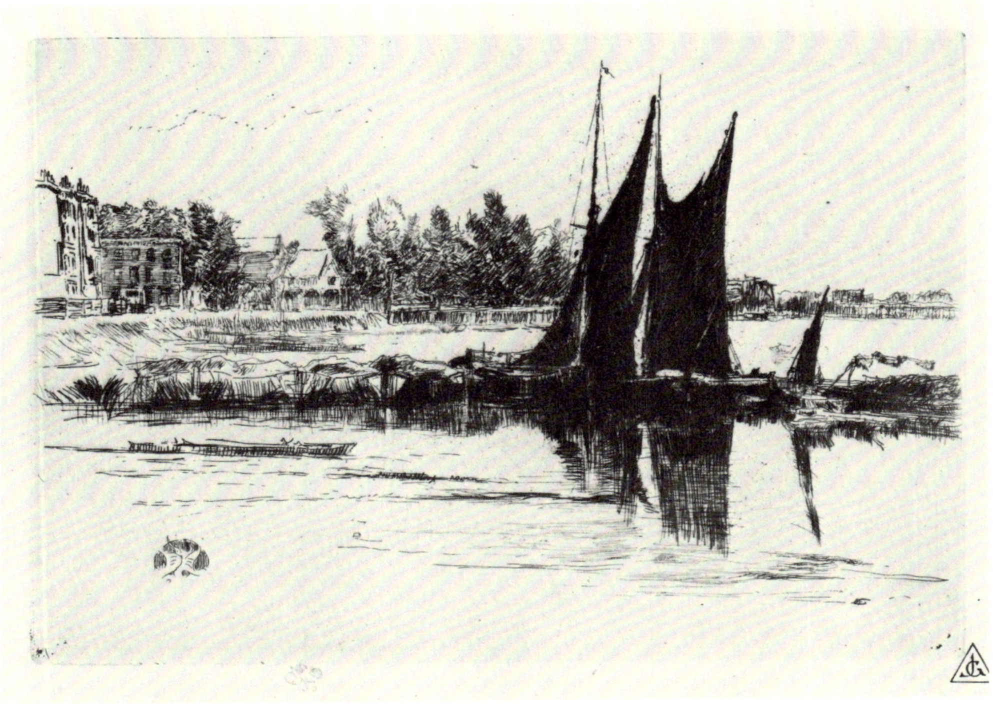

25. *The "Adam and Eve," Old Chelsea, 1879*

K. 175 2/2

11 13/16 x 6 7/8 in. (17.5 x 30 cm.)

Etching and drypoint

Black ink on lightweight Oriental paper

Signed in plate upper left with butterfly

Published by Hogarth and Son, 1879

Provenance: purchased from Robin Garton, 1983

Much more literally detailed than Whistler's other Thames and London subjects of this period, the *"Adam and Eve"* was probably designed to interest the general public (a wise move, given the artist's dire financial straits at the time). The print was actually documenting a London already lost and could not possibly have been worked from life because the area of the city where the popular Adam and Eve tavern was located was torn down around 1872, some years before Whistler depicted it. In fact, it is conceivable that the etching was worked from a photograph, a possibility that would account for its somewhat flat spatial character and the slightly stilted quality of the drawing.

Whistler himself considered the *"Adam and Eve"* to be a landmark print, marking, better than almost any other plate, a transition from his early, rather tight, and carefully delineated manner of working, as in the Thames Set, to his more suggestive and atmospheric handling of a scene, as in the Venetian etchings.

Whistler printed some impressions, but Wedmore records *"Adam and Eve"* was "issued by Hogarth at 6 pds., 6 s. But the printing was not of Mr. Whistler's kind. The impressions are often muddy."

NOTE: My thanks to Robert H. Getscher and Robin Spencer for suggesting the possibility of Whistler's having worked from photography.

LITERATURE: Fryberger, p. 31, no. 24; Getscher, pp. 19–20; Getscher and Staley, p. 64, no. 34; MacDonald, p. 19, no. 20; Mansfield, p. 109, no. 172; Naylor, p. xxvii, no. 72; Pennell and Pennell (1908) 1: 215, 280; Wedmore, p. 64, no. 144.

26. *Hurlingham, 1879*

K. 181 3/3

Etching and drypoint

5 7/16 x 7 7/8 in. (13.8 x 20 cm.)

Dark brown ink on medium-weight laid paper with watermark: 1814

Signed lower left with butterfly; signed in plate lower left with butterfly

Provenance: Jules Gerbeau (Lugt 1166); Otto Gerstenberg (Lugt 2785); purchased from Ira D. Gale, 1972

In *Hurlingham* the strong emphasis on the sailboats is somewhat unusual for the Thames etchings of the late 1870s. In retrospect, however, this focus sets the stage for some of the Venetian subjects, like *Nocturne* and *Fishing-Boat* (cat. nos. 59 and 64). One sees here too a particularly lovely landscape, evocative of wind rustling through trees and grasses. While equally lovely landscape details are found, for example, in *Old Putney Bridge* (cat. no. 28), there they are almost passed over in light of the overall power of the composition. To some extent, the rather scratchy line in *Hurlingham* is reminiscent of landscape elements in prints of two decades earlier (see fig. XIII).

Impressions are known in black ink as well as brown, generally on papers of Western origin. This impression bears the blindstamp of the Printsellers Association.

LITERATURE: Fryberger, p. 32, no. 25; Mansfield, p. 113, no. 178; Naylor, p. xxviii, no. 76; Wedmore, p. 65, no. 147.

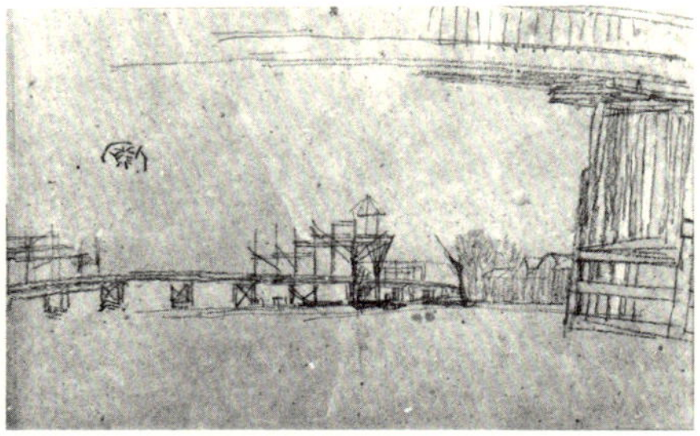

27a.
The New Albert Bridge and Old Battersea Bridge
Black chalk
7 15/16 x 11 3/8 in. (18.7 x 28.9 cm.)
Hunterian Art Gallery, University of Glasgow, Birnie Philip Gift

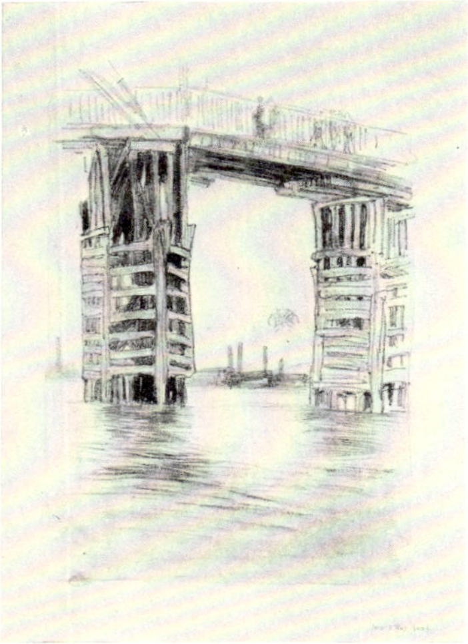

27b.
The Tall Bridge
Lithograph
11 x 7 1/8 in. (28 x 18.2 cm.)
Freer Gallery of Art

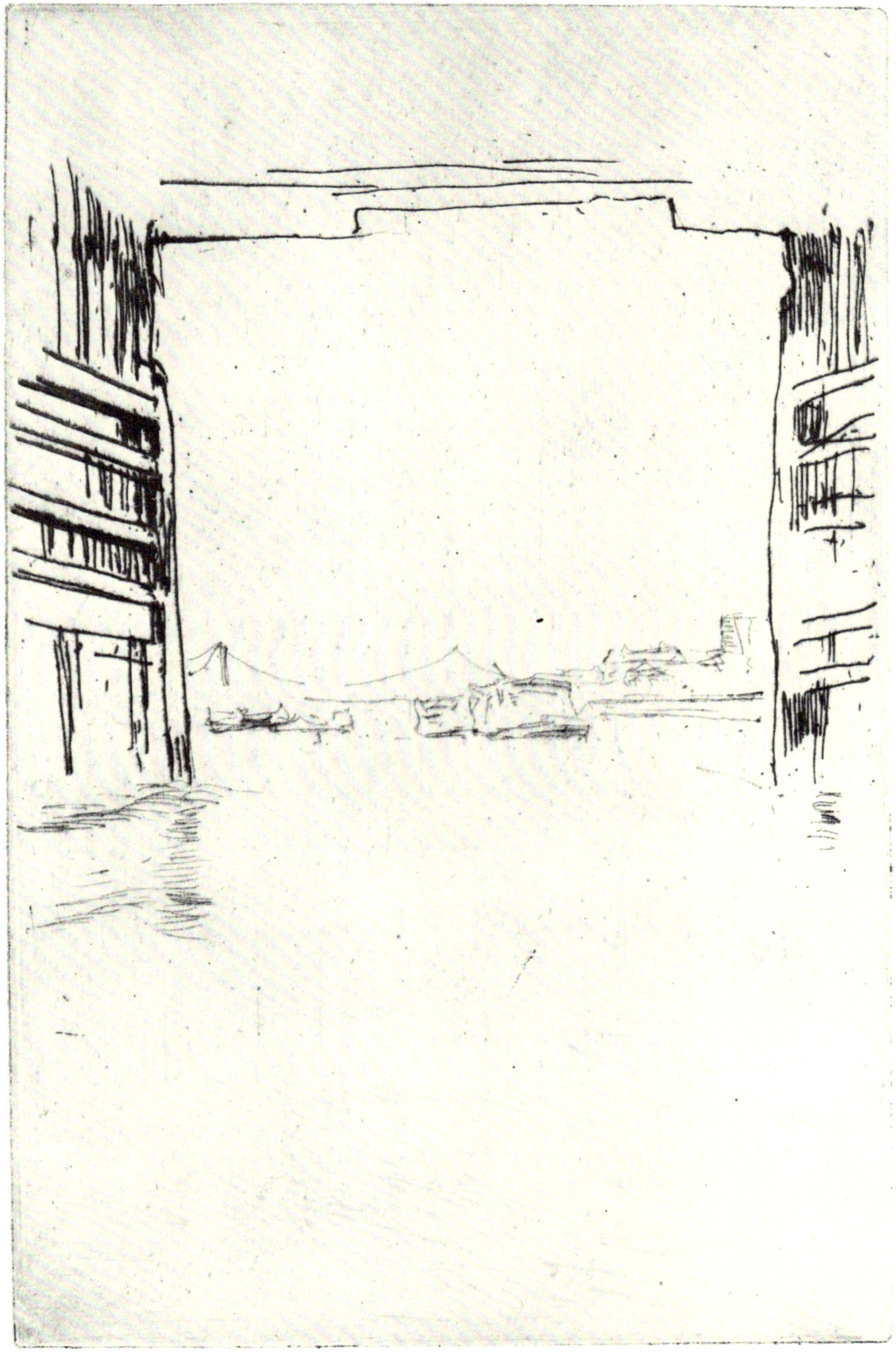

27. *Under Old Battersea Bridge,*

1879

K. 176 1/3

Etching and drypoint

8 7/16 x 5 5/16 in. (21.4 x 13.6 cm.)

Black ink on medium-weight laid paper with watermark: De Erven Dk. Blauw

Signed lower left with butterfly and **imp**

Provenance: Howard Mansfield (Lugt 1342); Harris G. Whittemore (Lugt 1384a); anonymous collector's stamp; purchased from Thos. Agnew & Sons, Ltd., 1981

Whistler's two Lindsey Row residences overlooked Old Battersea Bridge, and he was particularly attracted by its picturesque wooden structure. Replaced by the Albert Bridge in the early 1880s, during the 1870s Old Battersea was the subject of several of Whistler's paintings, drawings (fig. 27a), and prints.

Under Old Battersea Bridge, especially in its exceedingly sparse first state, seen here, is one of the most effective examples of Whistler's interest in the use of a framing structure to define an image. And in this state too, it offers a very cogent statement of the artist's assimilation of aspects of Japanese prints: broadly worked compositions in which a lack of depth and/or spatial ambiguity is evident. The composition is closely related to a lithograph of the previous year, *The Tall Bridge* (fig. 27b). Later states of the etching show considerable additions throughout.

First-state impressions are printed in black (to our knowledge without exception) on papers of Western origin. The copper plate is in the Hunterian Art Gallery, University of Glasgow.

LITERATURE: Mansfield, p. 110, no. 173; Naylor, p. xxviii, no. 73; John Sandberg, "'Japonisme' and Whistler," *Burlington Magazine* 106 (1964): 500–507; Wedmore, p. 59, no. 125.

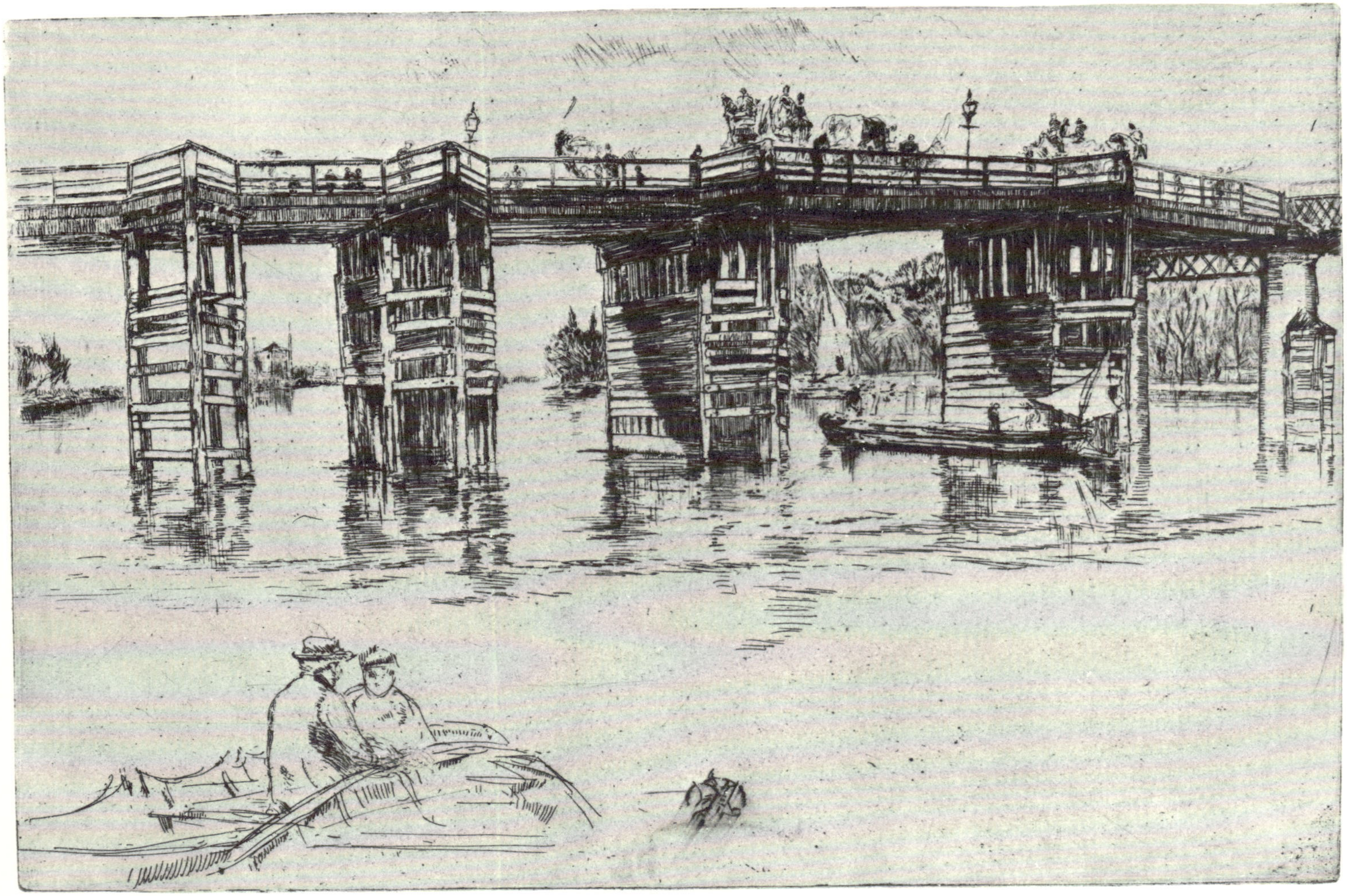

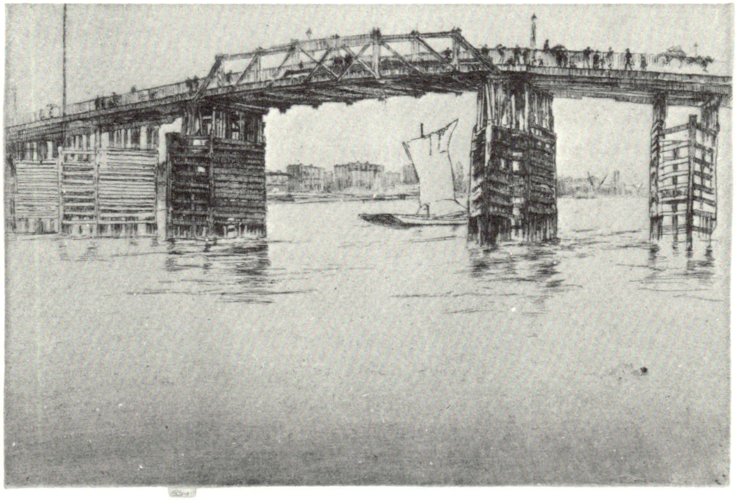

28a.
Old Battersea Bridge, *K. 177*
7 7/8 x 11 5/8 in. (15.6 x 29.5 cm.)
Julius L. and Anita Zelman

28. **Old Putney Bridge,** *1879*

K. 178 1/4

Etching and drypoint

7 15/16 x 11 5/8 in. (20.1 x 29.5 cm.)

Dark brown ink on medium-weight laid paper with watermark: Pro Patria

Signed lower right on tab with butterfly and ***imp****; signed in plate lower center with butterfly*

Published by the Fine Art Society, 1879

Provenance: C. W. Dowdeswell (Lugt 690); Sir John Day (Lugt 526); Otto Gerstenberg (Lugt 2785); anonymous collector's stamp; purchased from Associated American Artists, 1981

In its exquisitely composed integration of light, form, space, and human activity, *Old Putney Bridge* has much the same success as a very different image, *St. James's Street* (cat. 24). And in these respects *Old Putney* on the whole is a far more pulsating and active image than *Old Battersea Bridge* (fig. 28a) of some months later, with which it is frequently compared. Like the vertical *Under Old Battersea Bridge* (cat. no. 27), these two horizontal bridge images exemplify Whistler's understated use of the Oriental pictorial devices that so fascinated him. Both *Old Putney Bridge* and *Old Battersea Bridge* (the latter called by Wedmore "one of the noblest, most spacious, most refined of Mr. Whistler's visions of the Thames") were published shortly before the bridges were replaced by modern structures.

In this beautiful early impression the splendid delicacy of the distant landscape is at its brightest, allowing the flickering light to function most fully. In the second state additional work somewhat subdued this effect, even before the plate began to wear noticeably.

Some impressions are printed in black–most are in brown–generally on Western papers. Some in the fourth state were printed by Frederick Goulding and inscribed *F.G. imp.*

LITERATURE: Getscher, pp. 18–20; Getscher and Staley, p. 64, no. 35; MacDonald, p. 19, no. 21; Mansfield, p. 111, no. 175; Naylor, p. xxviii, no. 75; Wedmore, p. 64, no. 145.

29. **Drury Lane,** *c. 1881–82*

One of the Second Venice Set

K. 237 only

Etching

6 7/16 x 4 in. (16.3 x 10.1 cm.)

Brown ink on medium-weight laid paper with partial watermark: shield surmounted by crown

Signed in plate upper right with butterfly

Provenance: Jules Gerbeau (Lugt 1166); Walter S. Brewster (Lugt Supp. 2651a); Art Institute of Chicago (?); purchased from R. M. Light & Co., Inc., 1971

Whistler frequently attended theatrical performances, and one can imagine him taking time en route to or from Drury Lane Theatre to capture on copper this charming vignette. The piece is typical of the small etchings he did sporadically after his return from Venice almost to the end of his life. They feature street scenes in London and elsewhere and often include groups of children at play. This interest in children can readily be traced to Whistler's earliest etchings. Portraits of his nieces and nephews, for example, and the offspring of friends and associates (e.g., cat. nos. 9 and 12) show that the artist was captivated by children from the time of his youth; on the title page for his first set of etchings, Twelve Etchings from Nature (fig. XVII and XVIII), he depicted himself surrounded by youthful observers.

Even as seemingly slight a subject as *Drury Lane* rewards careful study. Note the marvelous gestures of the dapper men in conversation on the pavement in the rear and the woman behind the fence to their right.

Impressions are known in black ink and a variety of shades of brown generally on Western papers. *Drury Lane* was one of the five non-Venice subjects included in the Second Venice Set. The cancelled copper plate was delivered to Dowdeswells on January 17, 1887, and is now in the Art Institute of Chicago.

LITERATURE: Getscher, pp. 49–50; Getscher and Staley, p. 54, no. 26; GUL Whistler, NB1, p. 33; Mansfield, p. 163, no. 234.

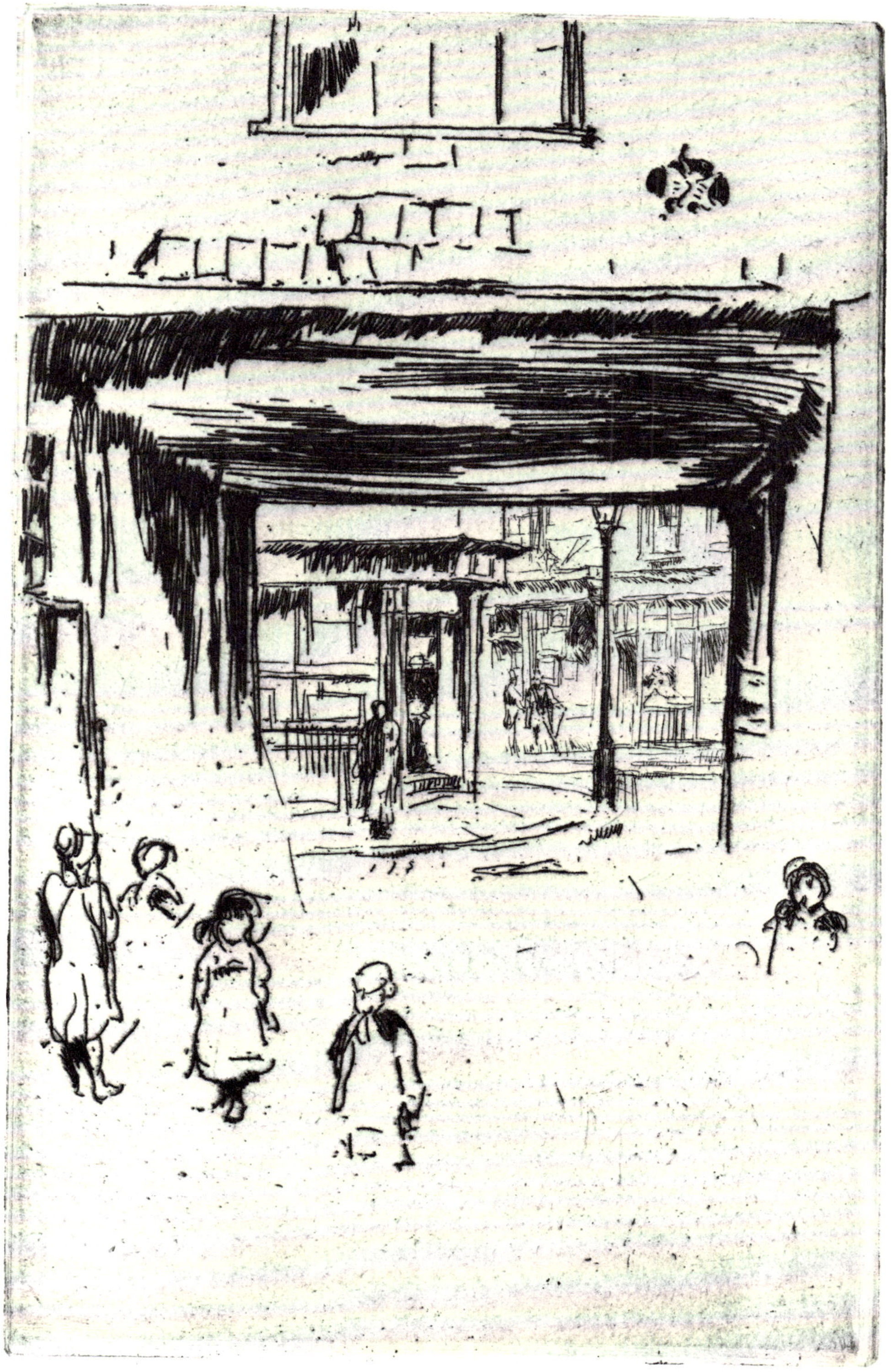

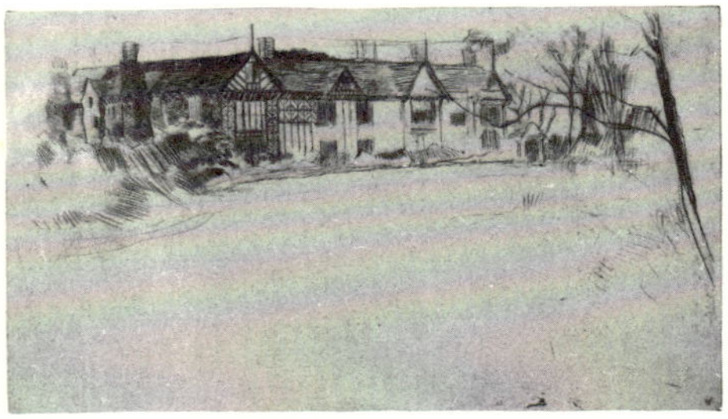

30a.
Speke Hall, No. 2, *K. 143*
7 x 12 in. (17.6 x 30.5 cm.)
National Gallery of Art,
Rosenwald Collection

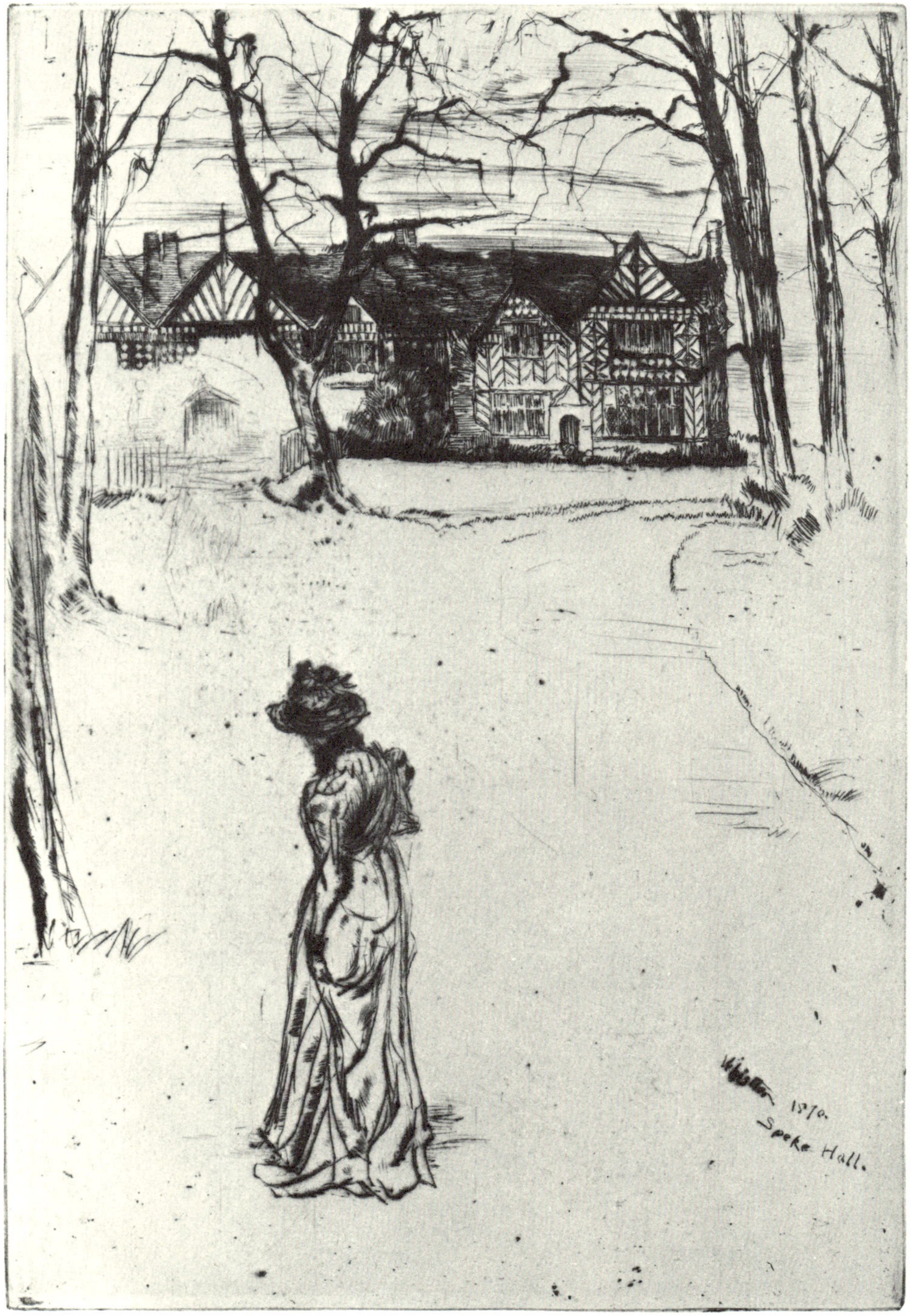

30. **Speke Hall, No. 1,** 1870

K. 96 1/10

Etching and drypoint

8 15/16 x 5 15/16 in. (22.5 x 15 cm.)

Black ink on medium-weight laid paper with watermark: De Erven Dk. Blauw

Signed, dated, and inscribed in plate lower right ***Whistler 1870 Speke Hall***

Provenance: Henry Harper Benedict (initials verso); anonymous collector's stamp; purchased from R. M. Light & Co., Inc., 1982

Speke Hall, No. 1 is the earlier of Whistler's two etchings of the mansion about eight miles from Liverpool which was occupied by the Leyland family during the early 1870s, when Whistler was a frequent visitor. Parts of the house date to the late fifteenth century.

A number of states of *Speke Hall, No. 1* in addition to Kennedy's ten are known, including one prior to the first recorded one, exhibited here. Property of the Liverpool City Libraries, it lacks touches of drypoint on the trees and the house and shows evidence of foul biting, which was removed before this impression was made. Margaret MacDonald has suggested that the plate probably was worked over a period of years. Changes centered on the figure in the foreground. The woman seen here was removed and replaced by another, depicted more fully in profile. In the last state, this second female figure likewise was burnished out.

About 1875, while Whistler was still struggling with *Speke Hall, No. 1,* he made a second version (first state, fig. 30a). Horizontal in format, *Speke Hall, No. 2* in its second, and final, state shows Whistler's efforts again to include figures.

The copper plate of *Speke Hall, No. 1* is in the Hunterian Art Gallery, University of Glasgow.

LITERATURE: MacDonald, pp. 31–32, nos. 60–61; Mansfield, p. 59, no. 95; Naylor, p. xxv, no. 48; *Speke Hall: A Guide to the Buildings and the Owners.* 2d. ed. (Liverpool: Merseyside County Museums, n.d.); Wedmore, pp. 12, 48, no. 86.

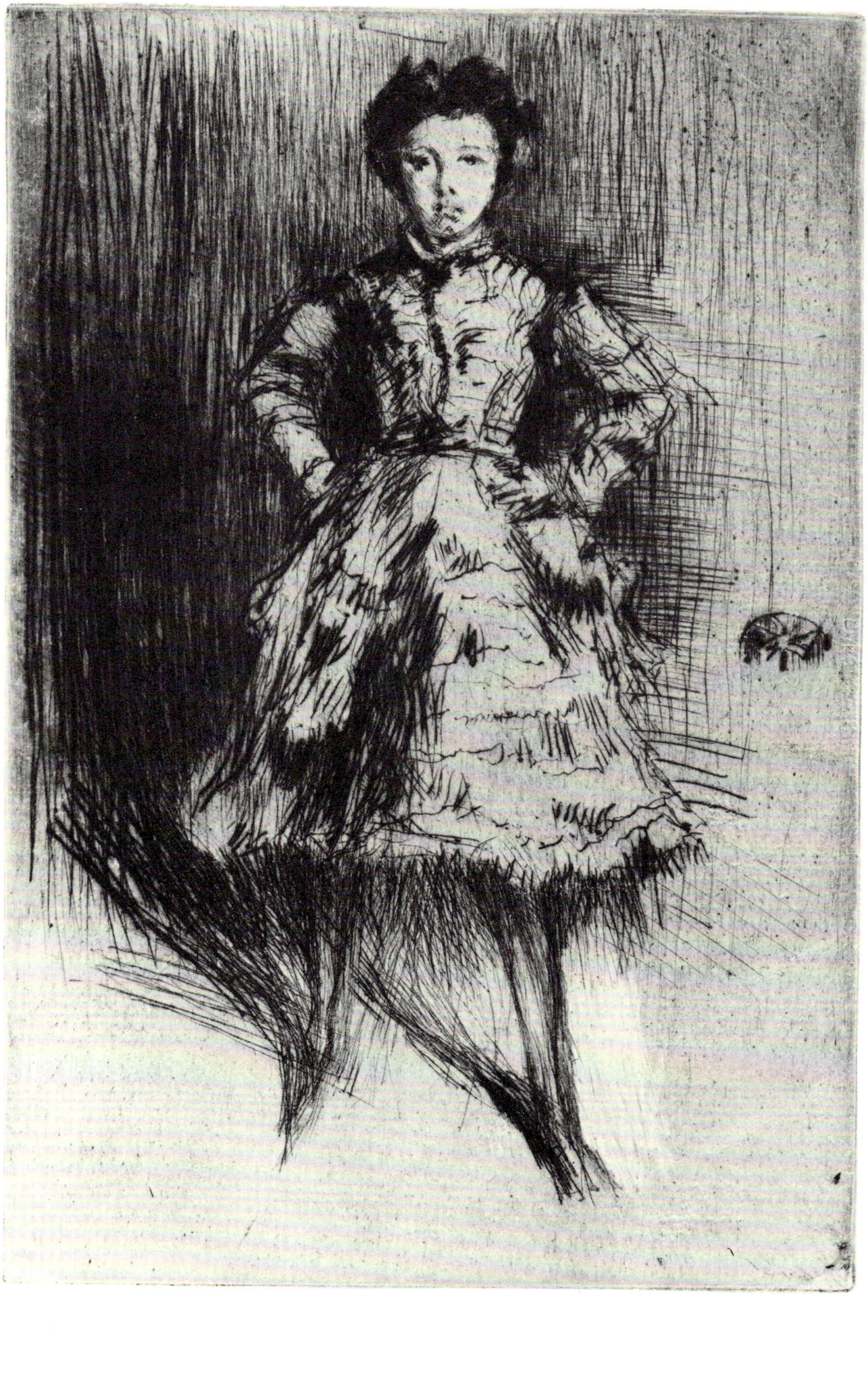

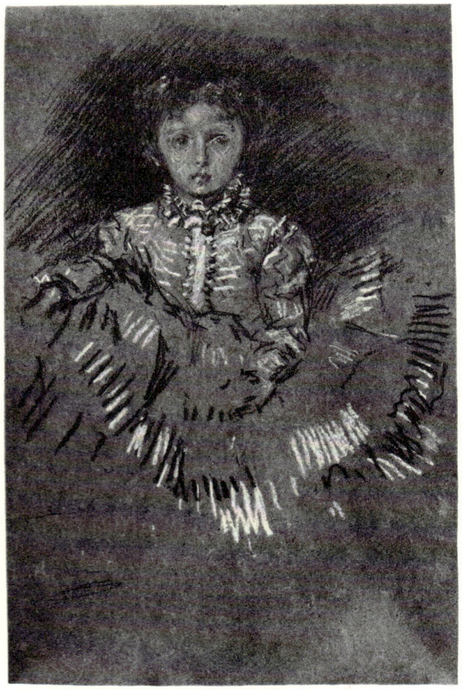

31a.
Study for a Portrait of Baby Leyland
Black and white chalk
11 x 7 1/16 in. (27.9 x 17.9 cm.)
Freer Gallery of Art

31. ***Elinor Leyland**, 1873*

K. 109 6/7

Drypoint

8 7/16 x 5 7/16 in. (21.4 x 13.8 cm.)

Black ink on medium-weight, antique laid paper (miscellaneous manuscript inscriptions in ink verso) with watermark: Arms of Amsterdam

Signed in plate right center with butterfly

Provenance: purchased from Kennedy Galleries, Inc., 1977

Whistler was thoroughly captivated by the Leylands' youngest daughter, Elinor, who would have been about twelve years old at the time this portrait was made. He also executed a number of drawing studies of the child (fig. 31a) and worked for several years on an oil portrait that never was completed.

Direct confrontation, important from the time of some of Whistler's earliest portrait prints (e.g., cat. no. 8), is the dominant aspect of this drypoint of young Elinor. The child's beauty is clearly evident, and one senses her self-awareness as she approaches womanhood.

The legs caused problems for Whistler, and they were removed and redrawn as the plate was developed; evidence of the burnishing is seen in the broad, light lines to the right of Elinor's left leg. After impressions of the present state were pulled, the head too was considerably reworked.

Impressions are generally printed in black on a variety of Western and Oriental papers. In this impression, the rich drypoint is enhanced by the use of plate tone in the shadow area. The copper plate, now in the Hunterian Art Gallery, University of Glasgow, was among those acquired by the Fine Art Society in 1880.

LITERATURE: MacDonald, p. 35, nos. 71–72; Mansfield, p. 67, no. 108; Naylor, p. xxv, no. 53; Thomas, no. 78; Wedmore, p. 51, no. 95.

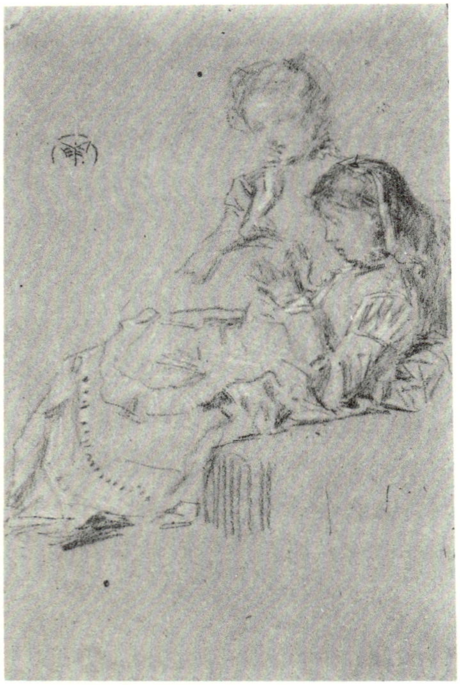

32a.
Two Leyland Sisters
Black and white chalk
11 1/4 x 7 1/16 in. (28.6 x 17.9 cm.)
Freer Gallery of Art

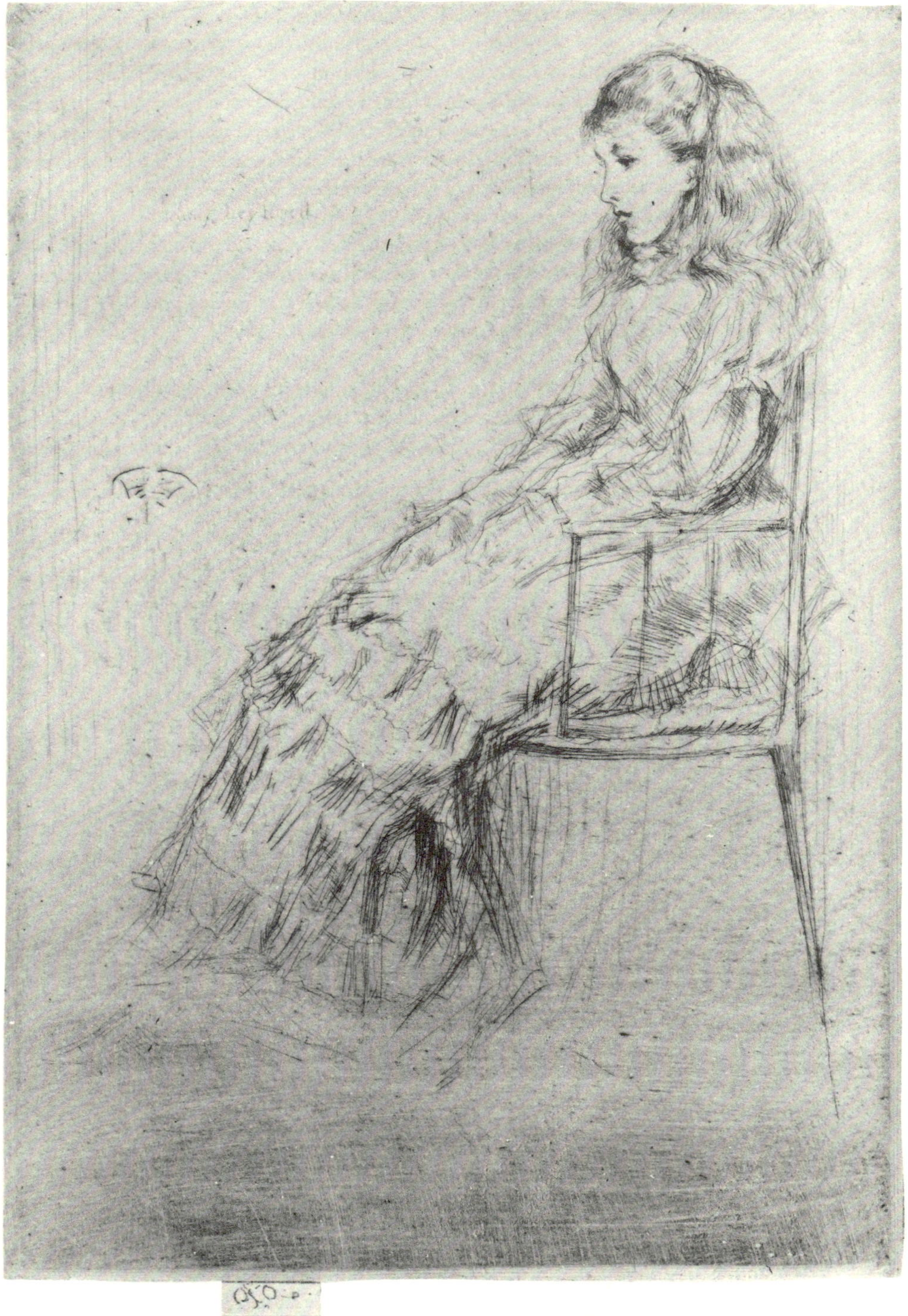

32. ***Fanny Leyland***, *1873*

K. 108 5/6

Drypoint

7 5/8 x 5 1/4 in. (19.4 x 13.3 cm.)

Brown ink on lightweight, antique laid paper with watermark: SH

Signed on tab lower left with butterfly and ***imp****; signed verso with butterfly and* ***imp****; signed in plate left center with butterfly*

Provenance: purchased from Kennedy Galleries, Inc., 1979

This is the least vigorous of the Leyland family drypoint portraits. Margaret MacDonald has accounted for this by suggesting that it may be based on a drawing (reproduced, Pennell and Pennell [1911], opp. p. 180) rather than on an encounter with the model. That drawing, however, is quite stilted when compared with Whistler's other drawings of the period (e.g., fig. 32a) and is also in the same direction as the etching rather than in reverse, which would be usual. It seems more likely, then, that the drawing is not a model for the print but actually a copy by some other artist of Whistler's etching.

Perhaps Whistler was responding to the personality of his sitter. The eldest of the three Leyland daughters, Fanny certainly appears to have been the most demure. She also is the one Whistler seems to have drawn least often, so would probably have known least well. The portrait, in any case, is a lovely example of what Wedmore described as Whistler's ability "to find a grace in the flutter of a flounce and frill."

This impression, printed in brown with a delicate layer of tone across the bottom and signed with the butterfly tab, was undoubtedly printed after Whistler's return from Venice. Earlier impressions tend to have far richer burr in Fanny's hair and on the shadows of her dress and to have been printed in black and on Oriental, rather than Western, sheets. The copper plate is in the Hunterian Art Gallery, University of Glasgow.

NOTE: My thanks to Margaret MacDonald for considering with me the possibility that the drawing in Pennell and Pennell is a copy of Whistler's print.

LITERATURE: MacDonald, p. 34, no. 67; Mansfield, p. 66, no 107; Thomas, no. 77; Wedmore, pp. 12, 51, no. 94.

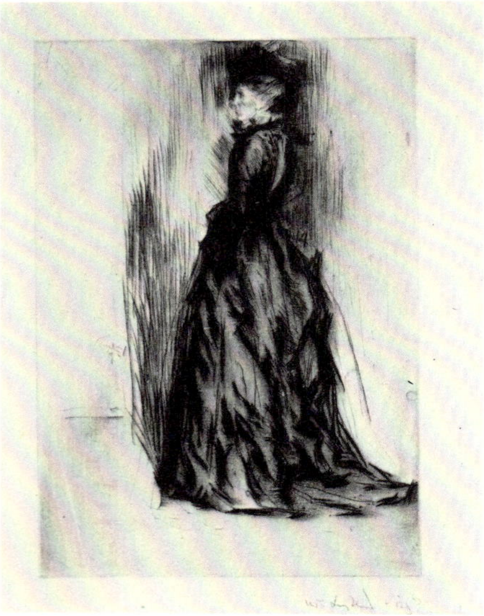

33a.
The Velvet Dress, *K. 105 5/5*
9 1/8 x 6 1/8 in. (23.2 x 15.6 cm.)
Freer Gallery of Art

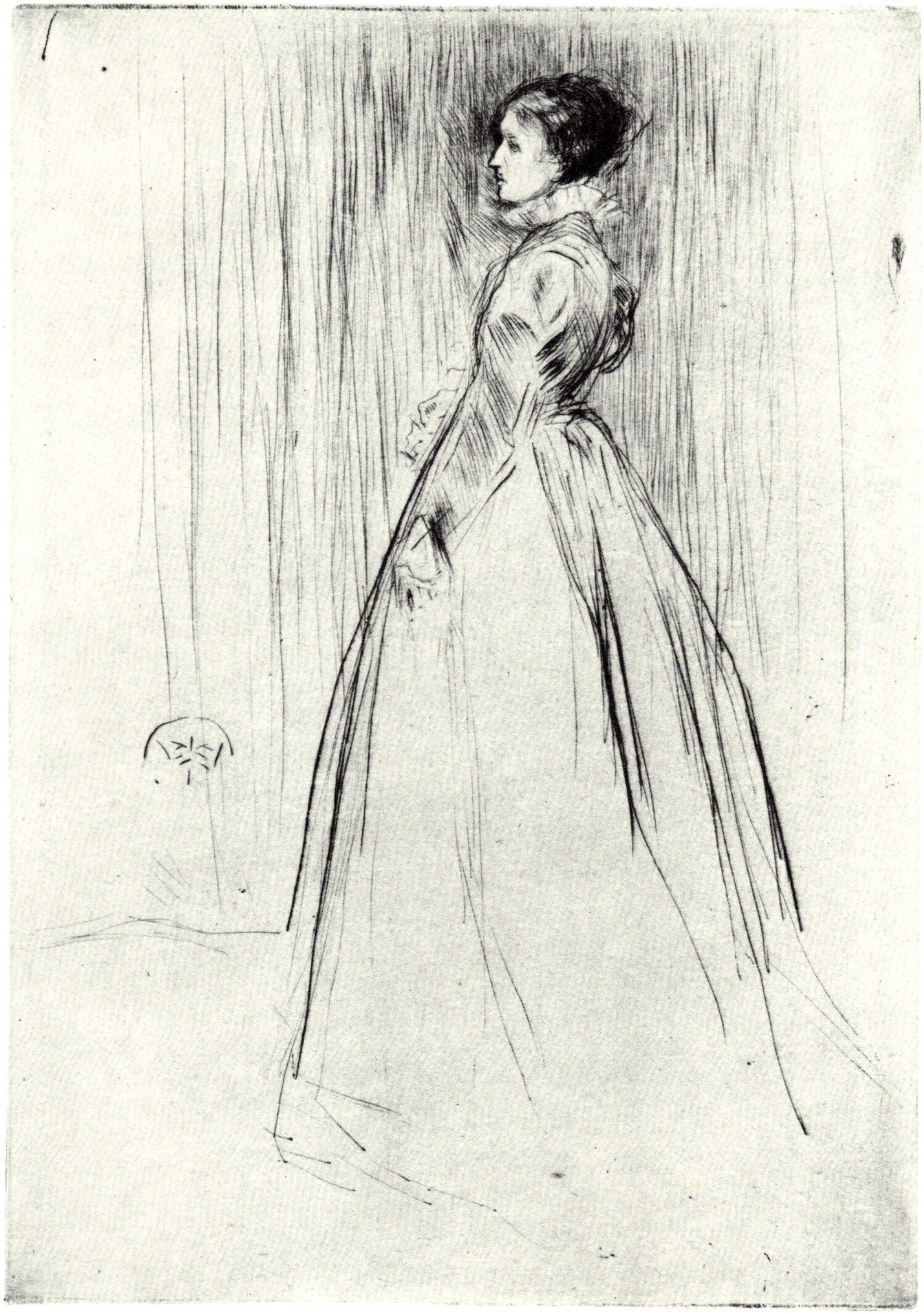

33. ***The Velvet Dress**, 1873*

K. 105 4/5

Drypoint

9 3/16 x 6 3/16 in. (23.3 x 15.7 cm.)

Black ink on lightweight laid Oriental paper

Signed in plate lower left with butterfly

Provenance: C. W. Dowdeswell (Lugt 690); Henry Studdy Theobald (noted verso); unidentified initials, J. W (?) or A. (?), in ink verso; purchased from R. M. Light & Co., Inc., 1980

Frances (Mrs. F. R.) Leyland is the subject of this and another drypoint portrait of 1873 (fig. IX) as well as numerous drawings and one of Whistler's most beautiful oil paintings, *Symphony in Flesh-colour and Pink: Portrait of Mrs. Frances Leyland* (Young et al., 106). In cataloguing *The Velvet Dress,* Thomas noted that "this and the following drypoints are in the artist's latest style, and though no less exquisite, graceful, and delicate than any previous ones, still differ totally in manner." They offer evidence of a beautifully controlled affinity between the artist and his medium. In the final state, the plate was thoroughly reworked into a full, dark, and dramatic image (fig. 33a).

Oriental papers are associated with the Leyland family drypoints, and impressions studied of *The Velvet Dress* support this. They have consistently been printed in black.

LITERATURE: MacDonald, p. 32, no. 63; Mansfield, p. 65, no. 105; Thomas, no. 76; Wedmore, p. 50, no. 91.

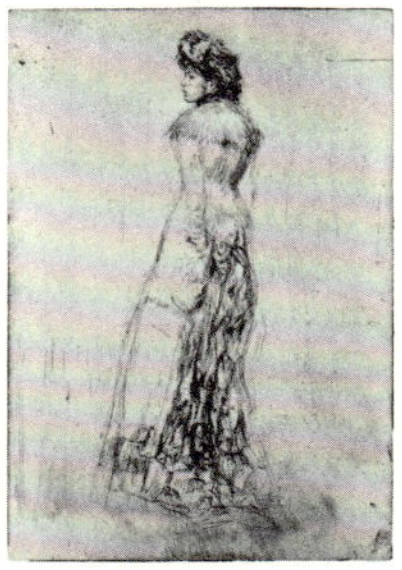

34a.
Maude, Standing, *K. 114 2/12*
8 7/8 x 5 7/8 in. (22.5 x 14.9 cm.)
Freer Gallery of Art

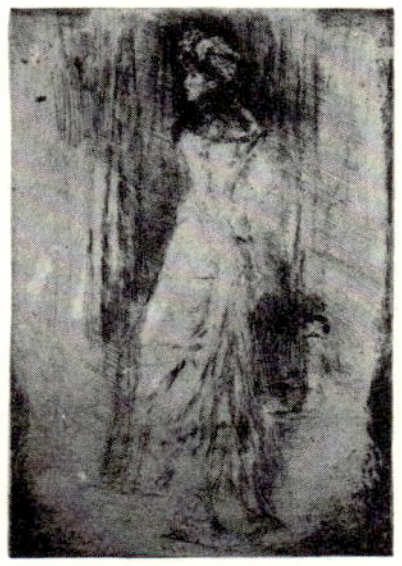

34b.
Maude, Standing, *K. 114 12/12*
8 7/8 x 5 7/8 in. (22.5 x 14.9 cm.)
Freer Gallery of Art

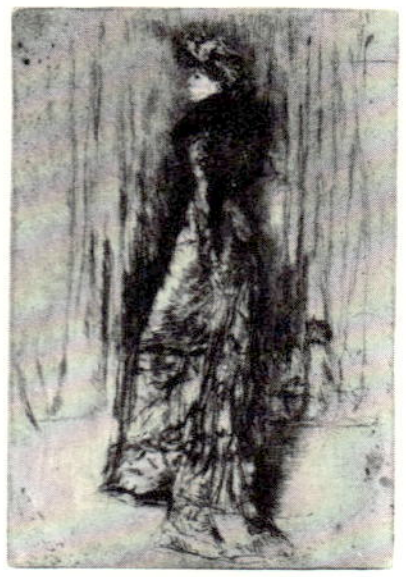

34c.
Maude, Standing, *K. 114 9-10/12*
Reworked with white chalk
8 7/8 x 5 7/8 in. (22.5 x 14.9 cm.)
National Gallery of Art,
Rosenwald Collection

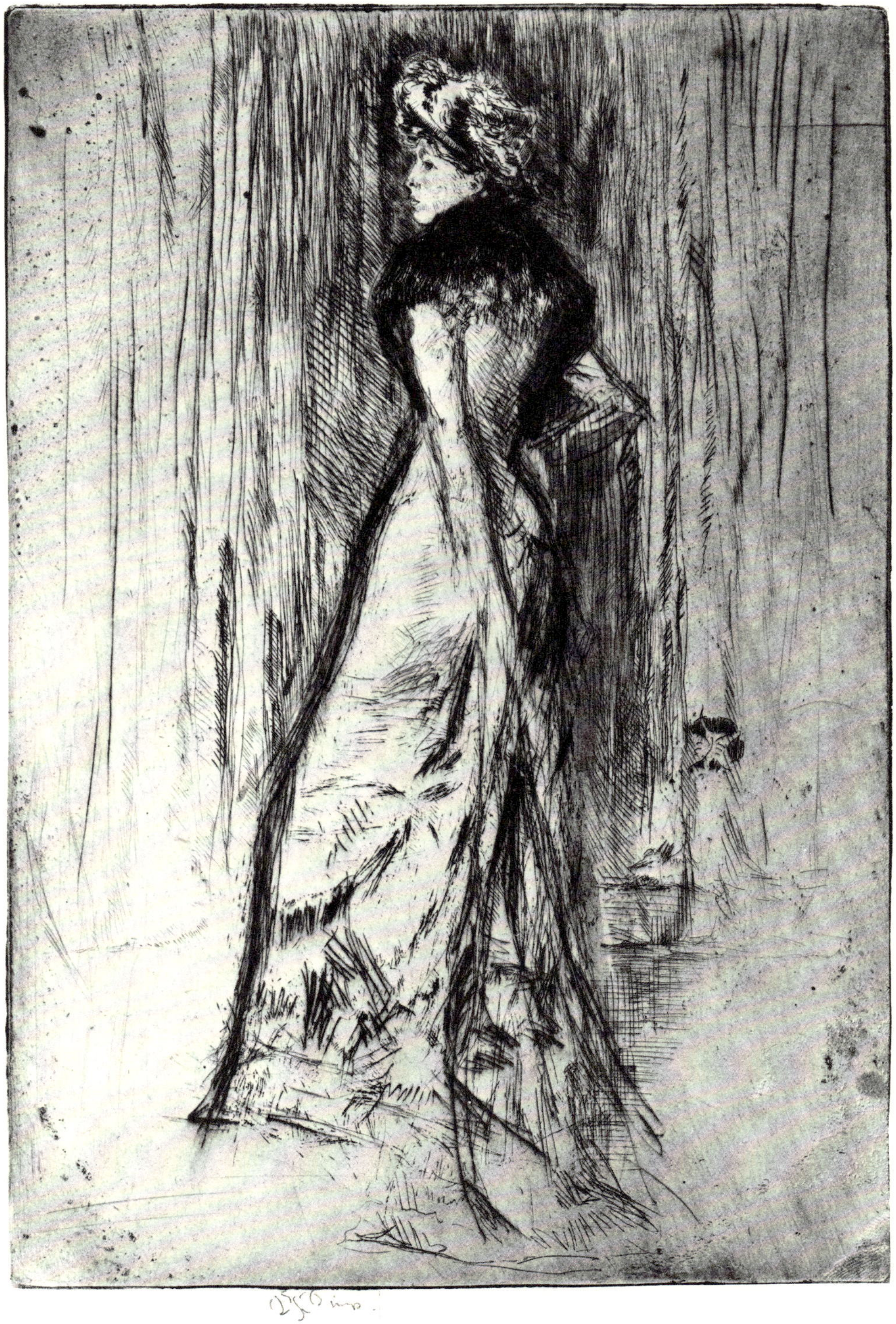

34. ***Maude, Standing,*** *1873*

K. 114 11/12

Etching and drypoint reworked with gray wash

9 x 5 15/16 in. (22.7 x 15.1 cm.)

Warm black ink on medium-weight, antique laid paper (miscellaneous manuscript inscriptions in ink verso) with watermark: T (?)

Signed on tab lower left with butterfly and ***imp****; signed in plate right center with butterfly*

Provenance: purchased from R. M. Light & Co., Inc., (Sotheby's, 12–13 November 1981, lot 479)

Beginning in the early 1870s as a stand-in model for Whistler's oil portrait of Frances Leyland (Young et al., 106) and for almost fifteen years, Maude Franklin was Whistler's mistress and model. She is the subject of many of his most beautiful oil paintings, drawings, and etchings. Margaret MacDonald has suggested that Whistler worried over this particular one for a period of several years, undoubtedly working the print through more states than the dozen listed by Kennedy. As a result of this reworking process (figs. 34a and 34b), we have several proofs of *Maude, Standing,* including the present one, with retouching by hand in various drawing media.

We can assume that by reworking a proof, the artist was trying to determine possible directions for further work on the plate. Often, however, drawn ideas are rejected, giving touched proofs like the one exhibited here and the National Gallery example (fig. 34c) no particular relation to the states of the print that follow. This makes the touched proofs all the more interesting, as they remain the only evidence of particular paths the artist considered.

In working *Maude, Standing* through so many states, Whistler made adjustments to most aspects of the plate: the pose, the costume, the atmosphere. In the examples reproduced here, there are substantial differences in the shadows on the dress and in the background immediately surrounding the figure. Maude's stance is typical of Whistler's many elegant standing portraits of the 1870s, oil paintings as well as etchings.

Impressions are known in brown ink as well as in black, generally printed on antique papers of Western origin.

LITERATURE: Donnelly and Thorp, pp. 14–15; MacDonald, p. 27, no. 49; Mansfield, p. 71, no. 113; Naylor, p. xxvi, no. 27; Wedmore, p. 52, no. 99.

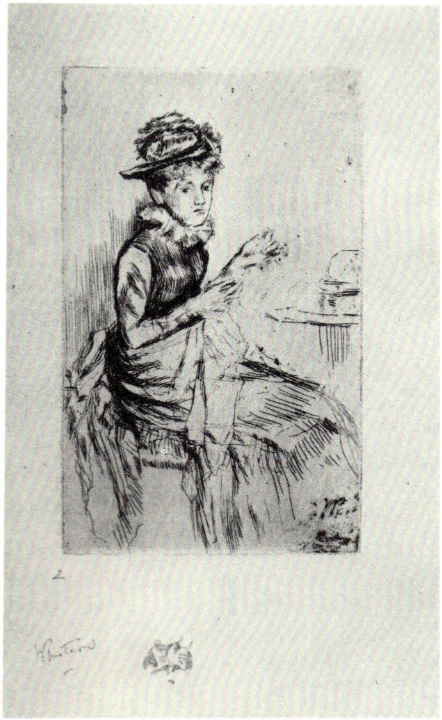

35a.
***Tatting,** K. 112*
5 x 3 in. (12.7 x 7.6 cm.)
National Gallery of Art,
Rosenwald Collection

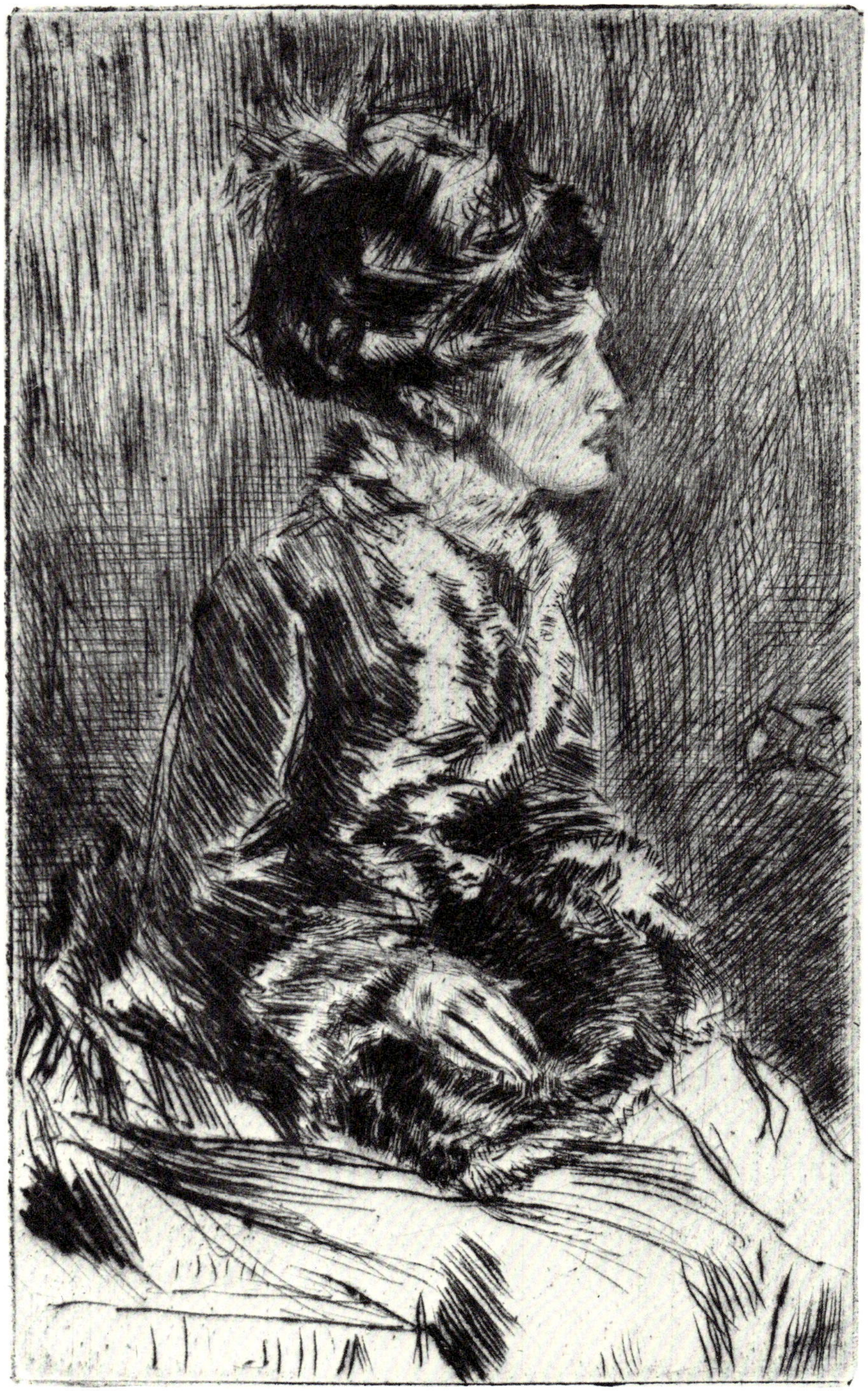

35. **The Muff**, *c. 1873**

K. 113 2-3/3

Drypoint

5 x 2 15/16 in. (12.5 x 7.5 cm.)

Black ink on medium-weight, antique laid paper with partial watermark: S (?)

Signed in plate right center with butterfly

Provenance: C. W. Dowdeswell (Lugt 690); Henry Studdy Theobald (Lugt 1376); Emma Regina Martin (initials verso); Robert Rice (not in Lugt); purchased from David Tunick, Inc., 1977

The Muff may be another study of Maude Franklin. It is a refined example of Whistler's use of subtle shifts in the direction of his strokes to imply solidity, most successfully in this instance in the hat and muff.

Impressions of *The Muff* were generally printed in black on Western papers. This appears to be an intermediate state, lacking some work in the upper right background area that appears in the final version, but showing some of the shadows near the woman's elbow that mark Kennedy's third state. Wedmore described this lovely print as "a scarce little drypoint, of elegant and refined triviality."

According to a prospectus issued in 1880 by Dowdeswells to advertise its publication in an edition of twenty-five in 1880, *Tatting* (fig. 35a) was meant to be a companion piece to *The Muff.*

LITERATURE: Mansfield, p. 70, no. 112; Naylor, p. xxvi, no. 56; Wedmore, pp. 12, 59, no. 126.

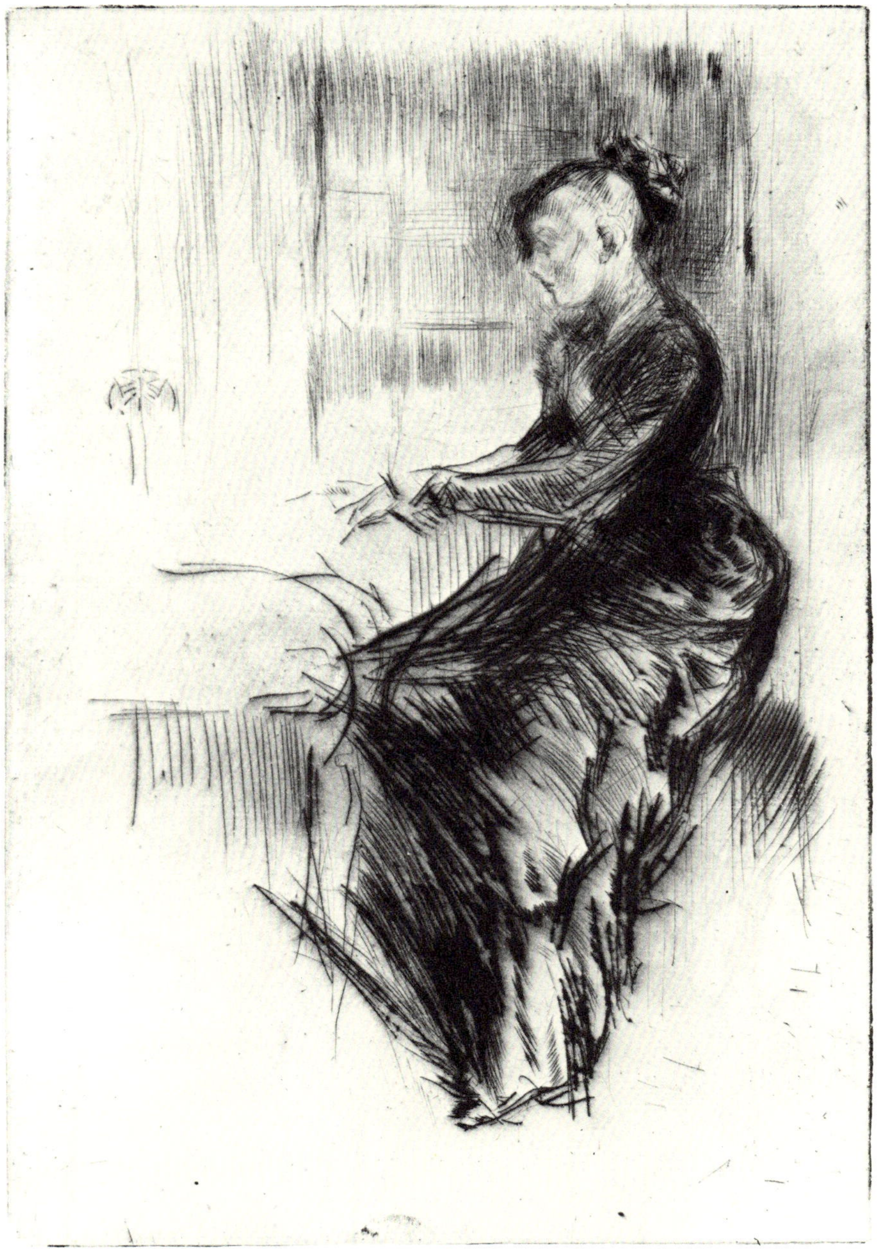

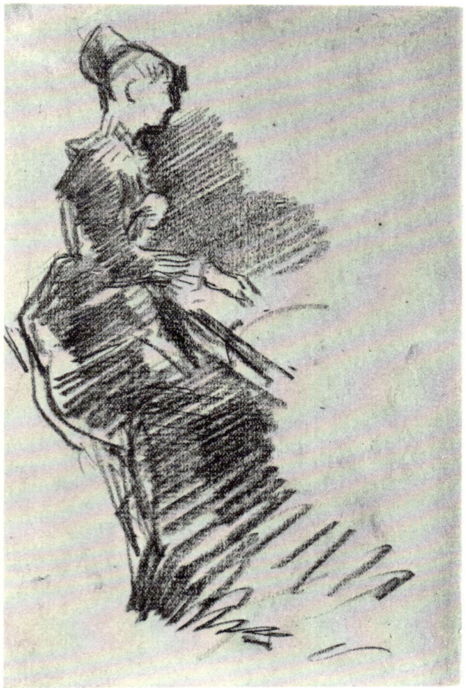

36a.
Woman Seated at the Piano
Black chalk
6 7/8 x 4 3/4 in. (17.5 x 11.2 cm.)
The Art Institute of Chicago

36. ***The Piano,*** *1875*

K. 141 4/6

Drypoint

9 3/16 x 6 3/16 in. (23.3 x 15.6 cm.)

Dark brown ink on medium-weight laid paper with watermark: De Erven Dk. Blauw

Signed lower right ***W.****; signed in plate upper left with butterfly; inscribed with symbol lower left* 

Provenance: Royal Library Windsor (Lugt 2535); purchased from Associated American Artists, 1977

The young woman at the piano is Miss Alice "Tinnie" Greaves, the sister of painter Walter Greaves. The Greaves family were neighbors of Whistler in Lindsey Row, and Walter was one of his great admirers. Whistler chose virtually to ignore the musical instrument for which the print is named, but his grasp of the figure's gesture allows us to be totally convinced of Miss Greaves's activity. Although the face is delicately rendered, portraiture clearly is not the focus of the artist's concern.

Additional lines in the background comprise most of the work on the plate after this state, although some additional lines also further define the dress. This is a lovely, rich impression of a subject that appears to be quite rare. In both ink color and paper type, it is typical of the few seen elsewhere. A small boatlike symbol at the lower left of the sheet may be a mark made by Beatrix Whistler, indicating her approval of the impression.

The cancelled copper plate was among those acquired by the Fine Art Society in 1880 and is now in the Hunterian Art Gallery, University of Glasgow. A preparatory drawing, which, like the print, is very broadly worked, is in the Art Institute of Chicago (fig. 36a).

LITERATURE: Mansfield, p. 85, no. 139; *Walter Greaves and The Nocturne,* exh. cat. (London: Michael Parkin Fine Art Ltd., 1974); Wedmore, p. 57, no. 117.

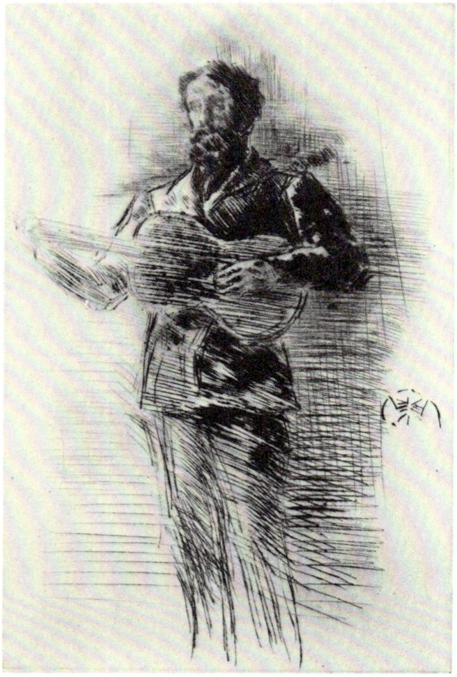

37a.
The Guitar Player, *K. 140 2-3/5*
10 7/8 x 7 in. (27.6 x 17.8 cm.)
National Gallery of Art,
Rosenwald Collection

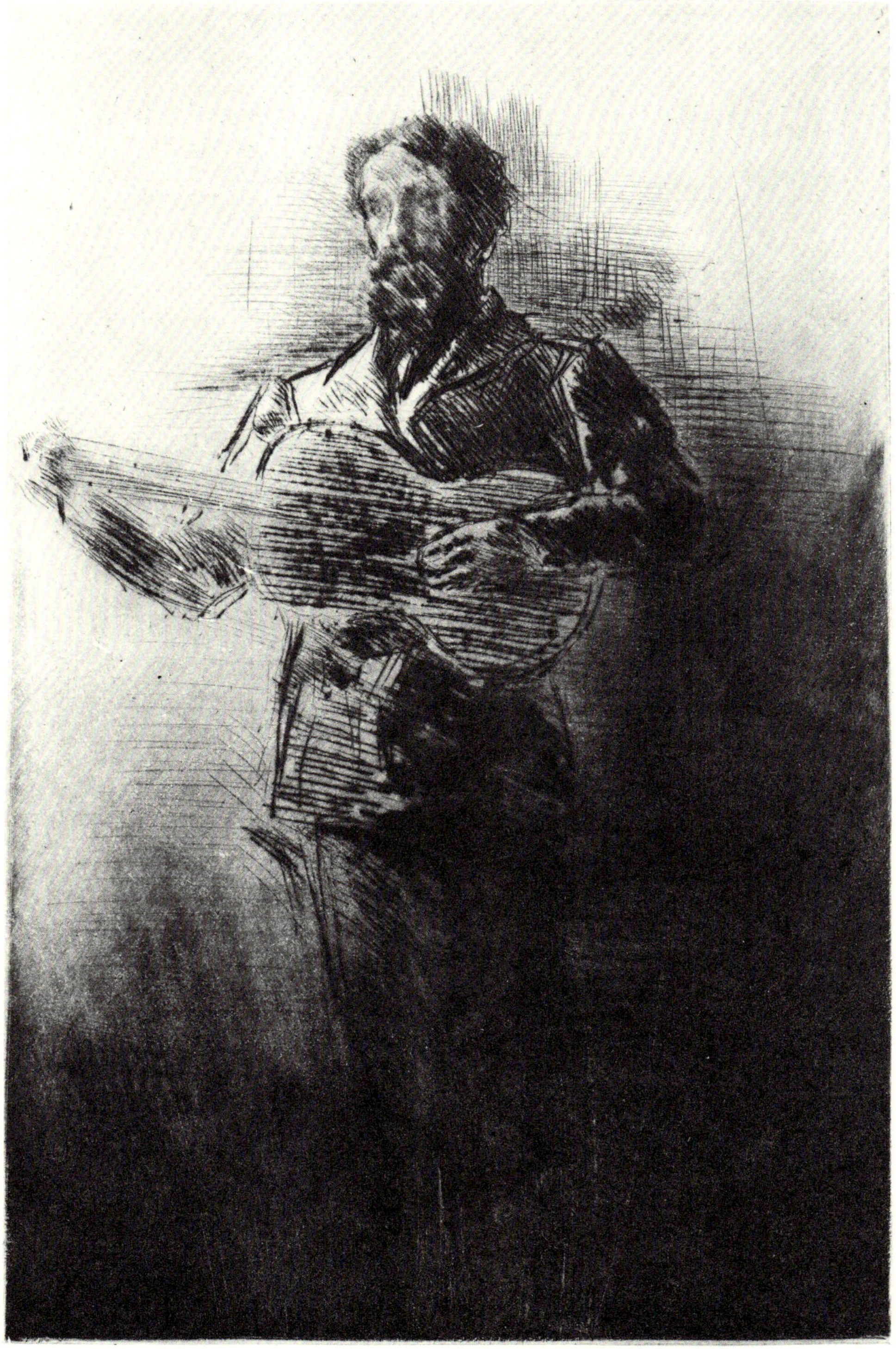

37. **The Guitar Player,** *1875*

K. 140 2-3/5

Drypoint

10 7/8 x 6 7/8 in. (27.6 x 17.5 cm.)

Black ink on lightweight, antique laid paper

Signed lower right with butterfly and ***imp;*** *signed in plate center right with butterfly*

Provenance: Edward G. Kennedy (Lugt 857); Thomas Glen Arthur (inscription verso); George W. Vanderbilt (?); anonymous collector's stamp; purchased from R. M. Light & Co., Inc., 1980

By 1875 Whistler had completed numerous portraits in drypoint, among the most beautiful those of the Leyland family (e.g., cat. nos. 31–33). Comfortable with the full-figure subject in general, he was undoubtedly totally comfortable with the medium as well. The musician here is Whistler's artist friend Matthew White Ridley, who is recorded as the lone figure in *The Storm* (cat. no. 6).

Although most impressions of *The Guitar Player* are modulated by some use of surface tone, this one is particularly beautiful in its dark richness. The use of plate tone provided the solution to a dilemma Whistler faced in some of his earlier portraits, for example, *Ross Winans* (cat. no. 16): how to deal with aspects of the image other than the head and face, aspects that were of secondary importance to him. In later pieces, such as the present one, the surface ink functions as a rich and mysterious atmosphere that envelops the figure.

Like most of the drypoint portraits, *The Guitar Player* is rather rare. Because few impressions were printed, generally they are rich in drypoint burr. Printed in either black ink or brown, in some examples the surface tone is used to emphasize the drawn areas alone (fig. 37a) rather than to establish broader atmospheric effects. Whistler himself valued the print rather highly. When he sent it with a dozen other subjects to Alfred Chapman in August 1878, it was by far the most expensive of the group (ten guineas compared with three that were the next highest price, six guineas, and the least expensive at two).

The copper plate is in the Hunterian Art Gallery, University of Glasgow.

LITERATURE: Getscher, pp. 14–16; Mansfield, p. 84, no. 138; Naylor, p. xxvi, no. 59; Wedmore, p. 58, no. 122.

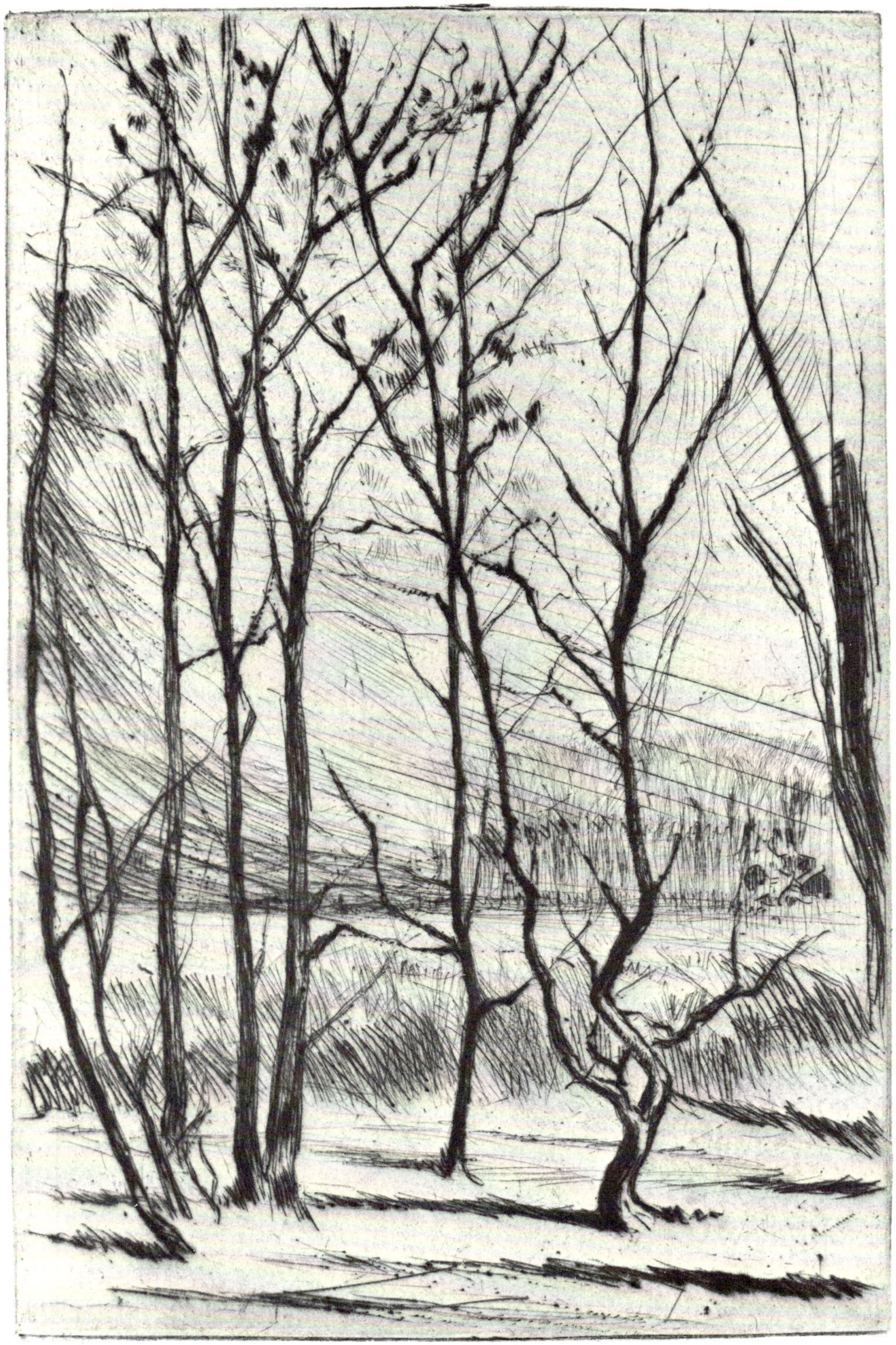

38. *The Dam Wood, 1875*

K. 145 3/3

Drypoint

6 15/16 x 4 7/16 in. (17.6 x 11.2 cm.)

Warm black ink on lightweight laid paper with watermark: Arms of Amsterdam

Signed lower right with butterfly and ***imp****; signed in plate center right with butterfly*

Provenance: Howard Mansfield (Lugt 1342); Harris G. Whittemore (Lugt 1384a); purchased from Linda M. Papaharis (Christie's, New York, 10–11 May 1982, lot 108)

The Dam Wood depicts a site near Speke Hall (see cat. no. 30). Kennedy's listing of only three states for the subject is incomplete. This does appear to be the final version, however, and several impressions seen elsewhere considered to be in the third state lack considerable work found here. The final work on the plate, essentially consisting of diagonal lines in the sky and the grasses, emphasizes the effects of wind, activating the air in the landscape. The rather rigorous lines added to the sky present a countercurrent to the descriptive qualities of the trees. The delicately drawn bank of trees at the right rear and the grasses blowing in the foreground foretell elements of landscape in the etchings Whistler was to make along the Thames a few years later (cat. nos. 26 and 28).

Another rather rare piece, *The Dam Wood* is seen printed in brown ink as well as black on a variety of papers. The copper plate is in the Hunterian Art Gallery, University of Glasgow.

LITERATURE: MacDonald, p. 32, no. 62; Mansfield, p. 88, no. 143; Wedmore, p. 57, no. 120.

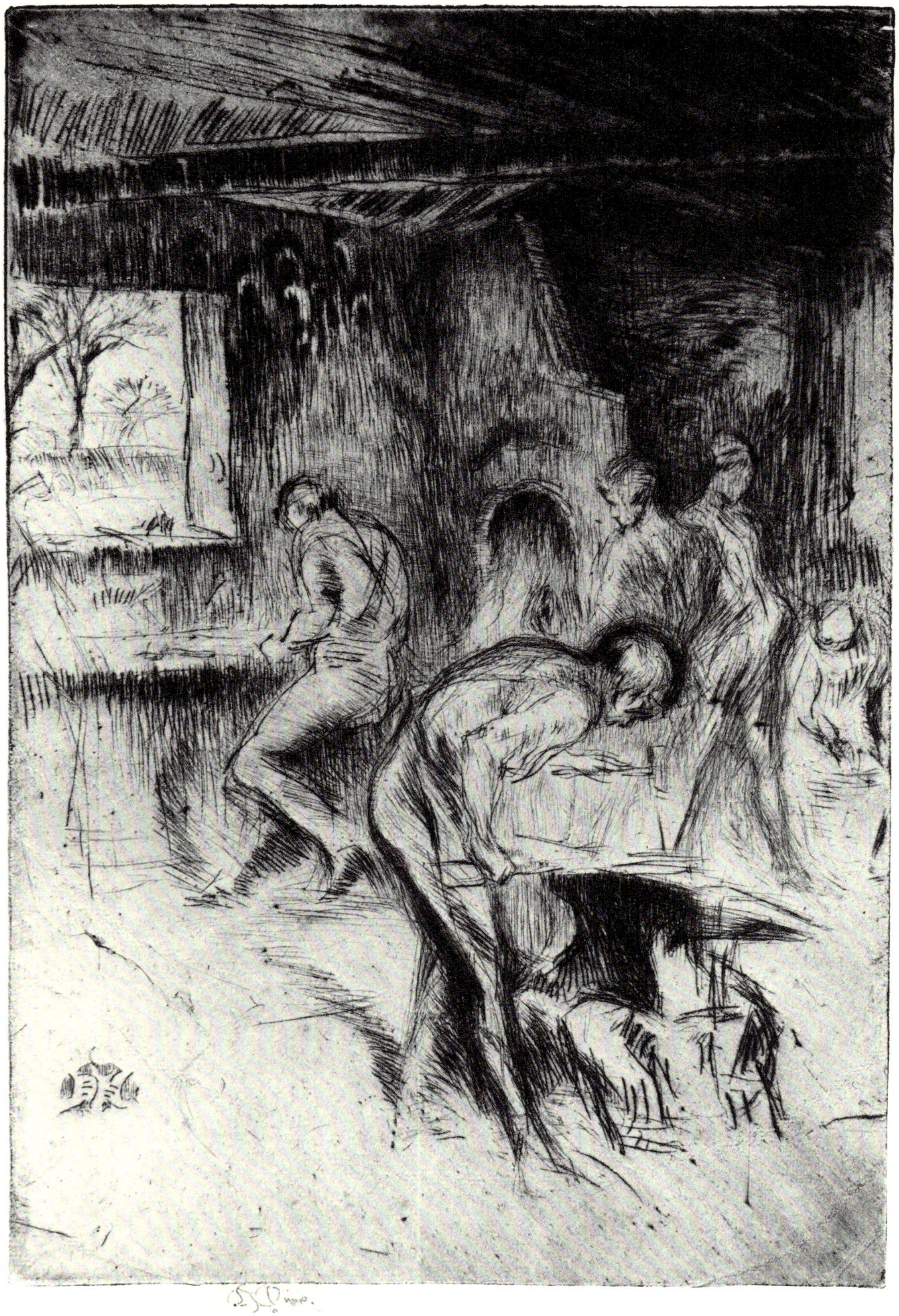

39. ***The Little Forge,*** *1875*

K. 147 8/8

Drypoint reworked with pen and brown ink

8 7/8 x 5 7/8 in. (22.6 x 15 cm.)

Dark brown ink on medium-weight laid paper (miscellaneous manuscript inscriptions in ink verso) with watermark: Arms of Amsterdam

Signed on tab lower left with butterfly and ***imp****; signed in plate lower left with butterfly*

Provenance: Walter Sickert (?); P. & D. Colnaghi & Obach, 1916 (note from old mat); purchased from Associated American Artists, 1977

Wedmore locates *The Little Forge* at Liverpool and dates the print to 1875. Margaret MacDonald has suggested that Whistler continued to work on the plate for several years. Comparison of this piece with *The Forge* of 1861 (cat. no. 7) is instructive. The earlier etching is centered around the character of the figures as revealed by facial features; in the Liverpool forge, gesture takes over this function. The broad, sweeping strokes that dominate Whistler's drawing style in 1861, emphasizing description, have been replaced in the late 1870s by brief, swift marks that work to build space and also define form. In the later piece, light is used in a less overtly dramatic fashion. The artist/viewer in 1861 was placed outside looking in; in the present piece, the artist/viewer is inside, close to the participants, and there is a window to facilitate looking out. A similar inside/outside structure appears later in *The Mill* (cat. no. 89).

This does appear to be the final version of the image, but more states than the eight listed by Kennedy are known. The butterfly on the tab is of the sort that Whistler used during the late 1880s. A notation on an old mat indicates that this impression was obtained by Walter Sickert directly from Whistler. It may have been printed and come into Sickert's possession while he was helping Whistler print the Venice etchings. The use of plate tone as seen here, particularly rich in the ceiling and in the semienclosed space at the rear, is fairly standard for this subject, although one also sees impressions that are relatively cleanly wiped. Impressions are known in black and in brown inks on paper of the general sort seen here. A study for the print in pen and brown ink is in the British Museum, and the copper plate is in the Hunterian Art Gallery, University of Glasgow.

LITERATURE: MacDonald, p. 36, no. 75; Mansfield, p. 89, no. 145; Wedmore, p. 56, no. 115.

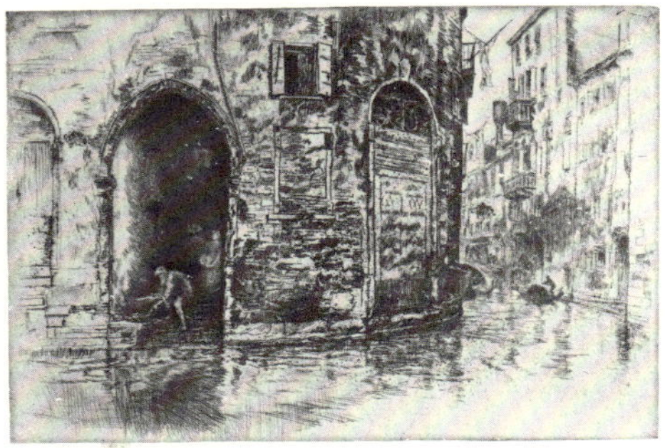

40a.
***Two Doorways,** K. 193 6/6*
8 x 11 ½ in. (20.3 x 29.2 cm.)
National Gallery of Art,
Rosenwald Collection

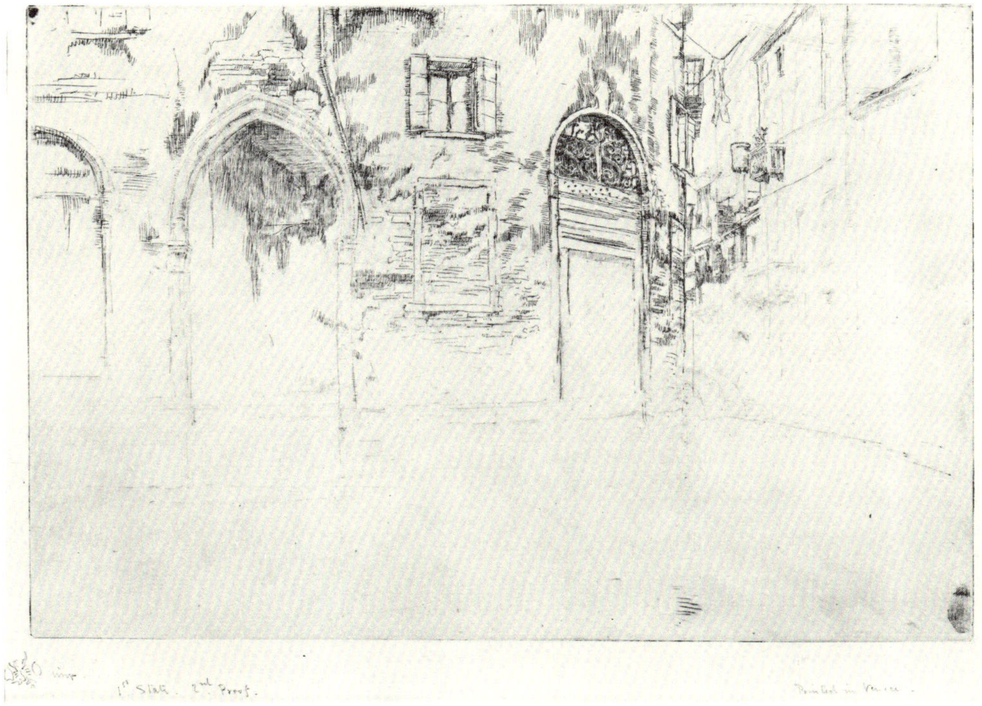

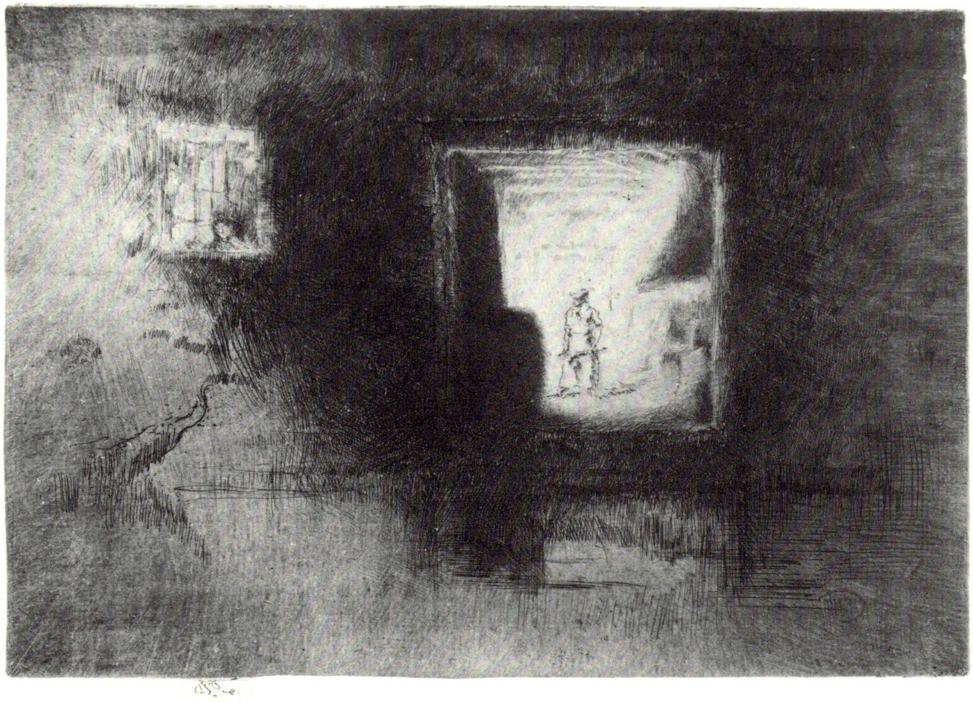

40. *Two Doorways, 1880*

One of the First Venice Set

K. 193 1/6

Etching and drypoint

8 x 11 9/16 in. (20.3 x 29.3 cm.)

Black ink on medium-weight laid paper with partial watermark: Van Gelder

Signed lower left with butterfly and **imp**; *annotated lower left* **1st state 2nd proof**; *annotated lower right* **Printed in Venice**

Provenance: anonymous collector's stamp; purchased from R. M. Light & Co., Inc., 1980

This wonderful first-state impression of *Two Doorways* gives little indication of the richness the image would eventually display (fig. 40a). It beautifully exemplifies, however, the early proofs of the Venice etchings, printed in situ. In black ink and very cleanly wiped, they showed Whistler a precise replication of the actual line drawing on the plate.

The first proof of this state (this being the second proof), printed on the same sort of paper, is in the Freer Gallery of Art. It is similarly signed and inscribed in precisely the same locations on the sheet as this one, an indication perhaps of Whistler's constant attention to matters of design. On the Freer impression, the wings of the butterfly signature are filled in, presumably a sign that it was signed by 1880, while the butterfly on the exhibited impression is of a sort not thought to have been used prior to 1882. Obviously, impressions are not necessarily signed at the time of printing; a likely occasion for signing is the time of sale.

In the second state, the bulk of the final composition was blocked in, including a gondola and two men in the foreground. Their anecdotal quality probably distracted from Whistler's essential interest in mood and composition, and they were removed before the third-state impressions were pulled. The edition was completed, and the copper plate was cancelled by mid-June 1892. The plate is now in the Hunterian Art Gallery, University of Glasgow.

LITERATURE: Fryberger, p. 37, no. 30; GUL Whistler, LB1/15; Mansfield, p. 125, no. 190; Naylor, p. xxix, nos. 85–87; Wedmore, p. 69, no. 158; Wiehl, p. 26, no. 36.

41. *Nocturne: Furnace, 1880*

One of the Second Venice Set

K. 213 6-7/7

Etching and drypoint

6 1/2 x 9 in. (16.6 x 23 cm.)

Brown ink on medium-weight, antique laid paper

Signed lower left on tab with butterfly and **imp**; *signed in plate center left with butterfly; inscribed verso with butterfly and* **ex** *(?)*

Provenance: purchased from R. E. Lewis, Inc., 1970

In theme, *Nocturne: Furnace* was prefigured by *The Forge* and *The Little Forge* (cat. nos. 7 and 39) and is mirrored by one of Whistler's very last etchings *The Flaming Forge, Ajaccio* (fig. xxxiii). But compositionally and in terms of mood, it is at the heart of the Venetian period, manifesting Whistler's delight in detached, semidistant observation as well as his enchantment with the atmosphere of night.

The use of surface tone in varying degrees to enhance the work in etching and drypoint is characteristic of the Venice subjects. This impression of *Nocturne: Furnace* is a particularly fine one with rich nuances developed throughout. Although the piece relies considerably upon its tonal wiping for dramatic power, the plate itself was also quite carefully worked in etching through several states, including a number, like this one, not recorded by Kennedy.

Whistler wrote enthusiastically of his late work on the plate to Walter Dowdeswell: "Did you see what a lovely state I have put your Nocturne Furnace in?" The plate was among those from which twelve impressions beyond the edition of thirty were printed. On February 25, 1887, the artist noted that the copper plate had been cancelled; it is now in the Art Institute of Chicago.

LITERATURE: Fryberger, p. 47, no 41; GUL Whistler, NB1, p. 33; *The Lessing J. Rosenwald Collection: A Catalog of Gifts of Lessing J. Rosenwald to the Library of Congress, 1943 to 1975,* Library of Congress, no. 1997 (Washington, D.C.: 1977); MacDonald, p. 43, no. 95; Mansfield, p. 148, no. 210; Wedmore, p. 76, no. 183.

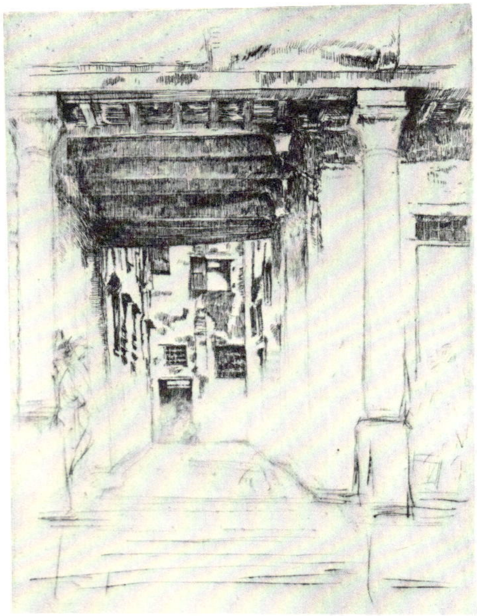

42a.
Venetian Court, *K. 230*
Unrecorded 3rd state
11 1/2 x 7 7/8 in. (29.2 x 20 cm.)
Freer Gallery of Art

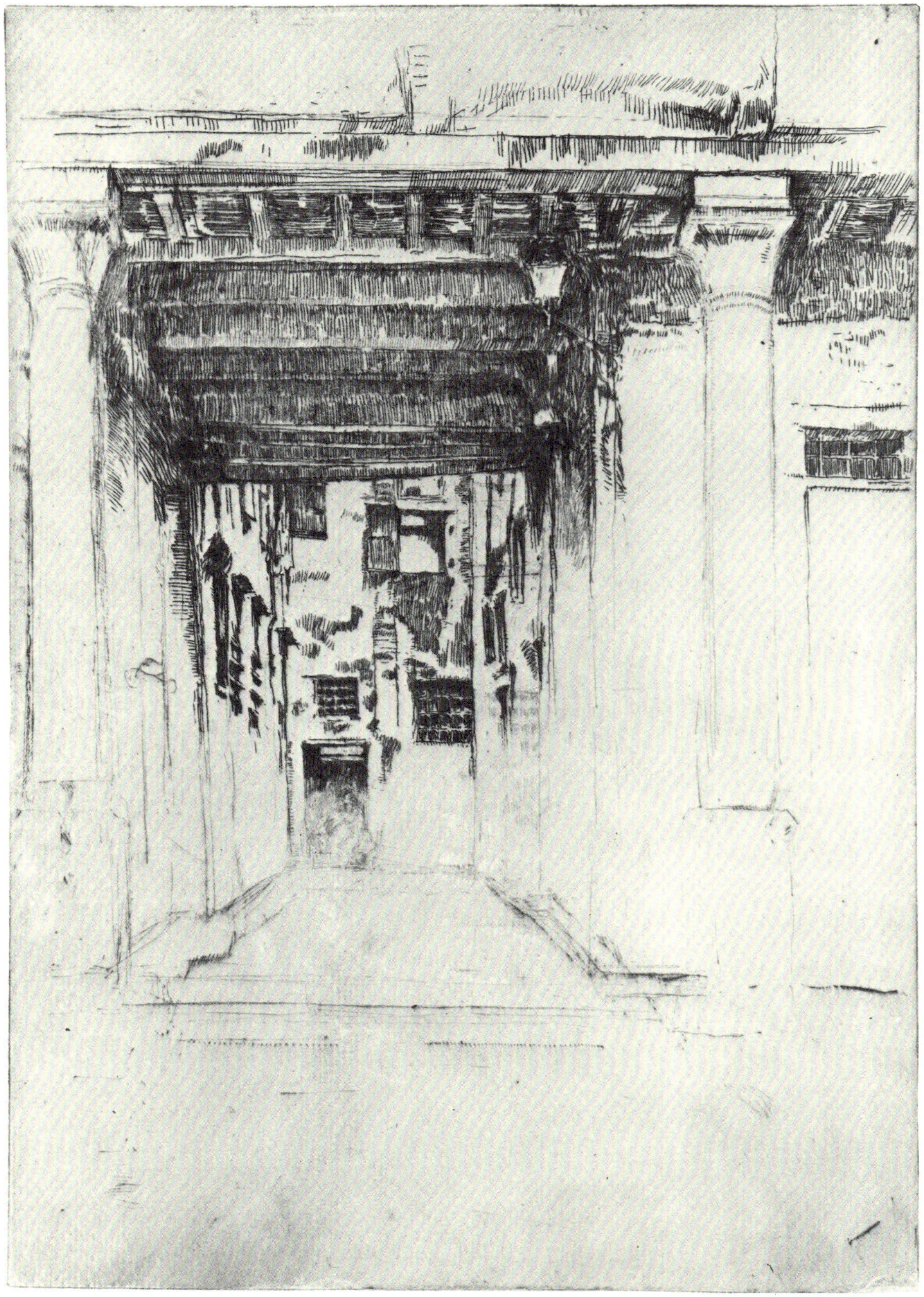

42. ***Venetian Court,*** *1879*

K. 230 1/2

Etching and drypoint

11 9/16 x 7 15/16 in. (29.3 x 20 cm.)

Black ink on medium-weight laid paper with watermark: calligraphic letters surmounted by shield with fleur-de-lis

Signed lower left with butterfly and ***imp****; inscribed lower left* ***1st state****; inscribed lower right* ***Venice 1879***

Provenance: Howard Mansfield (Lugt 1342); Harris G. Whittemore (Lugt 1384a); anonymous collector's stamp; purchased from R. M. Light & Co., Inc., 1980

Of all the Venetian scenes, *Venetian Court,* one of the earliest of them, is most reminiscent compositionally of *The Lime-Burner* (cat. no. 17). As a doorway within a doorway, it also suggests *Garden* (cat. no. 46), another Venice piece, of some months later.

The differences between this first state and the second are slight, the latter showing additional shading in the roof of the passageway. There is a third state, not described by Kennedy, in the Freer Gallery of Art in which additional work is added in a quite sketchy form (fig. 42a). Even with the indications of steps in the foreground, fuller bases for the columns, and very brief sketches of figures on both sides in the space between the columns and the main structure, there is a general lack of finish to the piece, noteworthy even for an artist who worked as sparsely as Whistler. It was not published in either Venice set.

The first-state impression exhibited here appears to be the one reproduced by Kennedy, and it may be unique. The second and third states too have each been seen in one impression only, both at the Freer Gallery of Art.

LITERATURE: Getscher, pp. 49–51; Mansfield, p. 160, no. 227.

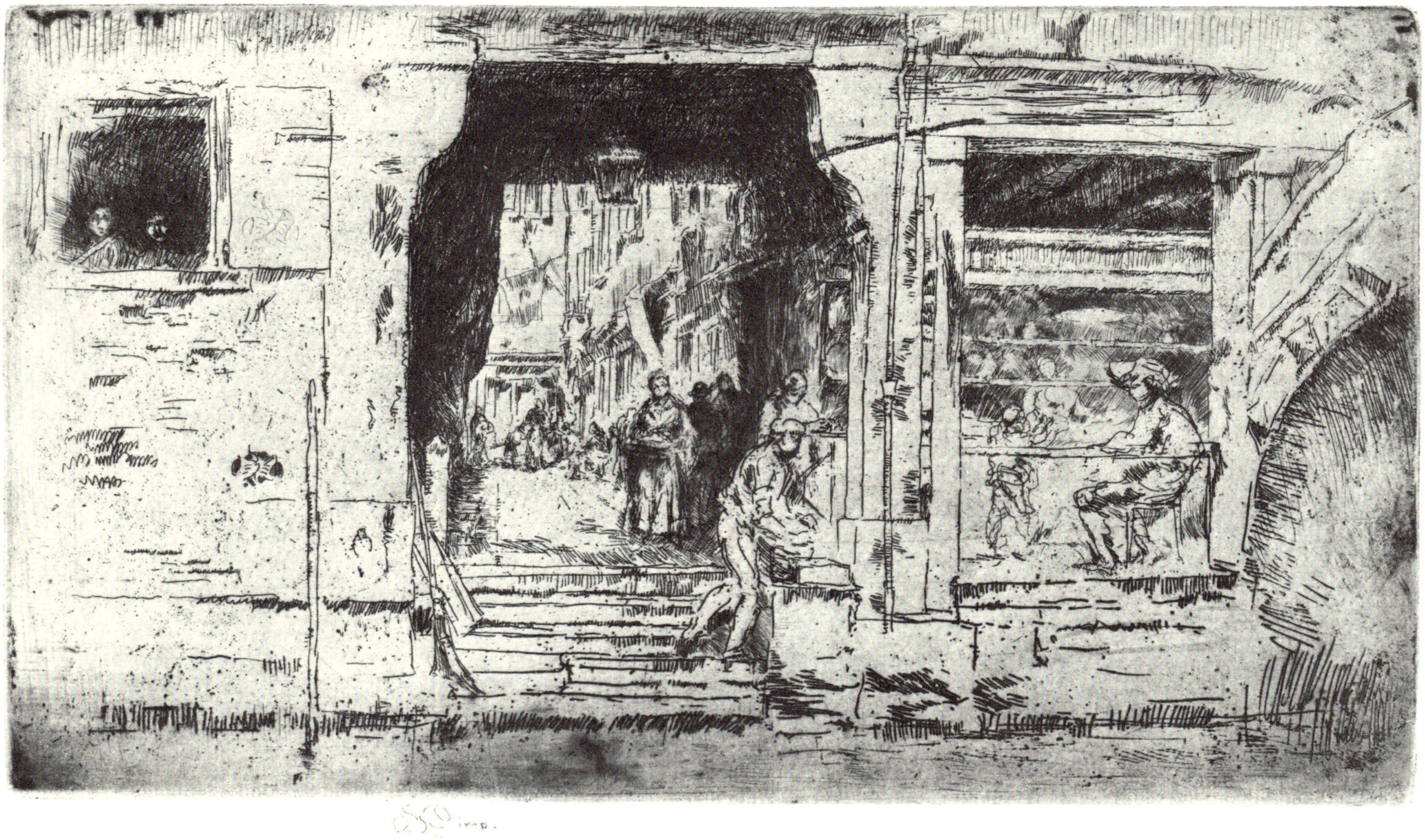

43. ***Fish-Shop, Venice,*** *1880*

K. 218 4-5/7

Etching and drypoint

5 1/8 x 8 13/16 in. (13.1 x 22.2 cm.)

Brown ink on medium-weight, antique laid paper with watermark: WW

Signed lower left on tab with butterfly and **imp**; *signed in plate center left with butterfly*

Provenance: purchased from R. E. Lewis, Inc., 1980

The *Fish-Shop, Venice* is one of the most fully structured and elaborated of the Venetian facades, most of them being of a more vignette-type composition. The subject combines elements found individually elsewhere: the window from which shadowy heads peer out at the artist/viewer; the passageway through which one moves into a teeming mass of public activity; and the framing doorway: a more private space with faceless figures. One experiences a summary of exchanges between the artist and the world.

The print was not published in either Venice set and therefore is relatively rare. This impression is a lovely one, typical in its use of plate tone, primarily in the water, to mirror the darkness of the passageway. Contrary to custom, impressions of the earliest recorded state were printed in brown, while impressions of the latest recorded state were printed in black, both generally on Western papers. The plate was put through several more states than the seven noted by Kennedy, the present impression showing one of them. The copper plate is in the Hunterian Art Gallery, University of Glasgow.

LITERATURE: MacDonald, p. 43, no. 94; Mansfield, p. 152, no. 215; Naylor, p. xxxi, no. 102; Wedmore, p. 77, no. 188.

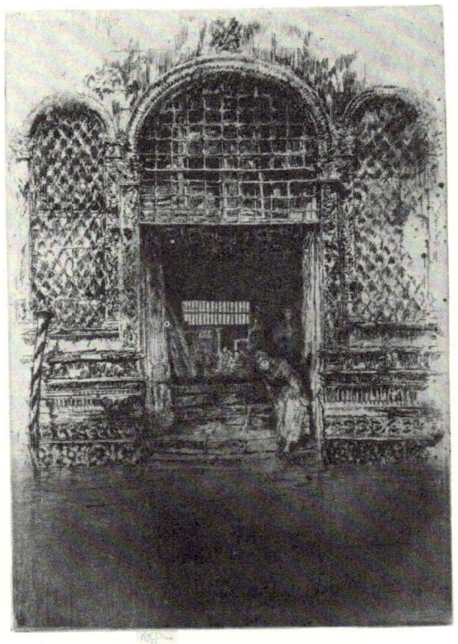

44a.
The Doorway, *K. 188*
11 1/2 x 8 in. (29.2 x 20.3 cm.)
Julius L. and Anita Zelman

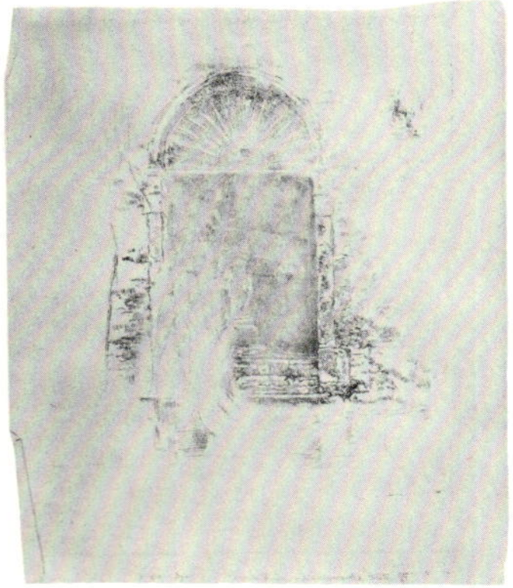

44b.
The Dyer, *K. 219*
Unrecorded 6th state, counterproof
11 7/8 x 9 3/8 in. (30.2 x 23.8 cm.)
Hunterian Art Gallery, University of Glasgow, Birnie Philip Bequest

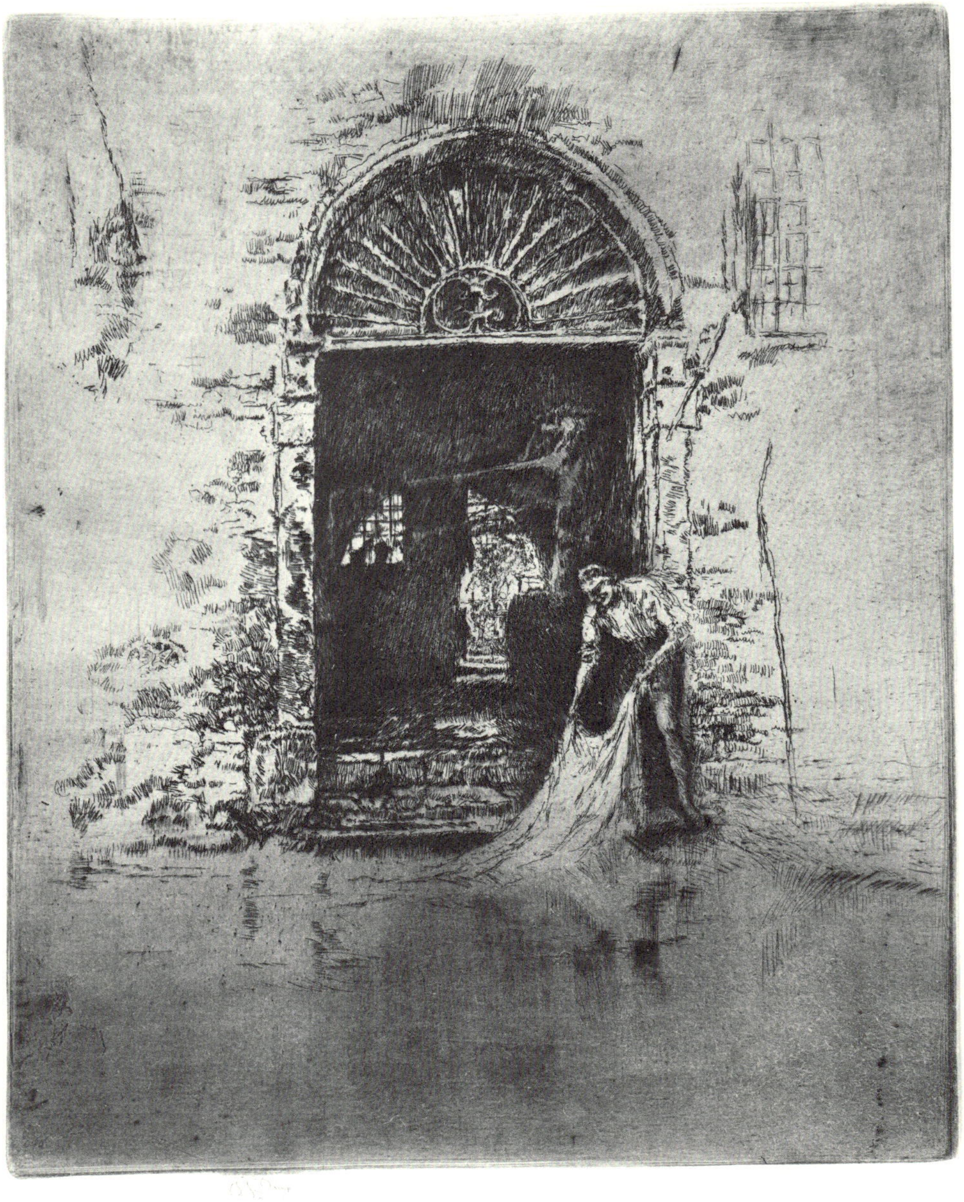

44. **The Dyer,** *1880*

K. 219 3/4

Etching and drypoint

9 7/16 x 11 13/16 in. (23.9 x 30.3 cm.)

Brown ink on lightweight, antique laid paper with watermark: Arms of Amsterdam

Signed lower left on tab with butterfly and ***imp****; signed in plate lower left with butterfly*

Provenance: purchased from R. M. Light & Co., Inc., 1983

Particularly distinctive to *The Dyer* is the outdoor view seen in the distance as one looks through the building. In general, Whistler's Venetian interior glimpses focus on the darkened space itself, emphasizing a sense of mystery.

This is a lovely impression of *The Dyer,* enhanced by a sensuous film of surface ink in the water. The print is rather similar in composition to *The Doorway,* one of the First Venice Set (fig. 44a), although it is less fully elaborated and the emphasis is on the monumentality of the figure rather than the ornate architecture. In Glasgow there are two states beyond the four known to Kennedy: the first shows the figure of the man removed, and the second shows that Whistler then tentatively replaced him with a figure of a much younger man.

Also in Glasgow is a counterproof of this final version (fig. 44b). This counterproof, a print taken from a wet proof rather than from the copper plate, shows the image reversed for a second time, that is, in the direction it appeared on the copper plate. The counterproof would have allowed Whistler more directly to consider additional work on the plate.

Although seriously considered for inclusion in the First Venice Set, *The Dyer* was not included in either of the Venetian publications and consequently is relatively rare. The copper plate is in the Hunterian Art Gallery, University of Glasgow.

LITERATURE: Getscher, pp. 52–53, 88–89; Getscher and Staley, p. 78, no. 47; Mansfield, p. 153, no. 216; Wedmore, p. 78, no. 189.

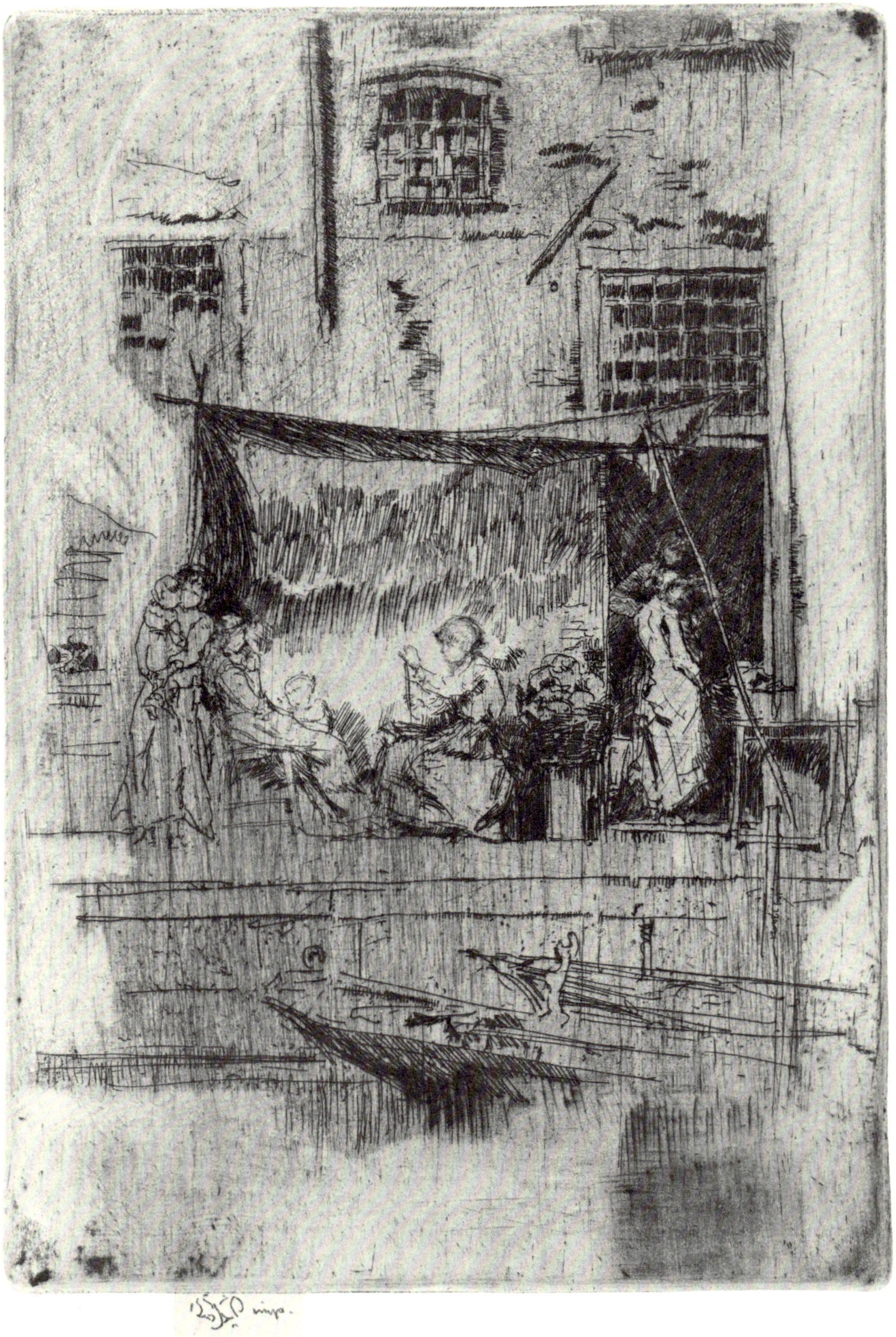

45. **Fruit-Stall,** 1880

One of the Second Venice Set

K. 200 2/7

Etching and drypoint

9 x 6 in. (22.8 x 15.2 cm.)

Warm black ink on medium-weight, antique laid paper

Signed lower left on tab with butterfly and ***imp****; signed in plate center left with butterfly*

Provenance: B. B. McGeorge (Lugt 394); T. J. Coolidge (initials verso); Henry Harper Benedict (Lugt 1298); Harris G. Whittemore (Lugt 1384a); Mrs. Edward Pulling (?); purchased from Kennedy Galleries, Inc., 1977

This early impression of the *Fruit-Stall* is a very instructive one, as it affords the opportunity to observe how a plate looks as it is worked. The gray, striated tonal areas throughout are the evidence of work with a scraper, while the whiter strokes (e.g., above and to the left of the window at center top and above, to the left, and moving below the window at the right) are the result of the burnisher's being used to polish areas that previously had been scraped. In addition, the drypoint work in the shadows of the gondolas in the foreground gives an exceedingly fresh and rich example of that method.

Whistler's essential conception of the *Fruit-Stall* is complete in this early state. Later states, of which there are more than Kennedy records, show revisions to the figures in the doorway, considerably more burnishing, and wear in the drypoint areas.

Brown and reddish-brown ink are most common for this subject as are Western papers. The cancelled copper plate was turned in to Dowdeswells on February 8, 1887, and is now in the Art Institute of Chicago.

LITERATURE: GUL Whistler, NB1, p. 34; MacDonald, p. 43, no. 93; Mansfield, p. 134, no. 197; Wedmore, p. 72, no. 166.

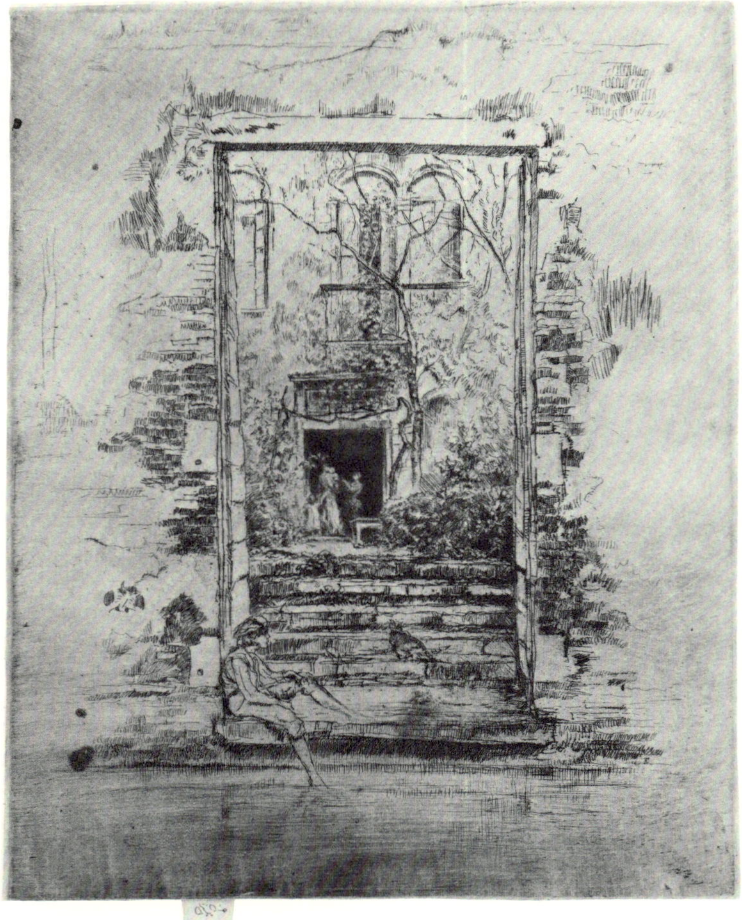

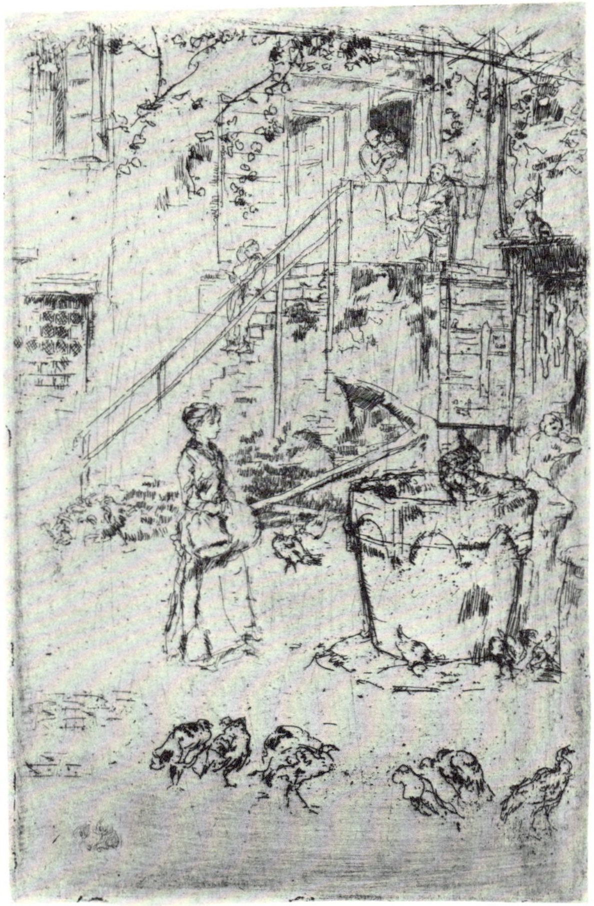

46. **Garden,** *1880*

One of the Second Venice Set

K. 210 7/8

Etching and drypoint

11 13/16 x 9 3/8 in. (30 x 23.8 cm.)

Warm brown ink on lightweight, antique laid paper

*Signed lower left on tab with butterfly and **imp**; signed in plate lower left with butterfly*

Provenance: purchased from Kennedy Galleries, Inc., 1977

Garden must have been among Whistler's favorites of the Second Venice Set. Writing to Walter Dowdeswell in September 1886, he asked, "How do you like the proof? Isn't 'The Garden' lovely?" Among its loveliest aspects is one of Whistler's most beautifully etched "landscapes." Although garden subjects with delicate, feathery foliage are found in several lithographs, nowhere else in etching does he so successfully articulate trees and shrubs in their individual diversity and in their capacity, pictorially, to function as a foil for architectural form. Moreover, in its essential serenity *Garden* stands equal to *Long Lagoon* (cat. no. 52).

Visually, on one level, the exterior wall practically dissolves, but as a support for the boy who leans against it and as a frame for the garden itself, it is a very strong element indeed. The woman holding the child, in many of the etchings a "throw-away line," here is central to the scene. In fact, the evolution of *Garden* through numerous states has been directed at clarifying their importance; the rich film of tone in the water, found in the finest impressions, although varying considerably in them, echoes and enhances the darkness surrounding these key figures.

Garden is also among the most successful examples in Whistler's etchings of his compression of pictorial space through subtle formal relationships. For example, the modulations of the exterior wall are closely allied, tonally and compositionally, to the shrubbery in the garden while those of the inner wall create a spatial tension, allying the wall simultaneously with the interior space beyond and the garden and exterior wall in front. The effect is one of shifting layers, constantly in flux. This quality of spatial ambiguity is one aspect of Whistler's approach that engages our interest today.

Garden was among the subjects printed in twelve extra impressions beyond the edition of thirty. On July 16, 1887, the copper plates for it and for *The Balcony* (fig. 82a) were the last two of the Second Venice Set to be cancelled and turned over to Dowdeswells. They are now in the Art Institute of Chicago.

LITERATURE: Bacher, p. 192; Fryberger, p. 46, no. 40; Getscher, pp. 52–53, 89–90; GUL Whistler, NB1, p. 35; *The Lessing J. Rosenwald Collection: A Catalog of Gifts of Lessing J. Rosenwald to the Library of Congress, 1943 to 1975*, Library of Congress, no. 1997 (Washington, D.C.: 1977); MacDonald, p. 44, no. 97; Mansfield, p. 146, no. 207; Naylor, p. xxx, no. 97; Wedmore, p. 75, no. 180.

47. **Turkeys,** *1880*

One of the Second Venice Set

K. 199 2/2

Etching and drypoint

8 3/16 x 5 1/8 in. (20.8 x 13 cm.)

Brown ink on medium-weight, antique laid paper

*Signed lower left on tab with butterfly and **imp**; signed in plate lower left with butterfly*

Provenance: purchased from R. E. Lewis, Inc., 1977

In capturing this charming courtyard scene, Whistler depended in large measure on an illustrative vision and an anecdotal response to life, unusual in even the most picturesque of the Venice views. The drawing, moreover, is strangely diffuse, adding up to neither a coherent composition nor a commitment to vignette. The additions in this second state are the butterfly and the series of slanting drypoint lines behind the head of the man at the right.

The ink color and paper type of this impression are typical. The cancelled copper plate, turned in to Dowdeswells on February 8, 1887, is now in the Art Institute of Chicago.

LITERATURE: GUL Whistler, NB1, p. 34; Mansfield, p. 134, no. 196; Wedmore, p. 72, no. 165.

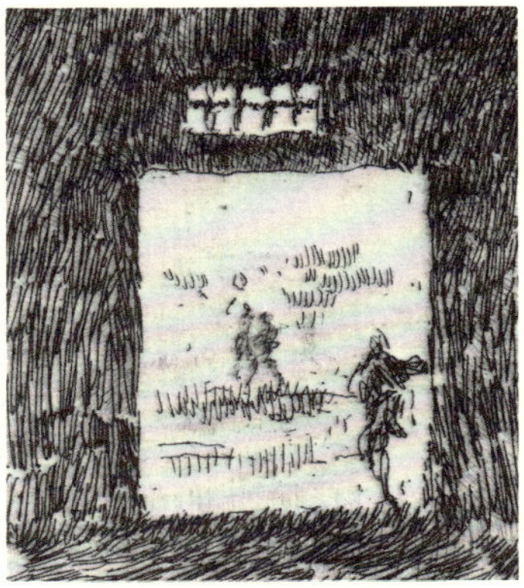

48a.
Doorway and Vine, *K. 196 3/9 (detail)*
9 1/4 x 6 11/16 in. (23.4 x 17 cm.)
National Gallery of Art, Gift of
Mr. and Mrs. J. Watson Webb in Memory of
Mr. and Mrs. H. O. Havemeyer

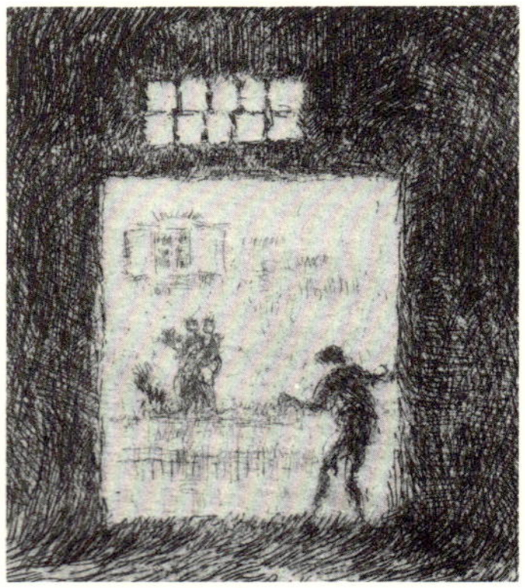

48b
Doorway and Vine, *K. 196 6/9 (detail)*
9 1/4 x 6 5/8 in. (23.4 x 16.9 cm.)
National Gallery of Art,
Rosenwald Collection

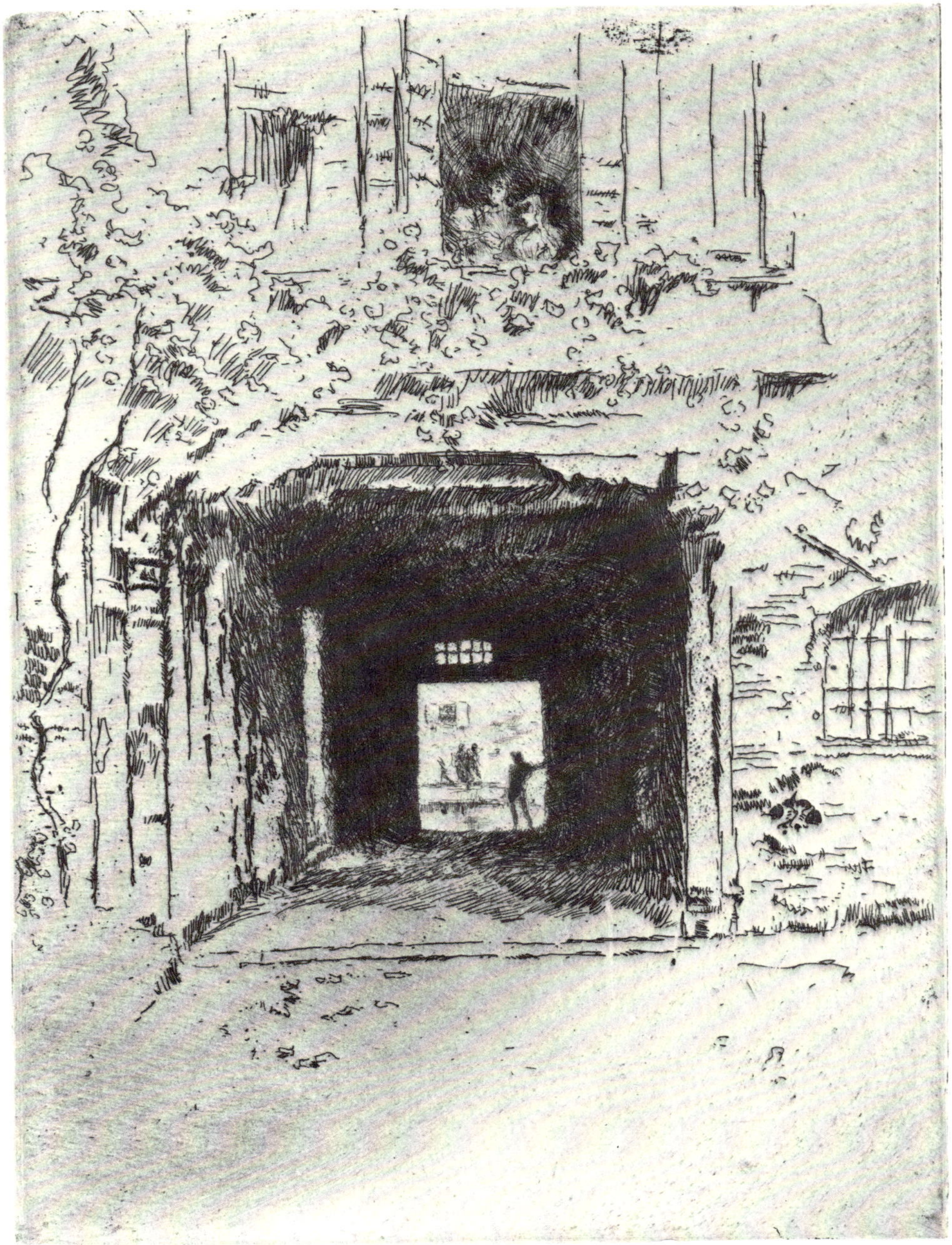

48. **Doorway and Vine,** 1880

One of the Second Venice Set

K. 196 9/9

Etching and drypoint

9 1/8 x 6 5/8 in. (23.2 x 16.8 cm.)

Brown ink on medium-weight laid paper with watermark: LVG surmounted by shield with fleur-de-lis surmounted by crown

Signed lower left on tab with butterfly and ***imp****; signed in plate lower right with butterfly*

Provenance: Otto Gerstenberg (Lugt 2785); purchased from Zeitlin & Ver Brugge Booksellers, 1970

The framed image intrigued Whistler as early as 1858 (see cat. no. 1). It takes a variety of forms in the Venetian pieces, one of them the double frame–window and passageway–seen here in *Doorway and Vine.* In addition, Whistler's almost casual assimilation of the broad compositional structures and the spatial compression of Japanese prints further enhances his framing strategy.

Several more states than the nine listed by Kennedy are known, but this is probably the image in its completed form. The scene was basically unchanged after Kennedy's third state: the figures in the window and at the far end of the passageway were reworked and clarified (see figs. 48a and 48b, both details different from the exhibited impression), and the dark shadow area was made more intense. These are the sorts of areas that generally engaged Whistler's attention as he worked the Venice series as a whole through its numerous states.

The foliage at the upper left, in keeping with the open and airy vignette image, is handled in a much more abbreviated manner here than a similar detail is handled in *Ponte del Piovan* (cat. no. 62), where the landscape element is part of a more fully and heavily worked composition.

Printed in twelve impressions beyond the edition of thirty, the cancelled copper plate was turned over to Dowdeswells on July 7, 1887. It is now in the Art Institute of Chicago.

LITERATURE: GUL Whistler, NB3, p. 39; Mansfield, p. 129, no. 193; Wedmore, p. 161, no. 70.

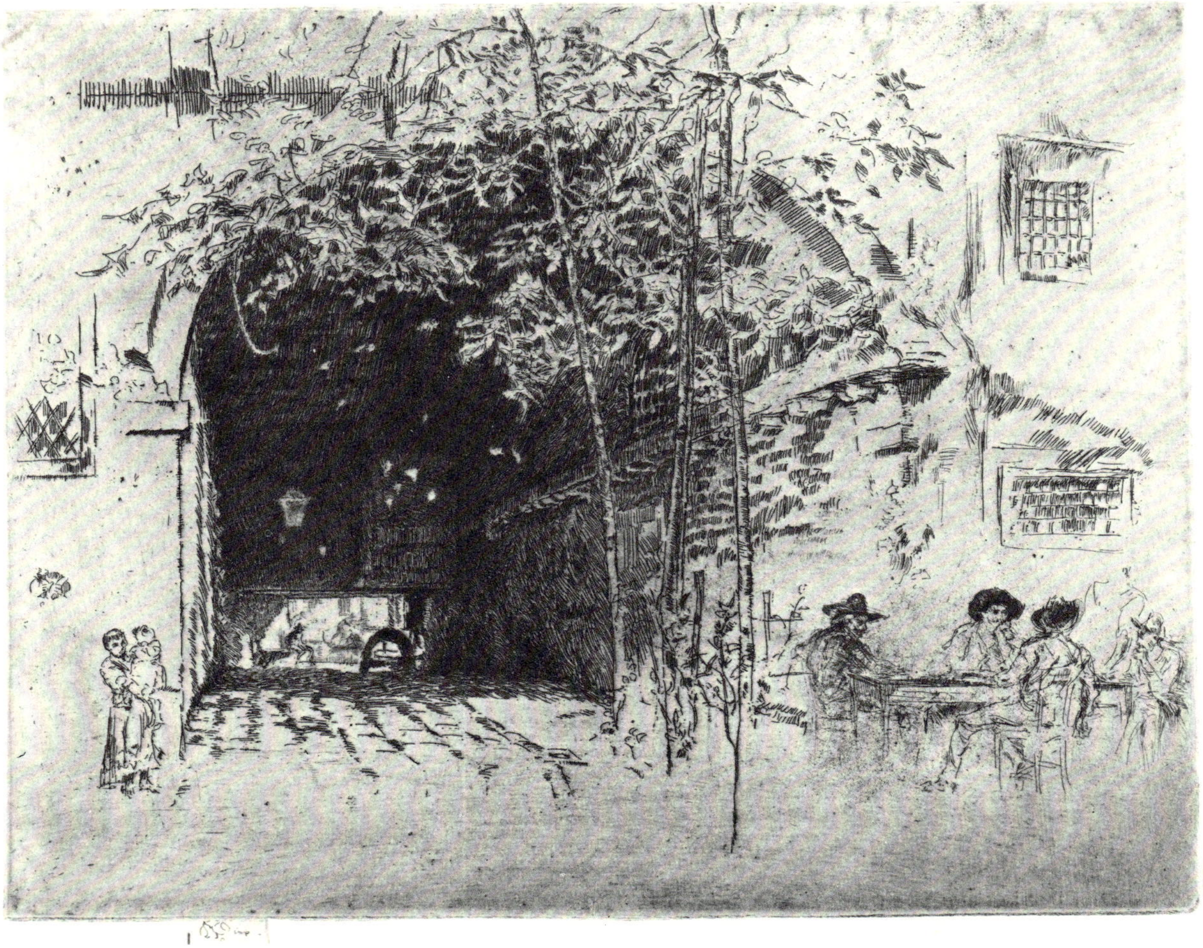

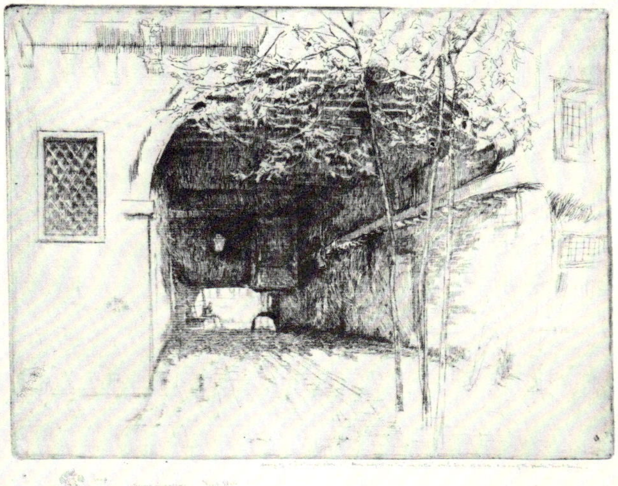

49a.
The Traghetto, No. 1, *K. 190*
9 3/8 x 12 in. (23.8 x 30.5 cm.)
Freer Gallery of Art

49. **The Traghetto, No. 2,** *1880*

One of the First Venice Set

K. 191 3-4/6

Etching and drypoint

9 1/2 x 12 in. (24.1 x 30.6 cm.)

Brown ink on lightweight, antique laid paper with watermark: Arms of Amsterdam

Signed lower left on tab with butterfly and **imp***; signed in plate lower left with butterfly*

Provenance: purchased from Zeitlin & Ver Brugge Booksellers, 1969

The Traghetto, No. 2 is Whistler's second etching of this subject. *The Traghetto, No. 1* (fig. 49a), which preceded *No. 2* by some months, was never published, however, and is known in a few proof impressions only. Otto Bacher recounts how the artist had overworked his first version of the image. In making a fresh start, Whistler inked the plate with white paint and made a proof to be used for transferring the image of *The Traghetto, No. 1* to a second copper plate. The acid-resist ground on the second plate was quite black, allowing the transferred white paint image to stand out. Whistler was able thereby to replicate the subject selectively. Using his first proof of the first plate as a model, he worked for days redrawing the image Despite this care in making a new start, he became dissatisfied. Between the second and third states, the artist almost entirely reworked the second *Traghetto* plate. This fourth state and the two later ones show only minor changes and additions however.

One must be amused by Whistler's sense of his own history. Having destroyed his first version of *The Traghetto,* he carefully annotated the proof of it acquired by Charles Freer, making certain that it was very clear what it was: *Proof of a destroyed plate–same subject as the "Traghetto" which took its place & is one of the Venice First Series.*

A lovely note in *Traghetto, No. 2* is the young woman standing, holding a child, an ensemble seen repeatedly in Whistler's work throughout the balance of his career.

Even beyond the early states, impressions are known in black as well as in brown on both Oriental and Western papers. The edition was completed and the copper plate cancelled by mid-June 1892; the plate is now in the Freer Gallery of Art.

LITERATURE: Bacher, pp. 169–84; Getscher, pp. 75–78; GUL Whistler, LB1/15; Mansfield, p. 122, no. 181; Naylor, p. xxix, no. 83; Wedmore, p. 68, no. 156; Wiehl, p. 25, no. 32.

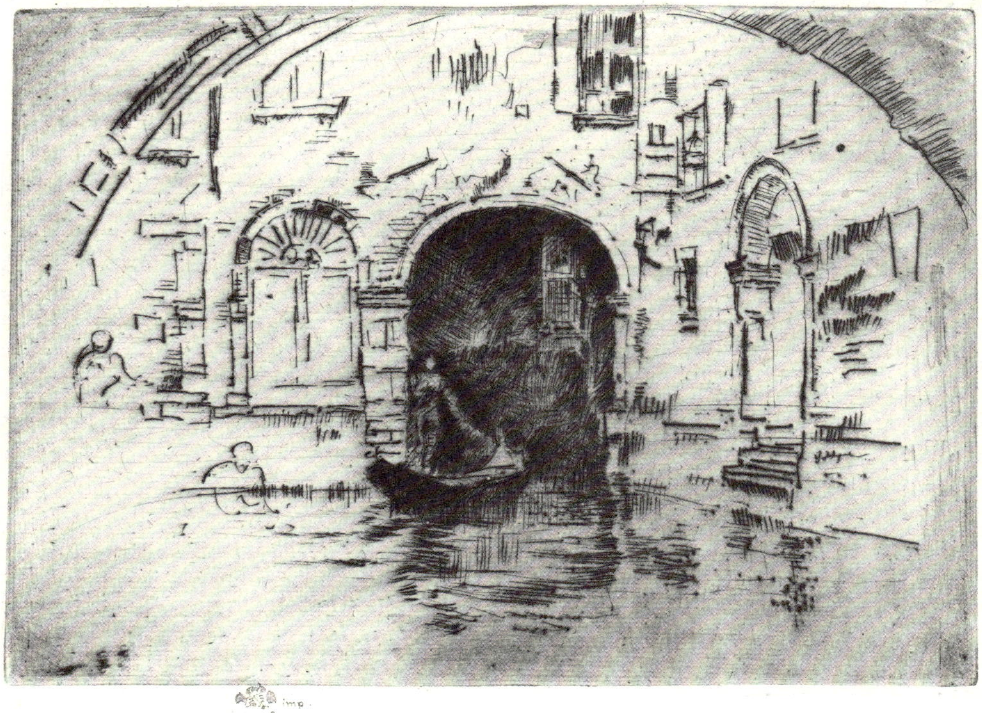

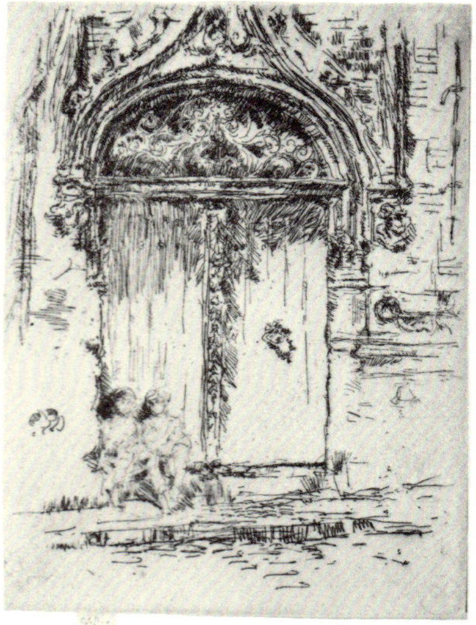

50a.
Hangman's House, Tours, *K. 376*
5 5/16 x 3 7/8 in. (13.5 x 9.8 cm.)
Freer Gallery of Art

50. **Stables,** *1880*

K. 225 2/3

Drypoint

6 7/16 x 9 1/8 in. (16.7 x 23.2 cm.)

Black ink on lightweight, antique laid paper with partial watermark

Signed lower left on tab with butterfly and ***imp****; inscribed verso lower left* ***1st proof*** *and lower right* ***Whistler***

Provenance: H. O. Havemayer (?); anonymous collector's stamp; purchased from Thos. Agnew & Sons, Ltd., 1982

Stables represents a shelter for gondolas. It is an extraordinarily selective piece in which the very minimum quantity of marks establishes a cohesive architectural composition. The darkened distance through the passageway shows us that this is actually another nocturne, despite its overall sense of brightness; the clear delineation of structures in this distant space further adds to the image's clarity of focus. It is interesting to compare the piece with some of the later etchings, like *Hangman's House* (fig. 50a), which focuses to an even greater degree on an isolated doorway/passageway image.

Not issued in either Venice set, *Stables* is exceedingly rare. Indeed, it is not found in such important collections of Whistler's prints as the Freer Gallery of Art and the Hunterian Art Gallery. It was, however, of interest to collectors during Whistler's lifetime. In 1889 Ernest Brown wrote him to send an impression for an unnamed buyer, requesting, "Please write on the back 'special proof' or something of that sort"–an interesting comment on the importance to Whistler personally of at least some of his inscribed proofs.

The type of butterfly signature on the tab of this impression, one with veined wings, indicates that it was printed and signed about 1880. The copper plate is in the Hunterian Art Gallery, University of Glasgow.

LITERATURE: GUL Whistler, F136; Mansfield, p. 157, no. 222; Wedmore, p, 79, no. 198.

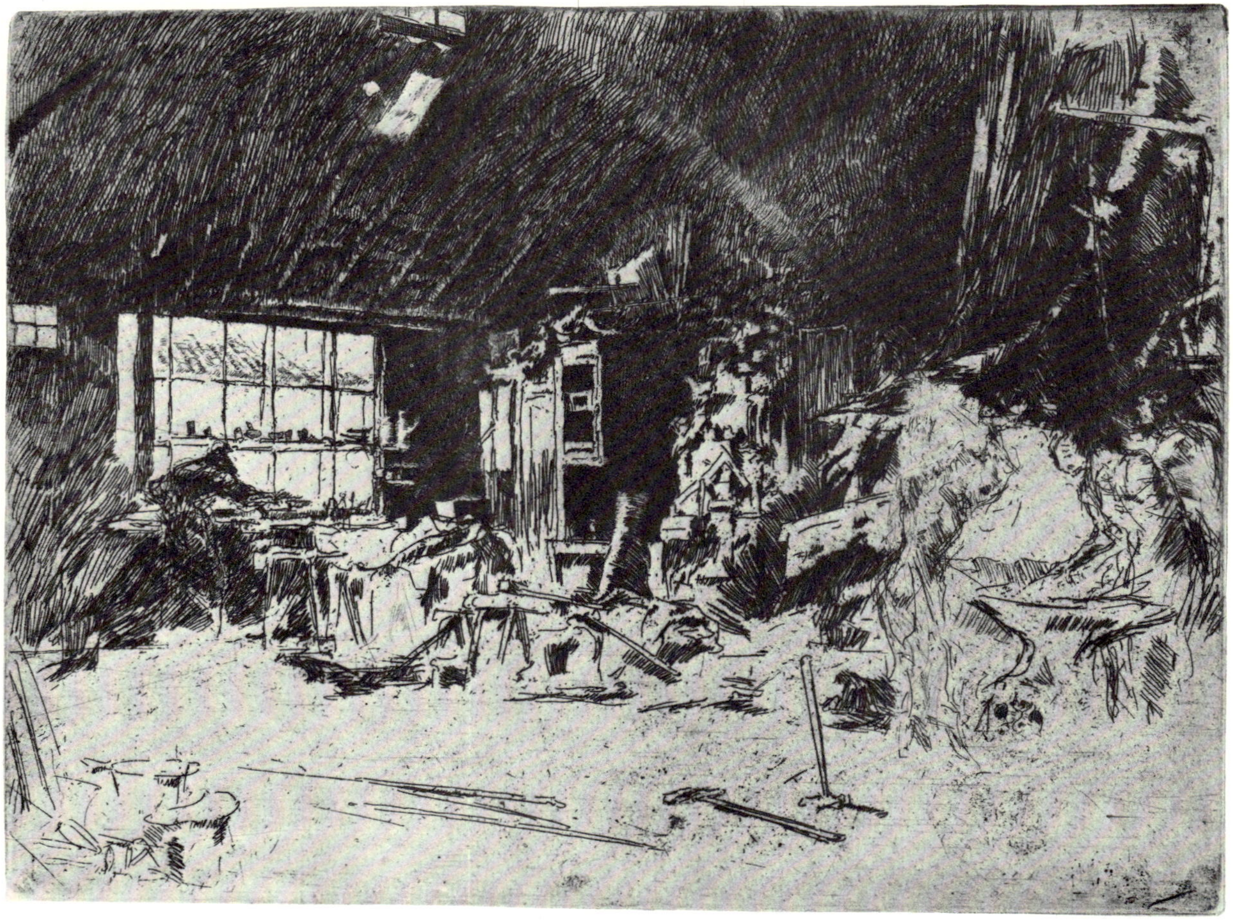

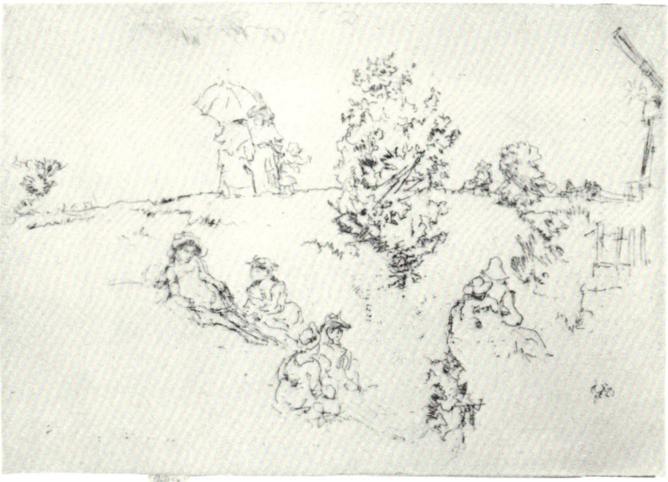

51a.
Ramparts, Sandwich, *K. 309*
5 x 7 in. (12.7 x 17.8 cm.)
Freer Gallery of Art

51. ***The Smithy,*** *c. 1880*

K. 240 2-3/5

Etching and drypoint reworked with pencil and pen and brown ink

6 3/4 x 8 7/8 in. (17.1 x 22.6 cm.)

Brown ink on medium-weight, antique laid paper

Signed in plate lower right with butterfly

Provenance: purchased from David Tunick, Inc., 1978

The Smithy presents particular problems. It has generally been placed in the mid-1880s and located, at least in one instance, in Belgium. But the print is totally unlike the swift, brief sketches, such as *Ramparts, Sandwich* (fig. 51a), which are characteristic of Whistler's etching during that period. In addition, the style of butterfly with which the plate is signed at the lower right, according to Margaret MacDonald, was used during a short period, 1878–81, at most. This, then, places the print right in the midst of the Venice sojourn, although it has never been associated with the prints done there.

The tile roofs seen through the window at the left suggest that part of the world as a possible site for this blacksmith subject. The handling of the line work fits nicely when compared with the shadow areas of such pieces as *Doorway and Vine* and *The Traghetto, No. 2* (cat. nos. 48 and 49). In addition, the figures at the right were reworked considerably (see below), as figures were in *The Dyer* and *The Doorway* (cat. no. 44 and fig. 44a), among other Venice subjects. A counterproof for the piece is known in Glasgow, relating it, with respect to working process, to *The Dyer* as well. Unfortunately, the copper plate does not conform to either of the types that are specifically associated by Getscher with Venice, but, then, not all of the plates do fit his categories. Documents concerning printing of *The Smithy* in the early 1880s have not been located; the earliest one found to date has an impression sold in 1886.

In summary, this piece may or may not have been done in Venice. If it was, the fact that Whistler had considerable trouble with the figures (and seems never really to have resolved them) could be a reason that it was one of the few Venice etchings not included in the 1883 exhibition at the Fine Art Society. Nevertheless it does seem clear, on the basis of stylistic evidence, that *The Smithy* dates from about the time of the Venice trip.

This appears to be an intermediate state, showing the man to the left of the butterfly as in state two, but with the third-state additions to the man at the right and to the ceiling beam. Reworked on this sheet with ink and pencil, particularly in the area of the figures, in the next state the sketchy standing figure to the left of the butterfly was removed. An impression of Kennedy's fifth state in the Freer Gallery of Art, however, shows him redrawn in pencil in a pose quite similar to the one seen here. The copper plate is in the Hunterian Art Gallery, University of Glasgow.

NOTE: Appreciation is due to Margaret F. MacDonald and Robert H. Getscher for their assistance in considering the possibility of placing this print in Venice.

LITERATURE: *An Exhibition of Etchings, Drypoints & Lithographs by James McNeill Whistler* (London: P. & D. Colnaghi & Co., 1971), p. 32, no. 103; Fryberger, p. 62, no. 66; GUL Whistler, NB1, p. 25; Mansfield, p. 164, no. 237; Naylor, p. xxi, no. 107; Wedmore, p. 79, no. 197.

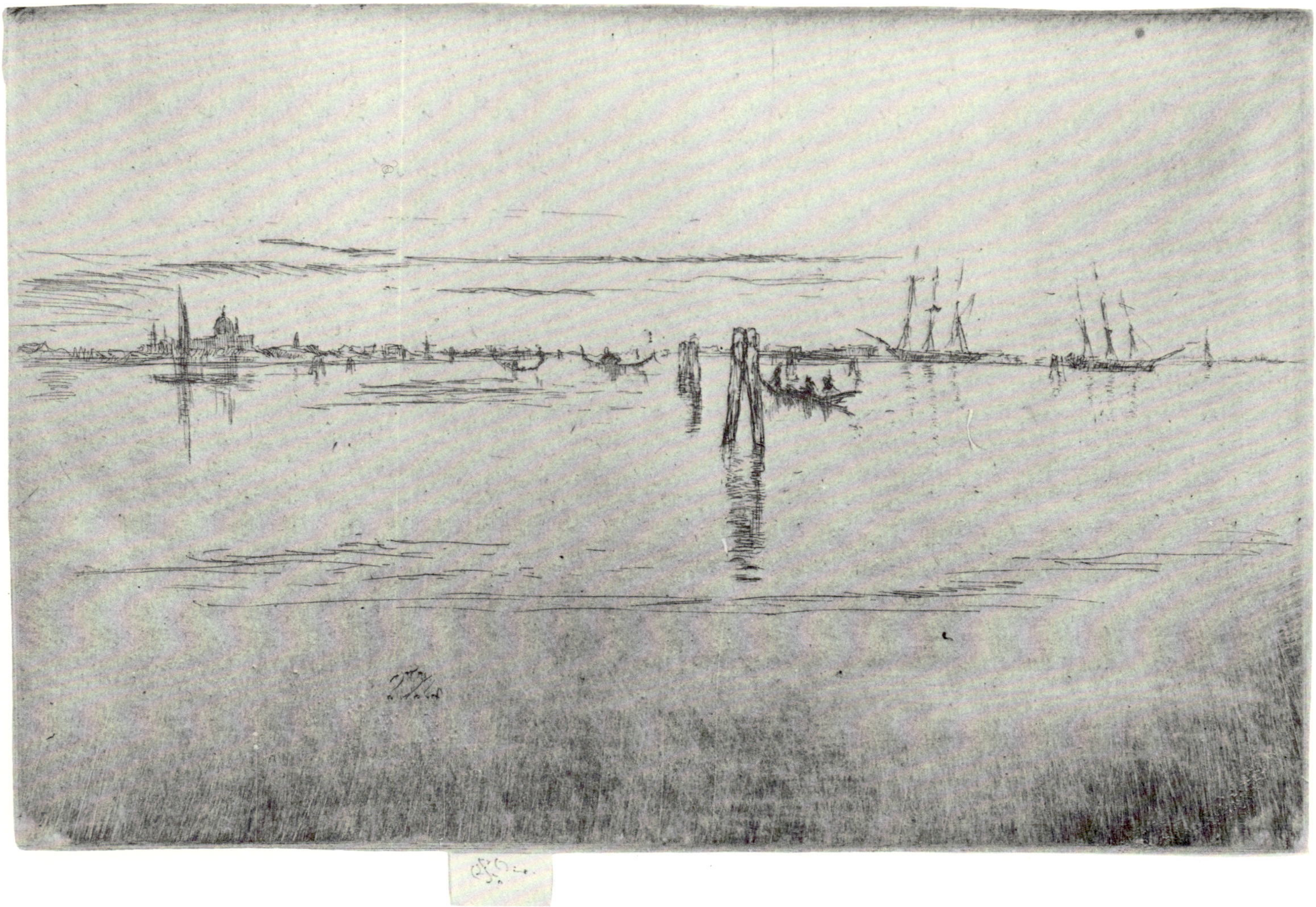

52. **Long Lagoon,** *1880*

One of the Second Venice Set

K. 203 2/2

Etching and drypoint

6 x 8 15/16 in. (15.2 x 22.6 cm.)

Warm brown ink on lightweight laid paper

Signed lower left on tab with butterfly and ***imp****; signed in plate lower left with butterfly*

Provenance: Otto Gerstenberg (Lugt 2785); purchased from Ira D. Gale, 1972

Long Lagoon is among the most serene of the Venice etchings. Drawn with the greatest economy, presumably very swiftly and with an exceedingly fine point, which produced the most delicate of lines, the plate was also lightly etched. In this impression, the whisper of plate tone in the foreground, wiped in a vertical direction, is the single counter to absolutely calm horizontality.

The butterfly at the lower left was the only addition to the second state. Impressions of the first state are known printed in black, but both states are frequently seen in brown, often the warm reddish-brown seen here, on papers of Western origin. The first fifteen of the twenty-six editions in the Second Venice Set were completed and the plates cancelled and turned in to Dowdeswells on January 17, 1887. *Long Lagoon* was among them. The copper plate is now in the Art Institute of Chicago.

LITERATURE: Fryberger, p. 44, no. 38; GUL Whistler, NB1, p. 33; Mansfield, p. 138, no. 200; Naylor, p. xxx, no. 92; Wedmore, p. 73, no. 169.

53a.
Upright Venice, *K. 205 1/4*
10 x 7 in. (25.4 x 17.8 cm.)
National Gallery of Art,
Rosenwald Collection

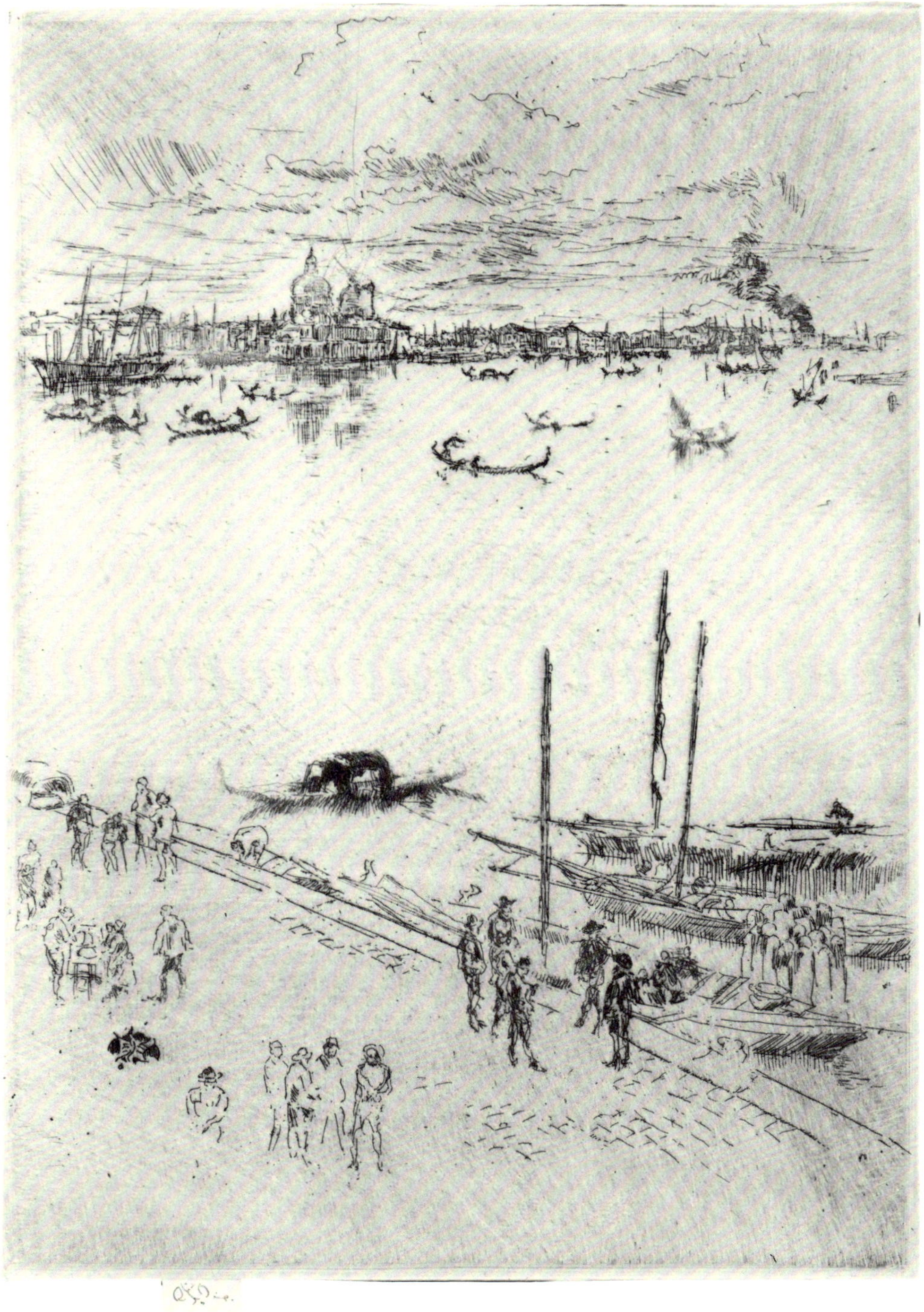

53. ***Upright Venice,*** *1880*

One of the Second Venice Set

K. 205 2/4

Etching

10 x 7 in. (25.2 x 17.8 cm.)

Brown ink on lightweight laid paper

Signed lower left on tab with butterfly and ***imp****; signed in plate lower left with butterfly*

Provenance: Otto Gerstenberg (Lugt 2785); purchased from Ira D. Gale, 1972

Lacking in the first state (fig. 53a), the entire lower half of *Upright Venice* first appeared in the second state of the image. Minor adjustments to the reflections of the gondolas are the only later changes. The foreground addition was not undertaken until some six months after the upper portion was completed. It is surprising in a way that the composition holds together, as it is actually comprised of two distinctly different aspects of Venice that Whistler most often approached individually: the city at a distance, sandwiched between sky and water (e.g., cat. no. 64), and the bustle of waterfront activity (e.g., cat. no. 62). It is Whistler's perfect composite Venetian view.

Impressions of both of the first two states are known printed in black ink, although the second, third, and fourth are more frequently seen in brown and on Western papers. After forty-two impressions were printed, the cancelled copper plate was turned over to Dowdeswells on January 17, 1887. It is now in the Art Institute of Chicago.

LITERATURE: Bacher, pp. 70–71; Getscher and Staley, pp. 72–73, nos. 40–41; GUL Whistler, NB1, p. 33; MacDonald, pp. 46–47, nos. 102–3; Mansfield, p. 140, no. 202; Naylor, p. xxx, no. 94; Wedmore, p. 74, no. 172.

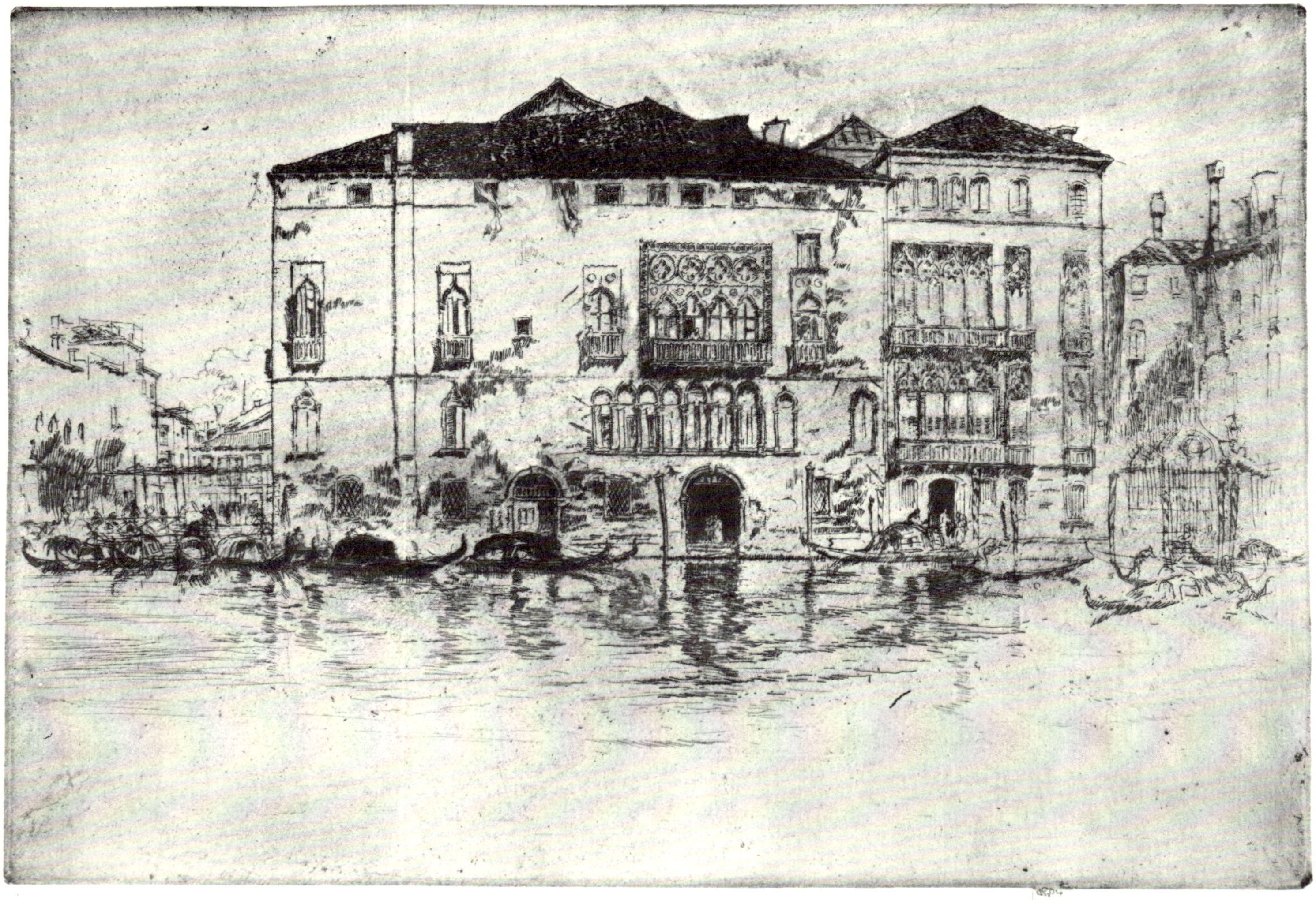

54. ***The Palaces,*** *1880*

One of the First Venice Set

K. 187 3/3

Etching and drypoint

9 3/4 x 14 1/16 in. (24.9 x 35.8 cm.)

Black ink on laid paper with watermark: 1814 surmounted by shield with fleur-de-lis surmounted by crown

Signed lower right on tab with butterfly and **imp***; annotated verso with two tiny circles*

Provenance: purchased from Kennedy Galleries, Inc., 1977

The Palaces is Whistler's largest etching. In its combination of internal scale, distance, and horizontality, it is distinctive among the Venetian scenes. More satisfying perhaps are those architectural pieces that seem to pull the viewer into them (e.g., cat. no. 46). This broad, full composition, however, would have given Whistler ideas for some of the Venetian vignettes, for the later shop fronts, and for the Amsterdam etchings of 1889, several of which focus on facades that are somewhat similar.

Third-state impressions like this show tonal areas actually etched into the plate: along the rooftops, for instance, and in the shadows in the water. This simply might be foul biting as the result of a weak ground, but it might also be an experiment with a sulphur tint.

Impressions of the final state of *The Palaces* are known in both black and brown inks, generally printed on Western papers. In the study of papers used by Whistler, watermarks are helpful in establishing relationships among impressions. Several impressions of *The Palaces* are on sheets that bear the watermark described; they may have been printed about the same time. The edition was probably completed by July 1892.

Tiny circles, sometimes one, two, or three, are seen on the verso of some Whistler prints. These circles are thought to have been a symbol identifying impressions the artist particularly liked. No document, however, has been located which verifies this. Impressions so annotated are not necessarily superior to others, and many very beautiful impressions were sent out of the studio with no annotations at all. If these annotations were a Whistlerian designation of quality, they were probably one more aspect of the artist's public relations campaign, allowing certain buyers to think they were getting something extraordinary.

LITERATURE: Fryberger, p. 34, no. 27; Getscher, p. 52; GUL Whistler, LB3/14; MacDonald, p. 45, no. 100; Mansfield, p. 118, no. 184; Naylor, p. xxviii, no. 81; Wedmore, p. 67, no. 153; Wiehl, p. 25, no. 30.

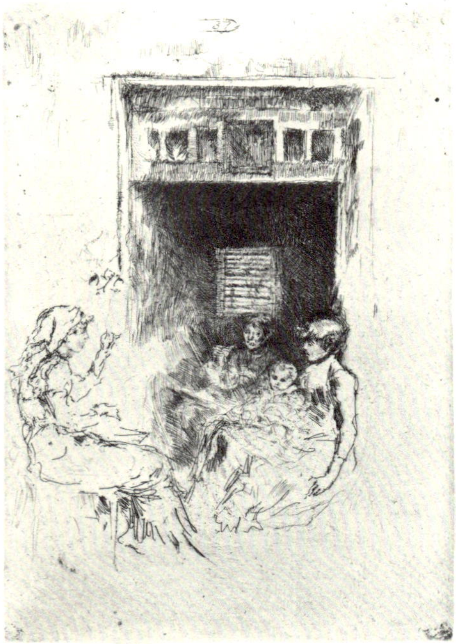

55a.
Bead-Stringers, *K. 198*
9 x 6 in. (22.9 x 15.2 cm.)
Julius L. and Anita Zelman

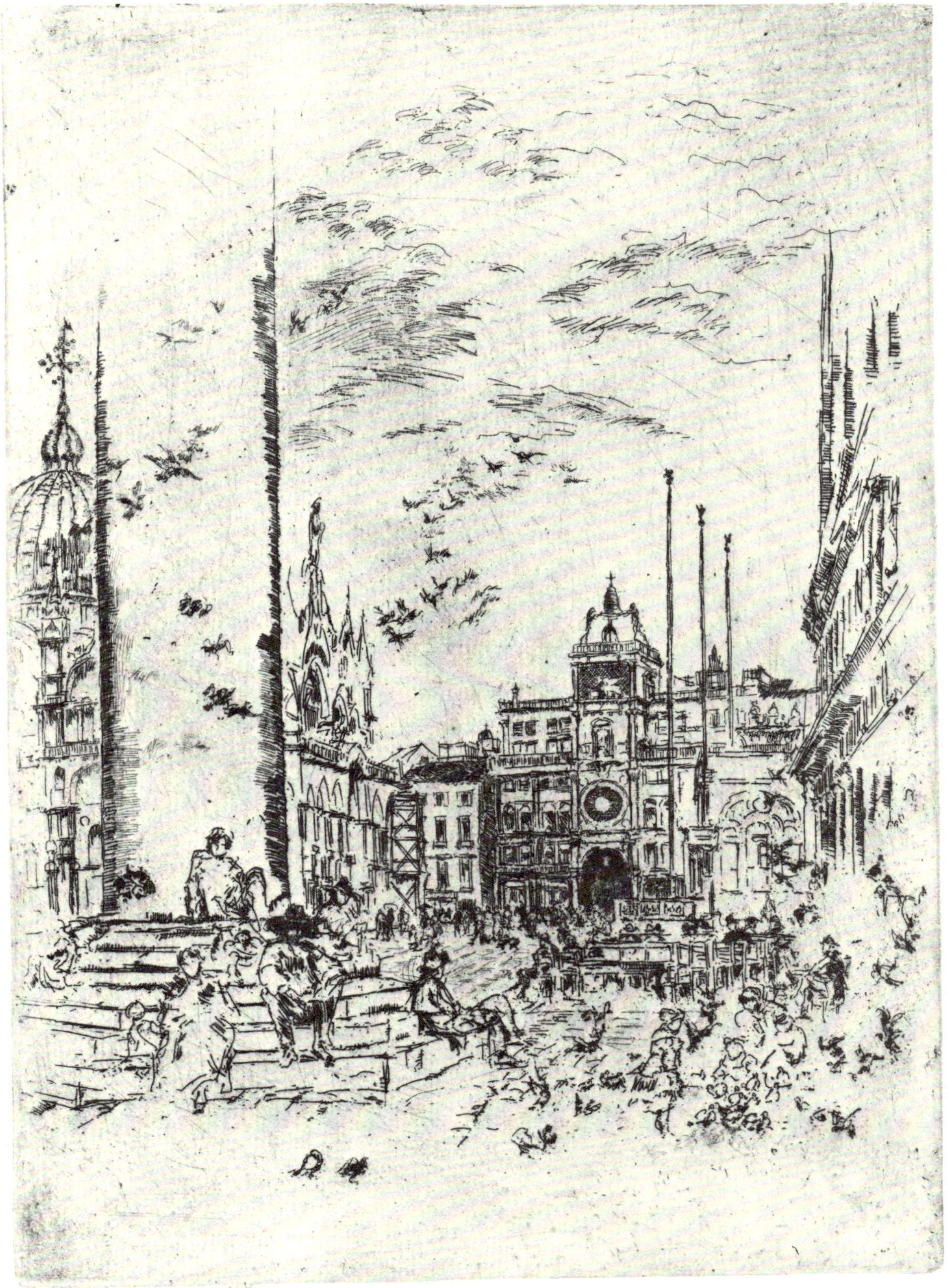

55. **The Piazzetta**, *1880*

One of the First Venice Set

K. 189 3/5

Etching and drypoint

10 1/8 x 7 3/8 in. (25.8 x 18.1 cm.)

Black ink on medium-weight, antique laid paper

Signed lower left on tab with butterfly and ***imp****; signed in plate lower left with butterfly*

Provenance: purchased from Kennedy Galleries, Inc., 1977

The Piazzetta is one of the very few popular Venetian tourist sights that Whistler depicted in his fifty etchings. Generally he was drawn to less frequently pictured byways, such as *Bead-Stringers* (fig. 55a).

The Piazzetta clearly shows how Whistler continued to work, as he did in *The Longshoremen* (cat. no. 19), with a diversity of drawing styles, albeit quite different ones. That is to say, he pointedly employed a range of means and skills to develop the complexities of his image. Some elements, the clock tower, for instance, and the man with a dark hat seated on the steps at the base of the column, are tautly and specifically defined. Others, such as the children feeding the birds at the lower right, are just suggested; while yet others, such as parts of the cathedral to the right of the column, are clearly described but with a looseness and spontaneity, in contrast to the clock tower, that makes them "feel" closer to the clouds that float through the sky than to anything solidly affixed to the ground. This diversity is probably one reason Whistler's art is attractive to us today, when facture is an important aspect of our aesthetic considerations.

Impressions of the third state are often seen printed in black like this one and relatively cleanly wiped, allowing the drawing to function independently of plate tone. The edition was completed and the copper plate cancelled by mid-June 1892. The plate is now in the Freer Gallery of Art.

LITERATURE: Getscher, p. 91; GUL Whistler, LB1/15; MacDonald, p. 42, no. 92; Mansfield, p. 120, no. 186; Naylor, p. xix, no. 82; Wedmore, p. 68, no. 155; Wiehl, p. 25, no. 29.

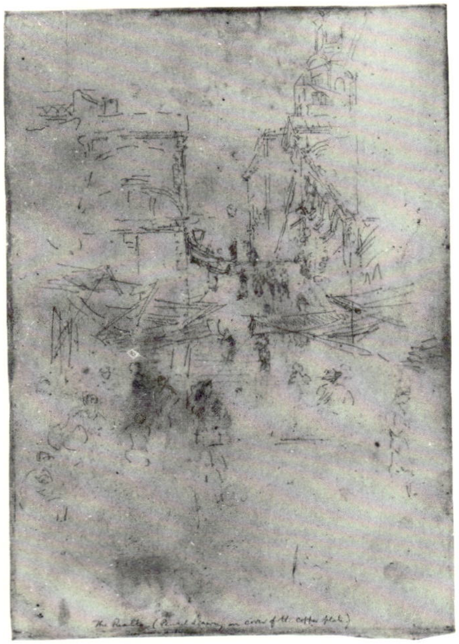

56a.
The Rialto
9 7/8 x 13 in. (25.1 x 33 cm.)
Pencil
Hunterian Art Gallery, University of Glasgow, Birnie Philip Bequest

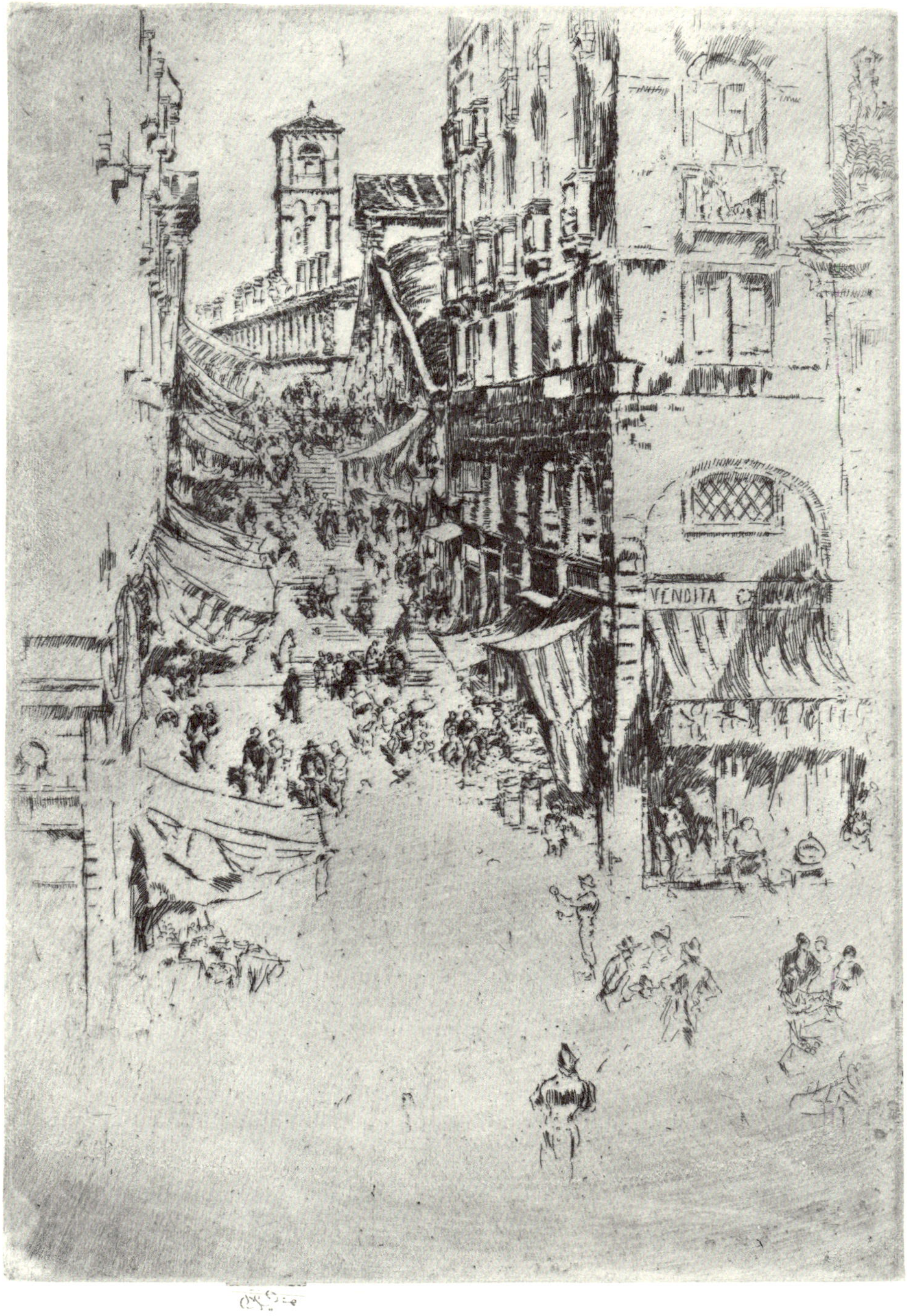

56. ***The Rialto,*** *1880*

One of the Second Venice Set

K. 211 2/2

Etching and drypoint

11 1/2 x 7 7/8 in. (29.3 x 20 cm.)

Brown ink on lightweight antique laid paper

Signed lower left on tab with butterfly

and ***imp***

Provenance: purchased from

Kennedy Galleries, Inc., 1977

One thinks immediately of *St. James's Street* (cat. no. 24) as an earlier model for this wonderful view toward the Rialto. Like the earlier London piece, this scene is dotted with figures in bright sunlight. A drawing (fig. 56a), related, but not specifically for the print, shows this to be one of the rare instances when Whistler drew on the plate in reverse so that the print would show the scene in the right direction. Between the first state and this second state, several small, very tentatively drawn figures in the foreground were removed, as was some foul biting. There is a third state, unknown to Kennedy, marked by the addition of Whistler's butterfly signature on the wall at the left.

The brown ink color, always dark, varies considerably from impression to impression, not unusual for the Venice subjects in general. The edition (forty-two impressions) of *The Rialto* was completed by mid-January 1887. The copper plate is now in the Art Institute of Chicago.

LITERATURE: Getscher, pp. 91–92; GUL Whistler, NB1, p. 33; MacDonald, p. 42, no. 90; Mansfield, p. 147, no. 208; Naylor, p. xxxi, no. 98; Wedmore, p. 76, no. 181.

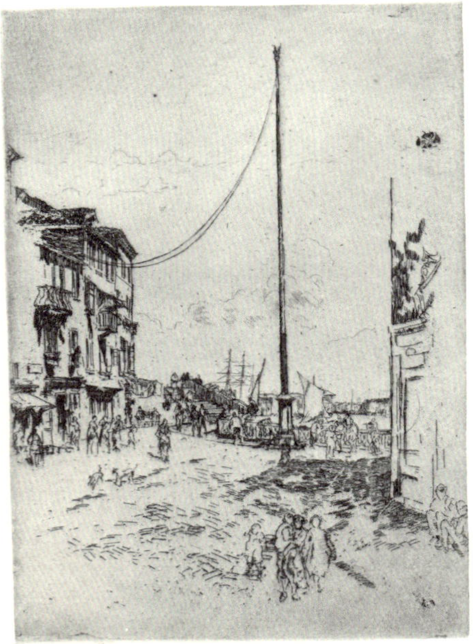

57a.
The Little Mast, *K. 185*
10 ½ x 7 ¼ in. (26.7 x 18.4 cm.)
Julius L. and Anita Zelman

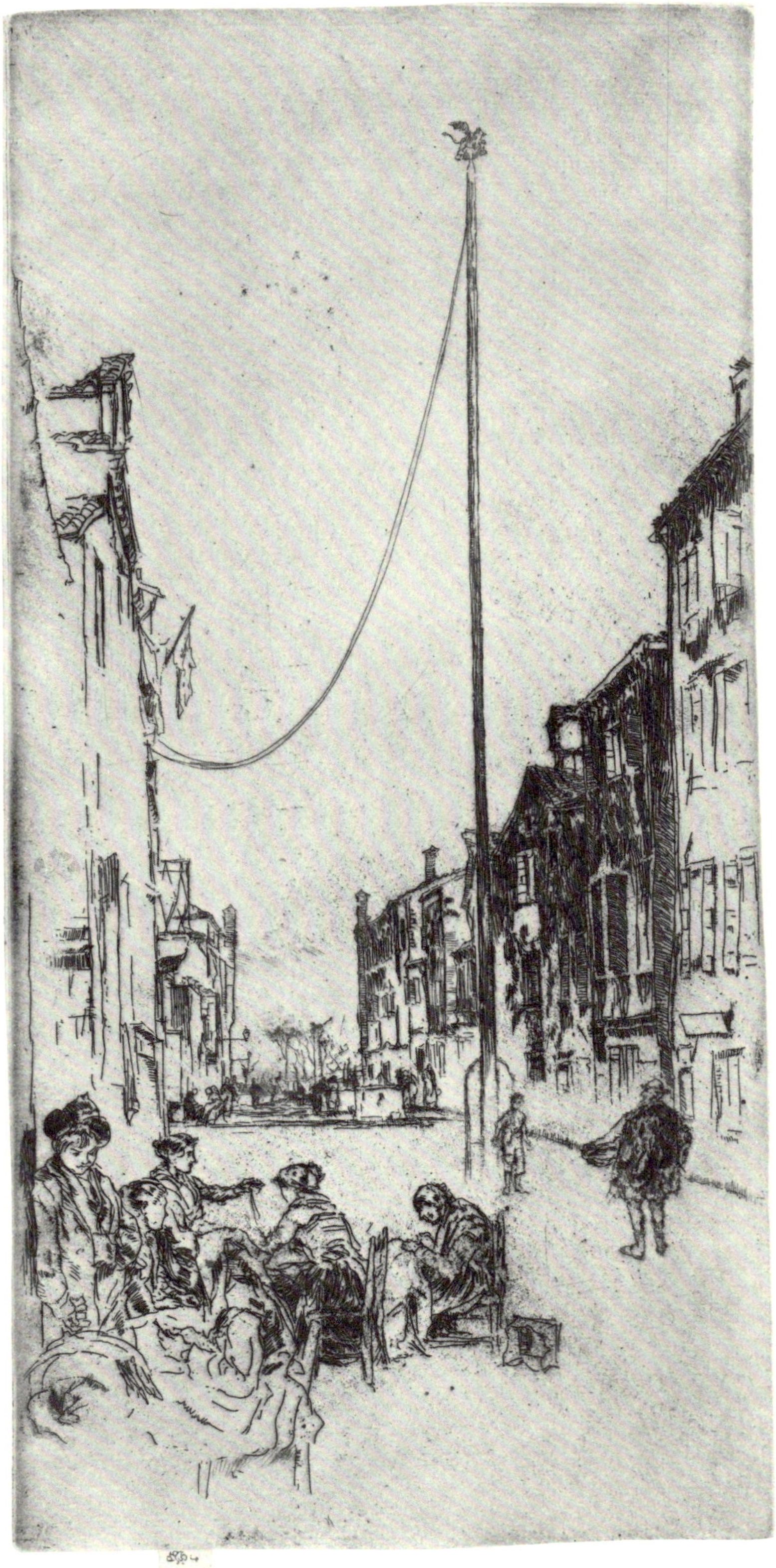

57. ***The Mast,*** *1880*

One of the First Venice Set

K. 195 6/6

Etching and drypoint

13 3/8 x 6 3/8 in. (33.8 x 16.1 cm.)

Brown ink on medium-weight laid paper with watermark: LVD surmounted by shield with fleur-de-lis surmounted by crown

Signed lower left on tab with butterfly and **imp**; *annotated verso with three tiny circles*

Provenance: purchased from Margaret Smith, 1969

This is the later of Whistler's two etchings that feature a mast, the earlier one (fig. 57a) being similar in conception to his broadly open city views such as *The Riva, No. 2* (cat. no. 63). Here the strong verticality of the format suggests a space that is relatively confined.

Of interest is Whistler's spontaneous, but specific delineation of the figures. Particular figures are the focus of many state changes Whistler made to the Venetian pieces. The point here is the coupling of specificity with Whistler's incredible spontaneity in working the figures. The group at the left is more fully described as a unit than one has come to expect. The young boy at the far left is particularly well described, while the man standing at the right, holding a basket, is rather fully developed as well.

The edition was completed and the copper plate cancelled by mid-June 1892. The plate is now in the Hunterian Art Gallery, University of Glasgow.

LITERATURE: Fryberger, p. 38, no. 32; GUL Whistler, LB1/15; Mansfield, p. 128, no. 192; Naylor, p. xxix, no. 89; Wedmore, p. 70, no. 160; Wiehl, p. 26, no. 37.

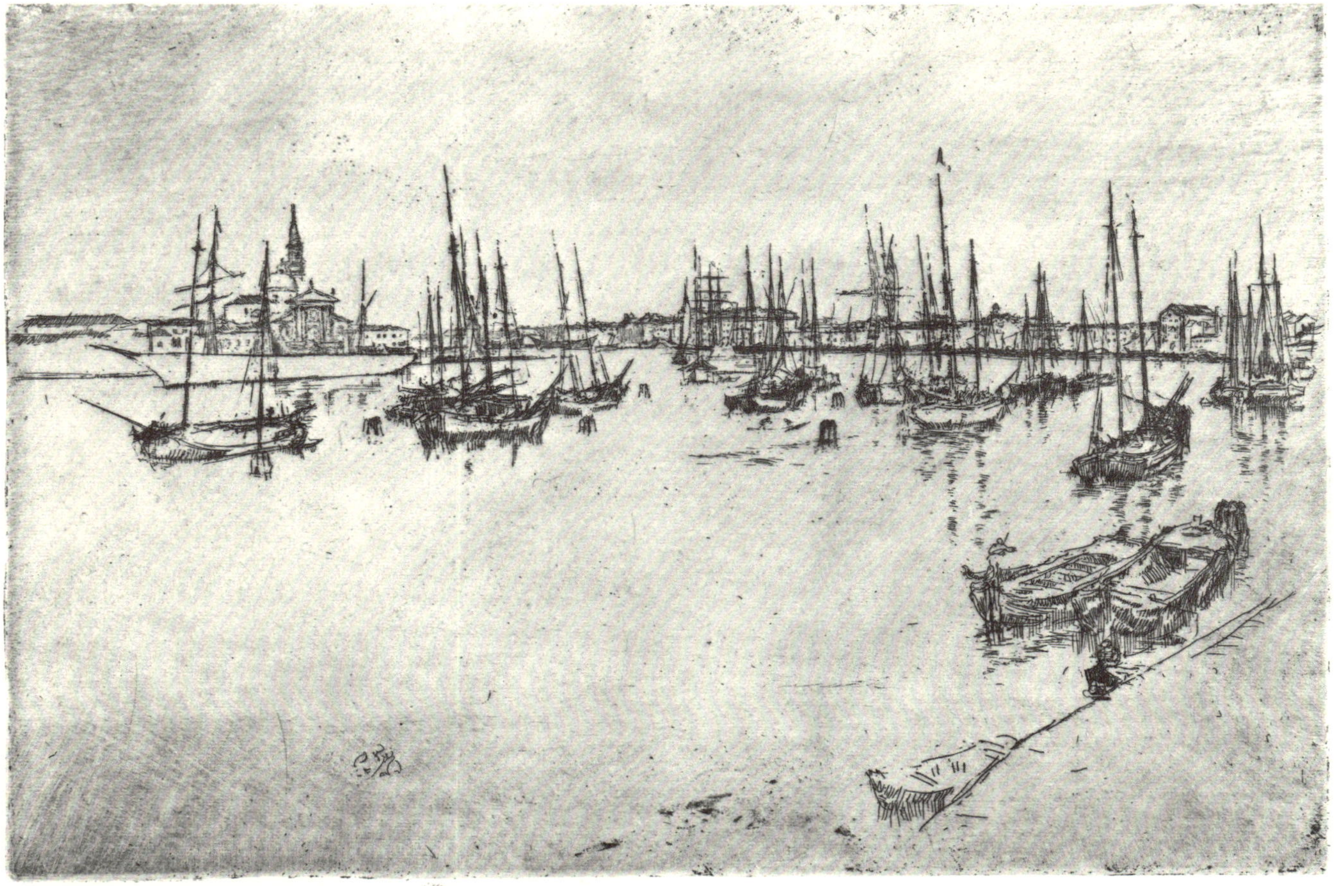

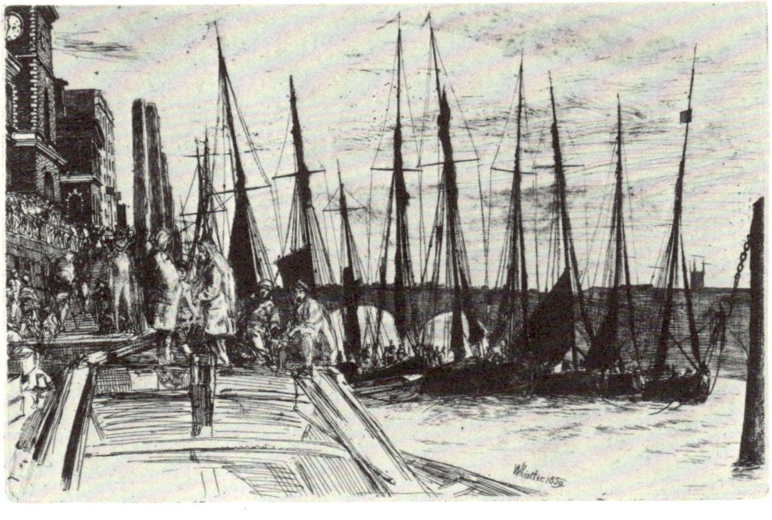

58a.
***Billingsgate,** K. 47*
5 7/8 x 8 7/8 in. (14.9 x 22.5 cm.)
Julius L. and Anita Zelman

58. **San Giorgio,** *1880*

One of the Second Venice Set

K. 201 4/4

Etching

8 3/16 x 11 5/16 in. (20.8 x 30.3 cm.)

Warm brown ink on lightweight, antique laid paper

Signed lower left on tab with butterfly and **imp**; *signed in plate lower left with butterfly*

Provenance: purchased from Kennedy Galleries, Inc., 1979

The early Thames etchings, like *Billingsgate* (fig. 58a), demonstrated Whistler's interest in the way the rigging of ships activated and defined pictorial space. Of all the Venetian pieces, *San Giorgio* best reflects his continuing attention in this regard: the vessels, rather than the architecture, dominate. The scene on the Giodecca Canal, where boats were moored, waiting for purchase, is looking toward the church of San Giorgio Maggiore.

Although a film of tone enriches the surface, the image is essentially dependent upon the drawing for its composition and atmospheric qualities. As a presentation of an aspect of life along Venetian waterways, it falls somewhere between the serenity of *Long Lagoon* (cat. no. 52) and the activity of *Riva, No. 2* (cat. no. 63). Whistler apparently worked on the plate intermittently for more than a month. Unlike the rest of the Venice plates, which were bitten with nitric acid, *San Giorgio* was bitten with Dutch mordant, not to Whistler's complete satisfaction.

San Giorgio was among the plates in the Second Venice Set from which twelve prints beyond the edition of thirty were printed. Impressions of the first two states are known in brown and black inks and of the later states in brown only, all of them on a variety of papers. *San Giorgio* was among the first fifteen cancelled copper plates turned in to Dowdeswells in mid-January 1887. It is now in the Art Institute of Chicago.

LITERATURE: Bacher, pp. 198–99; GUL Whistler, NB3, p. 33; Mansfield, p. 136, no. 198; Wedmore, p. 72, no. 167.

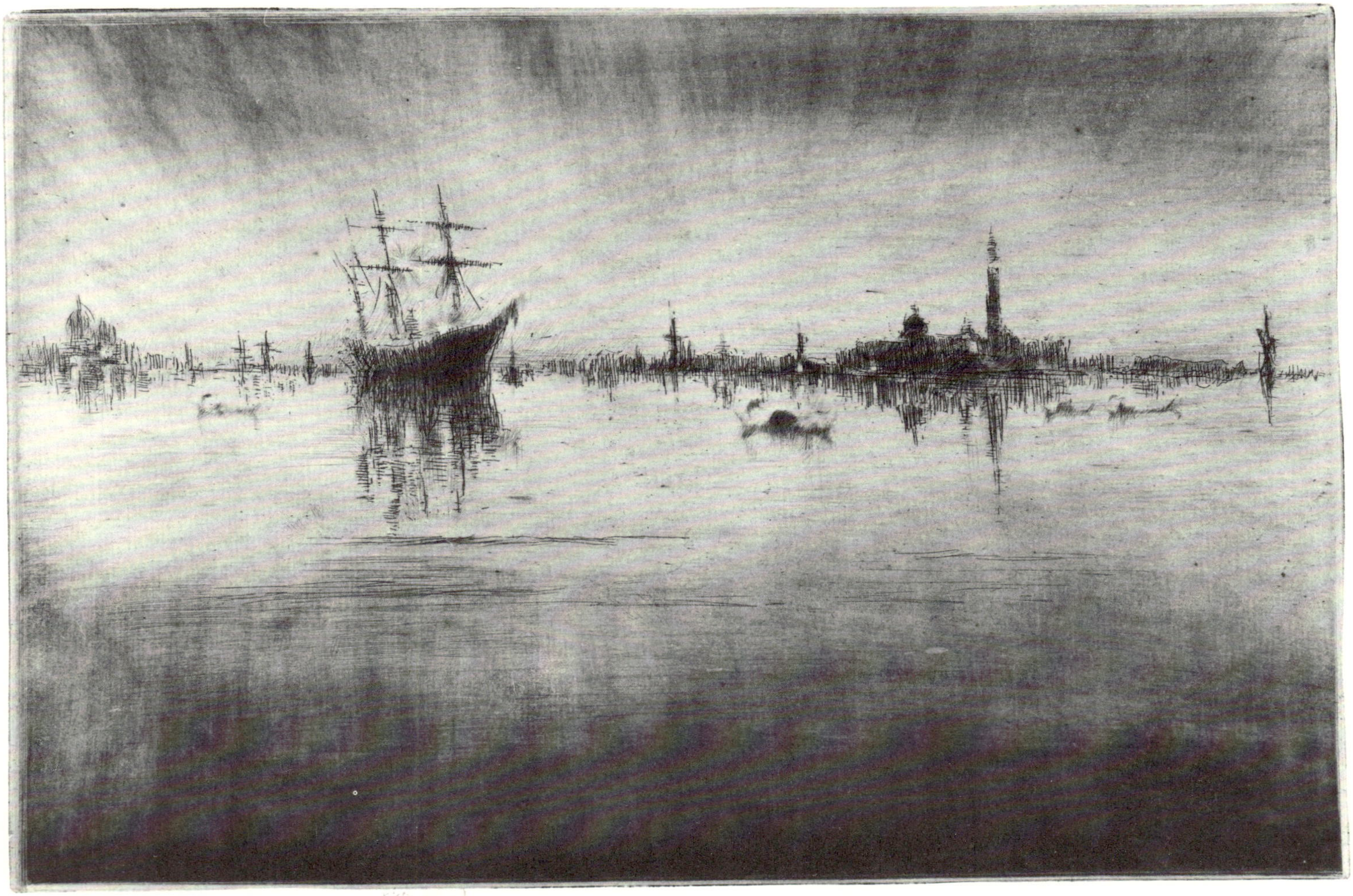

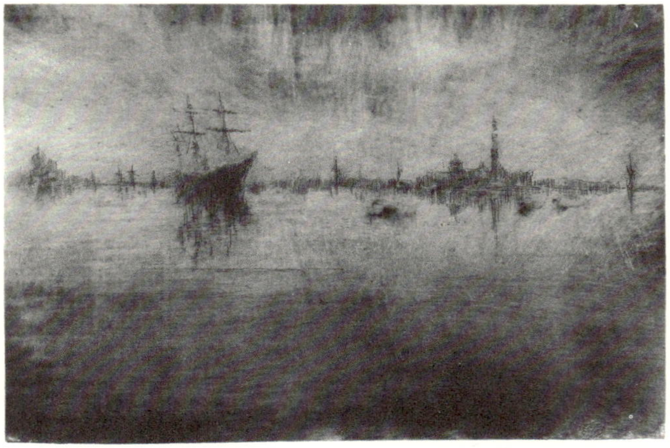

59a.
Nocturne, *K. 184 4/5*
7 7/8 x 11 5/8 in. (20 x 29.5 cm.)
National Gallery of Art,
Rosenwald Collection

59. **Nocturne,** *1879–80*

One of the First Venice Set

K. 184 4/5

Etching and drypoint

7 15/16 x 11 3/4 in. (20.2 x 29.8 cm.)

Warm brown ink on medium-weight, antique laid paper with watermark: IV

Signed lower left on tab with butterfly and ***imp***

Provenance: purchased from Thos. Agnew & Sons, Ltd., 1982

All of the etching work in *Nocturne* appears to have been completed in one stage. From then on, the image was developed with drypoint and through the use of plate tone.

The print caused quite a stir in the press. One reviewer wrote:

> *Nocturne* is different in treatment to the rest of the prints, and can hardly be called, as it stands, an etching; the bones as it were of the picture have been etched, which bones consist of some shipping and distant objects, and then over the whole of the plate ink has apparently been smeared. We have seen a great many representations of Venetian skies, but never saw one before consisting of brown smoke with clots of ink in diagonal lines. . . . A certain amount of judiciousness in printing is, of course, right, but when it comes to "painting" the plate with dilute ink it can scarcely be called etching. . . .

Of all the Venice etchings, *Nocturne* is printed with the greatest kind of variation between impressions. Indeed, depending upon the quality of the tonal wiping, the time of day appears to range from dusk to midnight (fig. 59a) to dawn. The implied quality of the air is diverse as well, ranging from calm to quite windy.

There are a number of states beyond those described by Kennedy. They evolved because Whistler reinforced the drypoint work as it wore down, taking the plate through many changes but not altering it substantively to any degree.

One sees impressions of this subject printed in black through Kennedy's third state; fourth- and fifth-state impressions are generally seen in brown. All states are printed on both Western and Oriental papers. The cancelled copper plate was turned over to the Fine Art Society on April 26, 1889.

LITERATURE: Fryberger, p. 34, no. 26; Getscher and Staley, p. 95, no. 59; GUL Whistler, F152; GUL Whistler, PC6, p. 15 (*British Architect,* 10 December 1880); MacDonald, p. 40, no. 84; Mansfield, p. 115, no. 181; Naylor, p. xxviii, no. 78; Wedmore, p. 66, no. 150; Wiehl, p. 25, no. 34.

60. ***Nocturne: Palaces,*** *1879–80*

One of the Second Venice Set

K. 202 6/9

Etching and drypoint

11 5/8 x 7 7/8 in. (29.6 x 20.1 cm.)

Dark brown ink on medium-weight laid paper with watermark: Pro Patria

Signed lower left on tab with butterfly and ***imp***

Provenance: purchased from William Weston Gallery, Ltd., 1980

Unlike the reception accorded *Nocturne* (cat. no. 59) just a few years earlier, the broad treatment of *Nocturne: Palaces,* exhibited in 1883, was praised even by critics generally unenthusiastic about the Venice etchings. It has remained a popular subject and was a source of inspiration for artists of the generation that followed Whistler, like D. Y. Cameron and James McBey. Although the print went through a number of states, as did *Nocturne,* they mainly functioned as reinforcements of areas that were wearing down rather than as substantive adjustments.

The radical image is actually somewhat sparsely laid in with line (fig. 60a) and depends almost entirely on plate tone for its dramatic structure. Although there is considerable tonal variety from impression to impression, there is essential consistency to its role in defining the buildings and time of day in contrast to impressions of *Nocturne,* where one finds the actual intentions of the image as a variable dependent on the surface wiping.

A night piece was among Whistler's earliest etchings (cat. no. 4), and nocturnes had been one preoccupation in his paintings through the 1870s. He also made a lithograph of a night subject, *Nocturne: The River at Battersea* (fig. 60b), in 1878, shortly before his departure to Venice. The Venetian etchings of night subjects, then, fit comfortably into a pattern.

Except for the earliest proofs, impressions are printed in brown on papers of Western origin. The edition (forty-two impressions) was completed and the cancelled plate turned in to Dowdeswells on January 27, 1887. The copper plate is now in the Art Institute of Chicago.

LITERATURE: Fryberger, p. 44, no. 37; Getscher, pp. 64–66; Getscher and Staley, p. 91, nos. 56–57; GUL Whistler, PC3, p. 44; GUL Whistler, NB1, p. 34; MacDonald, p. 40, no. 83; Mansfield, p. 136, no. 199; Naylor, p. xxx, no. 91; Wedmore, p. 73, no. 168; Wiehl, p. 29, nos. 55–56.

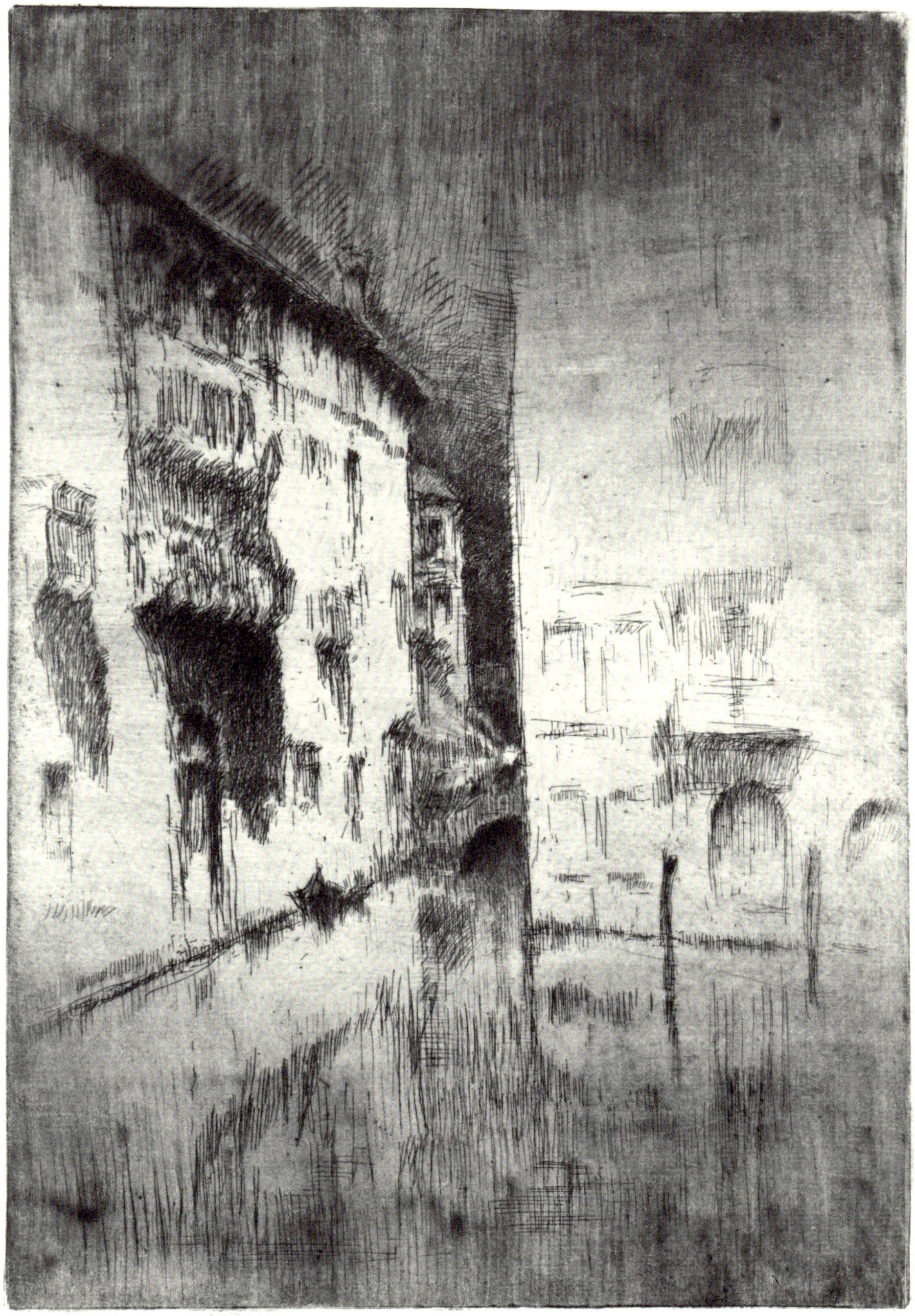

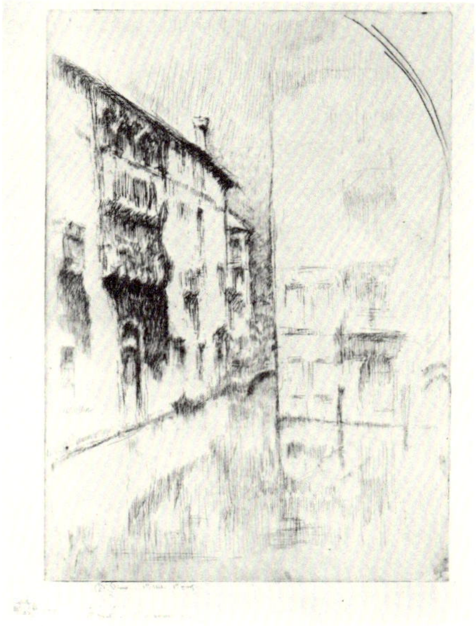

60a.
Nocturne: Palaces, *K. 202 1/9*
11 5/8 x 7 7/8 in. (29.5 x 20 cm.)
Freer Gallery of Art

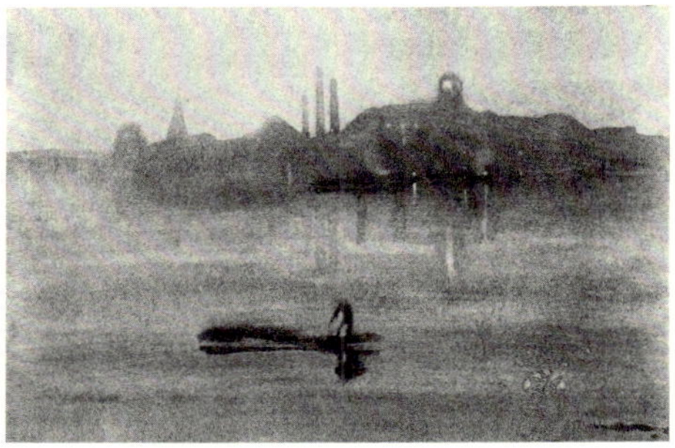

60b.
Nocturne: The River at Battersea
Lithograph
6 13/16 x 10 1/2 in. (17.3 x 26.7 cm.)
National Gallery of Art,
Rosenwald Collection

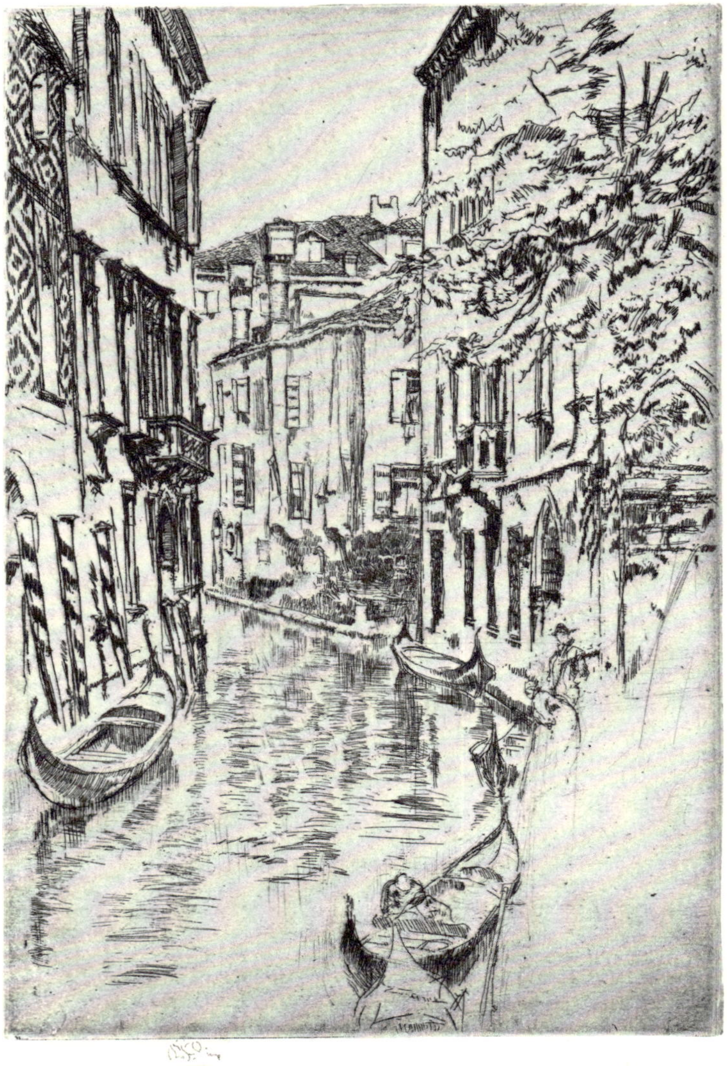

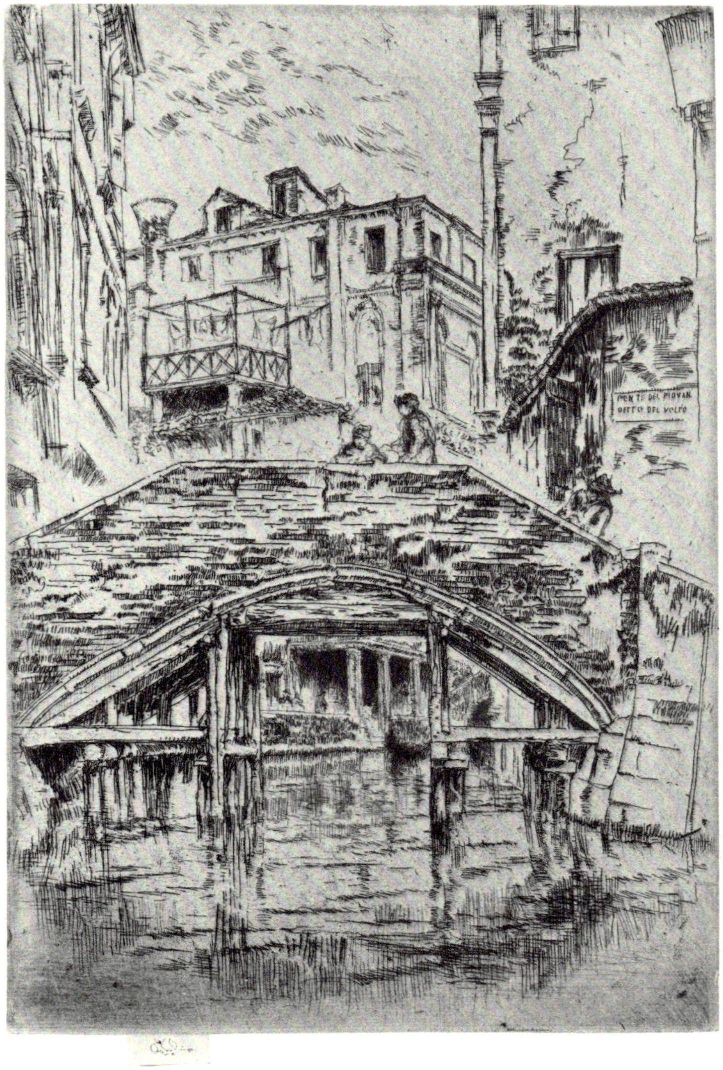

61. **Quiet Canal,** *1880*

One of the Second Venice Set

K. 214 4/5

Etching and drypoint

9 1/16 x 6 1/16 in. (23 x 15.5 cm.)

Warm black ink on lightweight, antique laid paper with partial watermark: shield with horn surmounted by crown

Signed lower left on tab with butterfly and ***imp***

Provenance: purchased from R. E. Lewis, Inc., 1980

Particularly distinctive in *Quiet Canal* is Whistler's beautiful handling of the upper right corner, filled with foliage that with equal measure is both described and implied. In the etchings it is among Whistler's most successful landscape elements and particularly handsome when contrasted with the geometric patterns, the stripes and the diamonds, which face it from across the canal.

This is a full, rich impression of what is possibly the final state of the print (Kennedy's state five actually may describe worn impressions of the present version). *Quiet Canal* was one of the plates from which twelve impressions were pulled beyond the thirty for the portfolios. It was among the first of the editions in the Second Venice Set to be completed: an impression of the cancelled plate was turned over to Dowdeswells on October 21, 1886, and the copper plate itself, the following January. The plate is now in the Art Institute of Chicago.

This impression is somewhat unusual in that, apart from the earliest proofs, the print is usually seen printed in brown, generally on Western papers.

LITERATURE: Bacher, p. 192; GUL Whistler, NB1, p. 33; *The Lessing J. Rosenwald Collection: A Catalog of Gifts of Lessing J. Rosenwald to the Library of Congress, 1943 to 1975,* Library of Congress, no. 1997 (Washington, D.C.: 1977); Mansfield, p. 149, no. 211; Naylor, p. xxxi, no. 100; Wedmore, p. 77, no. 184.

62. **Ponte del Piovan,** *1880*

One of the Second Venice Set

K. 209 6/6

Etching and drypoint

8 15/16 x 6 in. (22.6 x 15.2 cm.)

Brown ink on lightweight laid paper

Signed lower left on tab with butterfly and ***imp****; signed in plate center right with butterfly*

Provenance: purchased from Ira D. Gale, 1972

A few of the Venice scenes really are not "vistas" or "enclosed." *Ponte del Piovan* is one of them, having neither the majestic grandeur of the former nor the intimate mystery of the latter. In its spatial compression and reliance upon drawn surfaces and reflections rather than on plate tone to modulate the image, it moves toward the Amsterdam views of 1889.

Regarding states, in Glasgow there is an impression prior to Kennedy's first state, and the darker groups of vertical drypoint in the water lines at the bottom center of this impression are lacking in other sheets considered to be state six. This, then, would be an impression of at least an eighth state. Like *Quiet Canal,* the edition was completed by late October 1886, and the copper plate was among those turned over to Dowdeswells on January 17, 1887. The plate is now in the Art Institute of Chicago.

The subject was one of which an additional twelve prints were pulled beyond the thirty needed for the portfolios. As usual, the earliest impressions are printed in black, the others in brown. We have seen none of this subject on Oriental papers.

LITERATURE: Bacher, p. 191; GUL Whistler, NB1, p. 33; Mansfield, p. 145, no. 206; Wedmore, p. 75, no. 179.

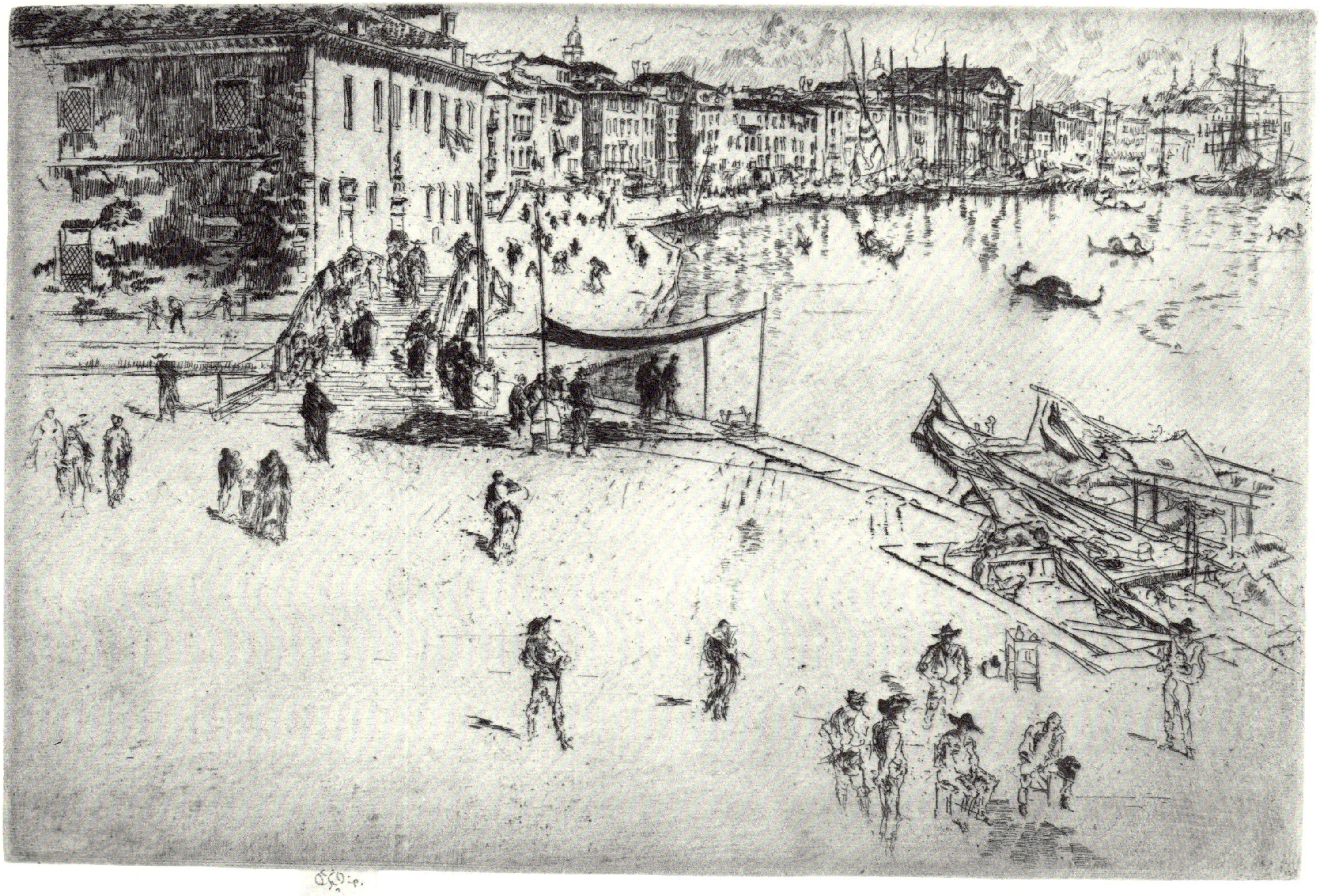

63. **The Riva, No. 2,** *1880*

One of the Second Venice Set

K. 206 1/2

Etching and drypoint

8 1/8 x 11 7/8 in. (20.5 x 30.1 cm.)

Warm brown ink on lightweight, antique laid paper

Signed lower left on tab with butterfly and ***imp****; signed in plate upper left with butterfly*

Provenance: purchased from R. E. Lewis, Inc. (Sotheby's, 10 November 1978, lot 379)

The Riva, No. 2 is the second of Whistler's views of the Riva degli Schiavoni. Possibly composed and drawn from more than one viewpoint, both depict the scene from virtually the same elevated vantage point (see fig. 64a). There are important differences however. In this version, the artist/viewer feels somewhat closer to the central activity, and a slightly larger band of sky with clouds helps to structure a more open composition. This openness is reinforced by relatively less articulation in the water and on the foreground pavement.

The image is almost complete in this first state, the later one being marked by the addition of only two slanting lines at the lower left corner. Except for the earliest proofs, the plate was printed in brown, generally on Western laid papers.

There is a related charcoal drawing in the Cleveland Museum of Art (reproduced, Fryberger, p. 36). The copper plate, now in the Art Institute of Chicago, was cancelled by early February 1887, after an edition of forty-two was pulled for Dowdeswells.

LITERATURE: Fryberger, p. 44, no.39; Getscher, pp. 92–96; Getscher and Staley, p. 73, no. 43; GUL Whistler, NB1, p. 34; Mansfield, p. 141, no. 203; Naylor, p. xxx, no. 95; Wedmore, p. 74, no. 175.

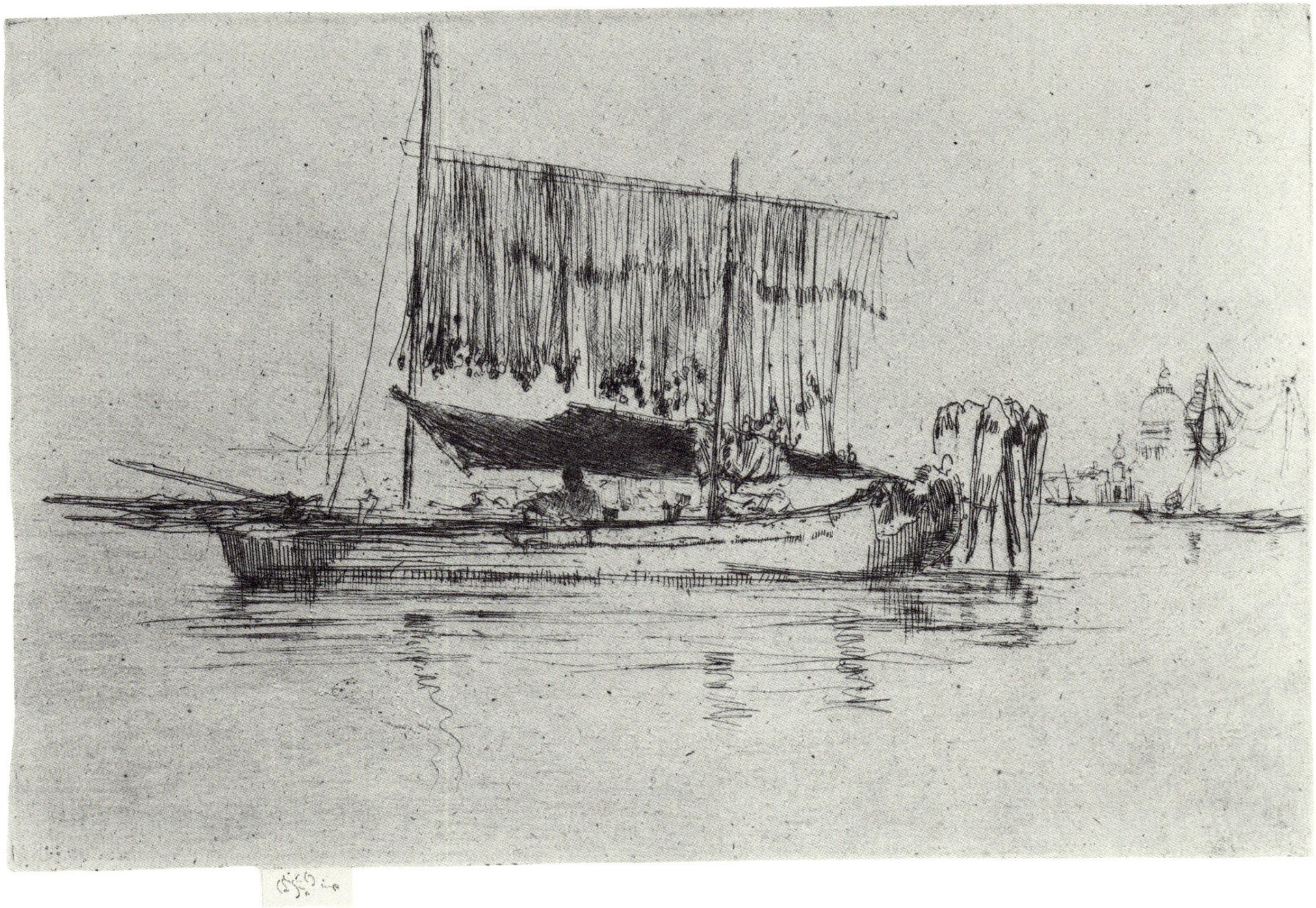

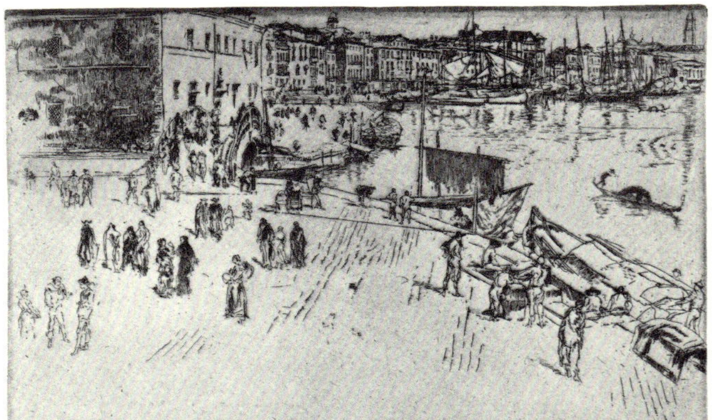

64a.
The Riva, No. 1, *K. 192*
7 ⁷/₈ x 11 ¹/₂ in. (20 x 29.2 cm.)
Julius L. and Anita Zelman

64. ***Fishing-Boat,*** *1880*

One of the Second Venice Set

K. 208 4/5

Etching and drypoint

6 3/16 x 9 1/8 in. (15.6 x 23.2 cm.)

Brown ink on lightweight, antique laid paper

Signed lower left on tab with butterfly and ***imp***

Provenance: purchased from R. E. Lewis, Inc., 1980

Fishing-Boat highlights one of the many vessels that captivated Whistler as he sought subjects for his etching series. The same sort of boat is central to another, more complicated Venice piece, *The Riva, No. 1* (fig. 64a).

One is reminded of *Two Ships* (cat. no. 21), and it is interesting to note the difference in mood of the two images. The boats on the Thames become a metaphor for London dockside hustle, whereas the fishing boat here exudes the poetic atmosphere and faded valentine qualities of Venice.

That the figure in the boat is in shadow is the important evidence that this is the fourth state. The first two states are known printed in black, the others, printed in brown, all generally on Western papers. The edition was among the earliest to be completed; a proof of the cancelled plate was turned over to Dowdeswells on December 15, 1886, and the plate itself, the following month. The copper plate is now in the Art Institute of Chicago.

LITERATURE: GUL Whistler, NB1, p. 33; *The Lessing J. Rosenwald Collection: A Catalog of Gifts of Lessing J. Rosenwald to the Library of Congress, 1943 to 1975,* Library of Congress, no. 1997 (Washington, D.C.: 1977); MacDonald p. 47, no 104; Mansfield, p. 144, no. 205; Naylor, p. xxx, no. 96; Wedmore, p. 75, no. 178.

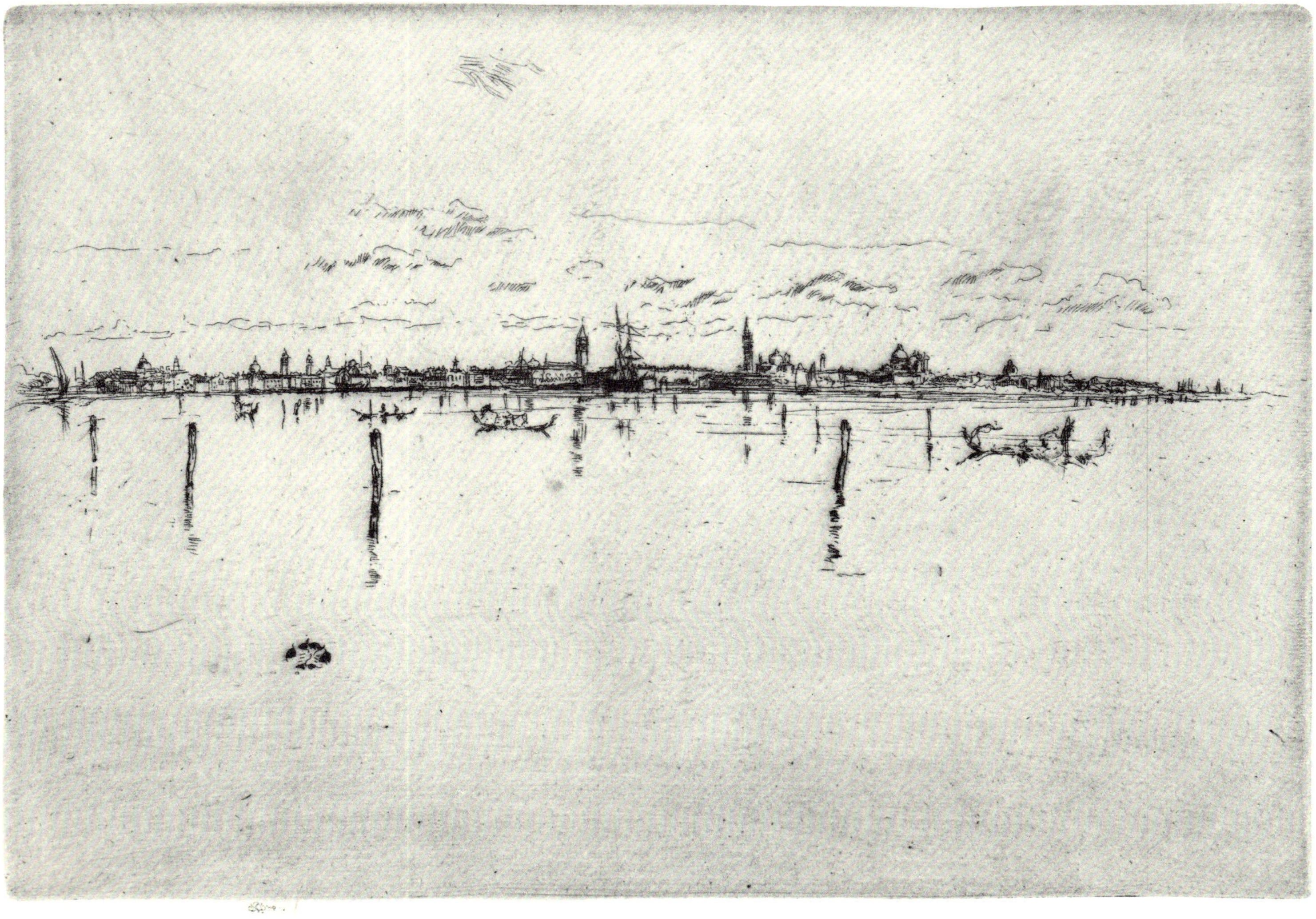

65. *Little Venice, 1880*

One of the First Venice Set

K. 183 only

Etching

7 5/16 x 10 3/8 in. (18.7 x 26.4 cm.)

Brown ink on lightweight, antique laid paper

Signed lower left on tab with butterfly and **imp**; *signed in plate lower left with butterfly*

Provenance: purchased from Lumley Cazalet Ltd., 1982 (cat. 1, no. 50)

One contemporary critic observed that " 'The Little Venice' is one of the slightest of the [First Venice Set]; but in its expression of that sense of solitude and isolation which is caused by a first view of the Queen of the Adriatic . . . it is as powerful as any of the twelve."

Generally, impressions of *Little Venice* were wiped so that a light, overall plate tone gave warmth to the image with some emphasis in the foreground. This light use of tone might be compared with the tonal wiping for *Nocturne* (cat. no. 59), which similarly is a sparsely drawn image. Here the use of etching alone, rather than etching and drypoint, gives a sharpness to the line, and the details of architecture are clearly depicted. Close scrutiny is well rewarded. In *Nocturne*, by contrast, the mood of the piece is gleaned from a more distant viewing; delicate and precise drawing, while there to no small degree, is not the point.

Impressions prior to this state show considerable evidence of scraper work, presumably in the process of eliminating foul biting. These impressions, unknown to Kennedy, are at the University of Glasgow and in the Freer Gallery of Art. This probably was one of the last of the Venetian etchings, as it was not actually bitten with acid until after Whistler's return to London. The cancelled plate was delivered to the Fine Art Society on April 15, 1889, thus signaling the end of the edition printing. *Little Venice* was one of the first to be completed. Impressions are known in both brown ink and in black on many sorts of papers.

LITERATURE: Getscher, pp. 74–75; Getscher and Staley, p. 75, no. 44; GUL Whistler, PC6, p. 13 (*St. James' Gazette*, 9 December 1880); Mansfield, p. 115, no. 180; Naylor, p. xxviii, no. 77; Wedmore, p. 65, no. 149; Wiehl, p. 24, no. 28.

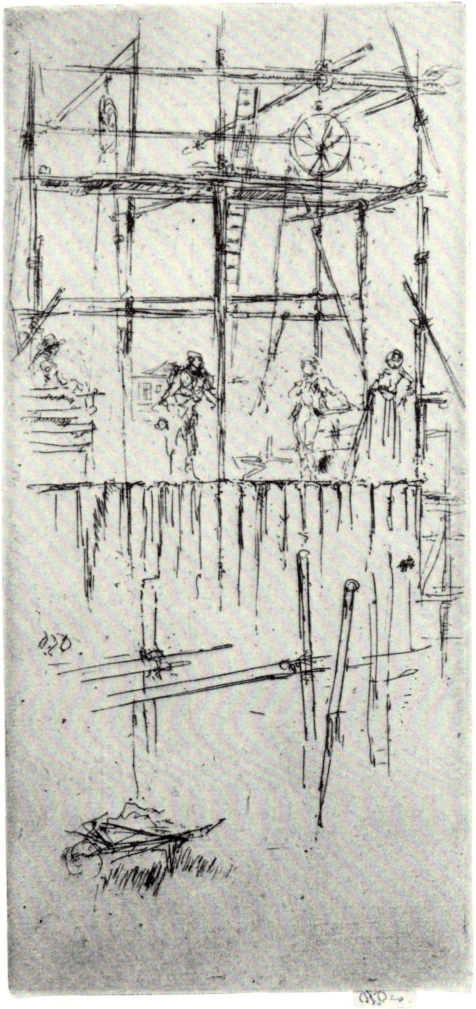

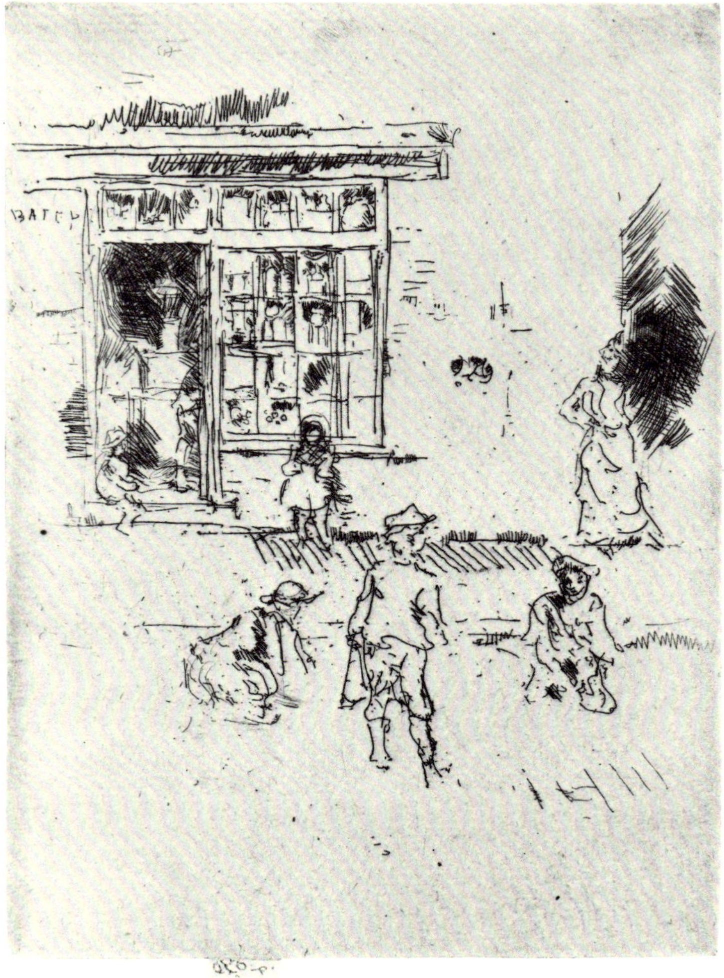

66. ***Savoy Scaffolding***, *c. 1887*

K. 267 only

Etching

6 15/16 x 3 3/16 in. (17.6 x 8 cm.)

Warm black ink on lightweight, antique laid paper

*Signed lower right on tab with butterfly and **imp**; signed in plate lower left with butterfly*

Provenance: purchased from Linda M. Papaharis (Christie's, New York, 26 March 1981, lot 363)

The prints of about 1887, of which there are approximately one hundred, are characterized by small scale and swift execution. Many were completed in only one state.

The Savoy Hotel under construction presented an unusual subject for Whistler, but he unerringly turned a work site into an elegant and graceful composition. Reproduced in 1900 in *Homes of the Passing Show*, the etching is described as having been drawn from Mr. D'Oyly Carte's office window as Whistler remarked that he "must draw it now, for it would never look so well again!"

Many impressions are printed in brown ink rather than the warm black seen here. The copper plate is in the Hunterian Art Gallery, University of Glasgow.

LITERATURE: *Homes of the Passing Show* (London: Savoy Press, 1900), p. 18; MacDonald, p. 22, no. 30; Mansfield, p. 175, no. 263; Naylor, p. xxxii, no. 112.

67. ***Marbles***, *c. 1887*

K. 284 3/3

Etching and drypoint

5 1/4 x 3 3/4 in. (13.2 x 9.6 cm.)

Warm black ink on medium-weight laid paper with partial watermark: Pro Patria

*Signed lower left on tab with butterfly and **imp**; signed in plate center right with butterfly*

Provenance: purchased from Lucien Goldschmidt, Inc., 1978 (cat. 47, no. 176)

Marbles points up Whistler's continuing attention to light: in the shading on the little boy at the right, on the sidewalk, behind the woman, and as it accentuates the objects seen through the shop window. Like *Drury Lane* (cat. no. 29), *Marbles* features a group of children, always a subject of interest to the artist.

Whistler by now had perfected a shorthand language that allowed him to portray each figure convincingly through a few swift gestural marks. *Marbles* essentially was complete in the first state, details of shadows being the only later additions.

In this bright impression one can see very light lines practically forming shadow figures for the woman standing at the right and the child kneeling at the left. These *pentimenti* are probably remnants of initial "thinking," preliminary gestures through the etching ground that Whistler covered over before biting the plate with acid. Also, in some first-state impressions, if the print is turned upside down, the remains of a woman's head wearing a rather elaborate hat can be seen quite clearly in what would then be the upper right corner. It is not unusual to find plates reused in this way (see also cat. no. 12).

The subject is known printed in brown as well as in black. The copper plate is in the Hunterian Art Gallery, University of Glasgow.

LITERATURE: Mansfield, p. 181, no. 280.

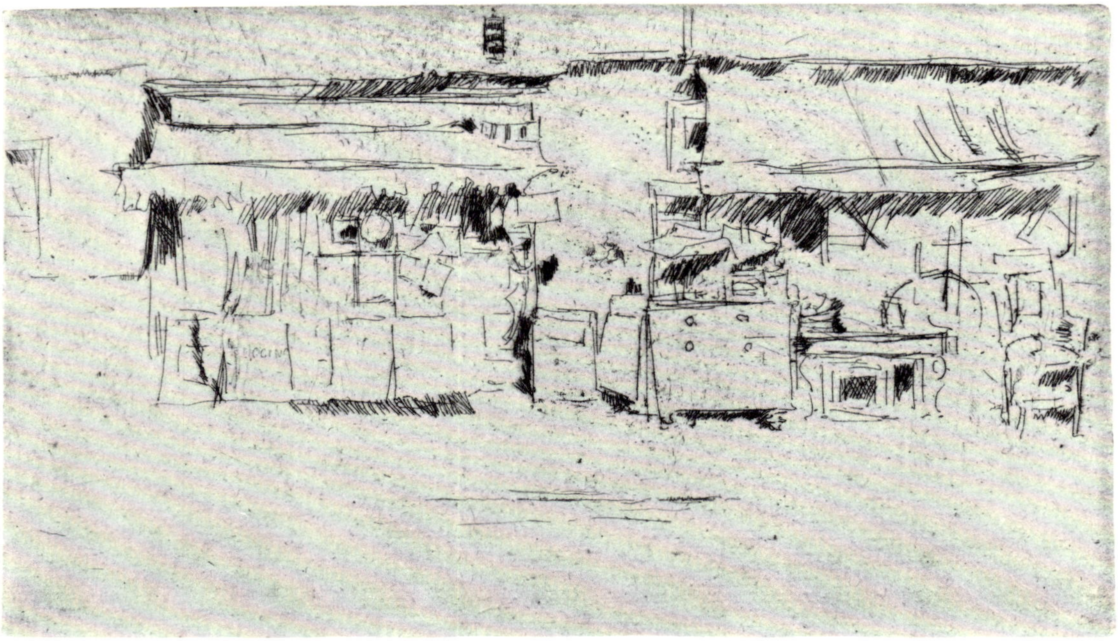

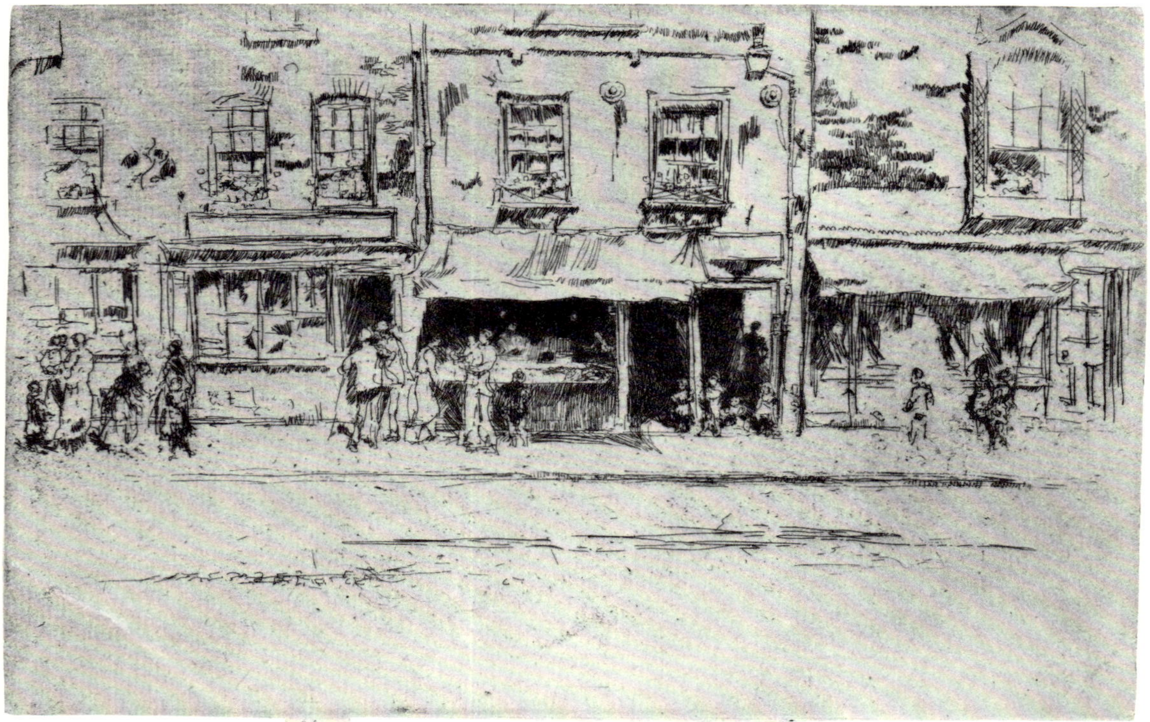

68. **Furniture-Shop,** *c. 1887*

K. 266 only

Etching and drypoint

3 3/4 x 6 7/16 in. (9.5 x 16.3 cm.)

Warm black ink on lightweight laid paper

Signed verso lower right with butterfly and ***imp****; signed in plate at center with butterfly*

Provenance: purchased from R. M. Light & Co., Inc., 1981

During the 1880s rows of shop fronts such as this were the subjects of numerous Whistler etchings, lithographs, drawings, and paintings. Among them *Furniture-Shop* is unusual in its lack of figures. It is essentially a drawing of shadows.

The plate is recorded by Kennedy in one state only, but Wedmore cites an alternative possibility in his very personalized catalogue description: "Two open shops slightly indicated. Under the stretched awning of the one to the right is a jumble of second-hand furniture. I have a very early proof. I hear the plate has since been worked on." The only evidence of work further considered is some light drypoint on the chair at the far right (and it is likely that this preceded, rather than followed, the rest of the work on the plate).

The print appears to be rare, and impressions are known in brown ink as well as in black. The copper plate is in the Hunterian Art Gallery, University of Glasgow.

LITERATURE: Mansfield, p. 175, no. 262; Wedmore, p. 88, no. 216.

69. **The Fish-Shop, Busy Chelsea,** *1887*

K. 264 2/2

Etching

5 1/2 x 8 1/2 in. (14 x 21.7 cm.)

Brown ink on medium-heavy-weight laid paper

Signed lower left on tab with butterfly and ***imp****; signed in plate upper left with butterfly*

Provenance: purchased from Sotheby Parke Bernet & Co. (14 December 1978, lot 330)

One is reminded of Whistler's earlier fish shop etching, one of the more complex of the Venice facades (cat. no. 43). The fish shop here, Maunder's, is depicted in another etching (K. 279) as well as in a lithograph (Way 28). Whistler printed *The Fish-Shop, Busy Chelsea* in an edition of about fifty to be sold on behalf of the Society of British Artists during his tenure as its president. Contradicting Wedmore and Mansfield, who have dated this edition to 1886, a printing record for part of 1887 shows these fifty impressions were printed June 6–26 of that year.

In contrast to *Furniture-Shop* (cat. no. 68), this is one of Whistler's more highly developed London shop scenes. Careful attention is paid to balancing the composition and to architectural details, like window boxes, and to his own butterfly signature, which becomes a decorative element at the left. Groups of figures are gracefully spaced across the pavement with occasional emphases, such as the man in silhouette to the right of center and the lone child to his right, framed by a veritable halo of white.

The print is recorded in two states; the man at center behind the counter is unshaded in the earlier one. In both ink color and paper type this impression is typical. The copper plate is in the Hunterian Art Gallery, University of Glasgow.

LITERATURE: Fryberger, p. 53, no. 50; GUL Whistler, NB2, insert between pp. 120–21; MacDonald, p. 25, no. 42; Mansfield, p. 173, no. 259; Naylor, p. xxxii, no. 111; Wedmore, p. 82, no. 214.

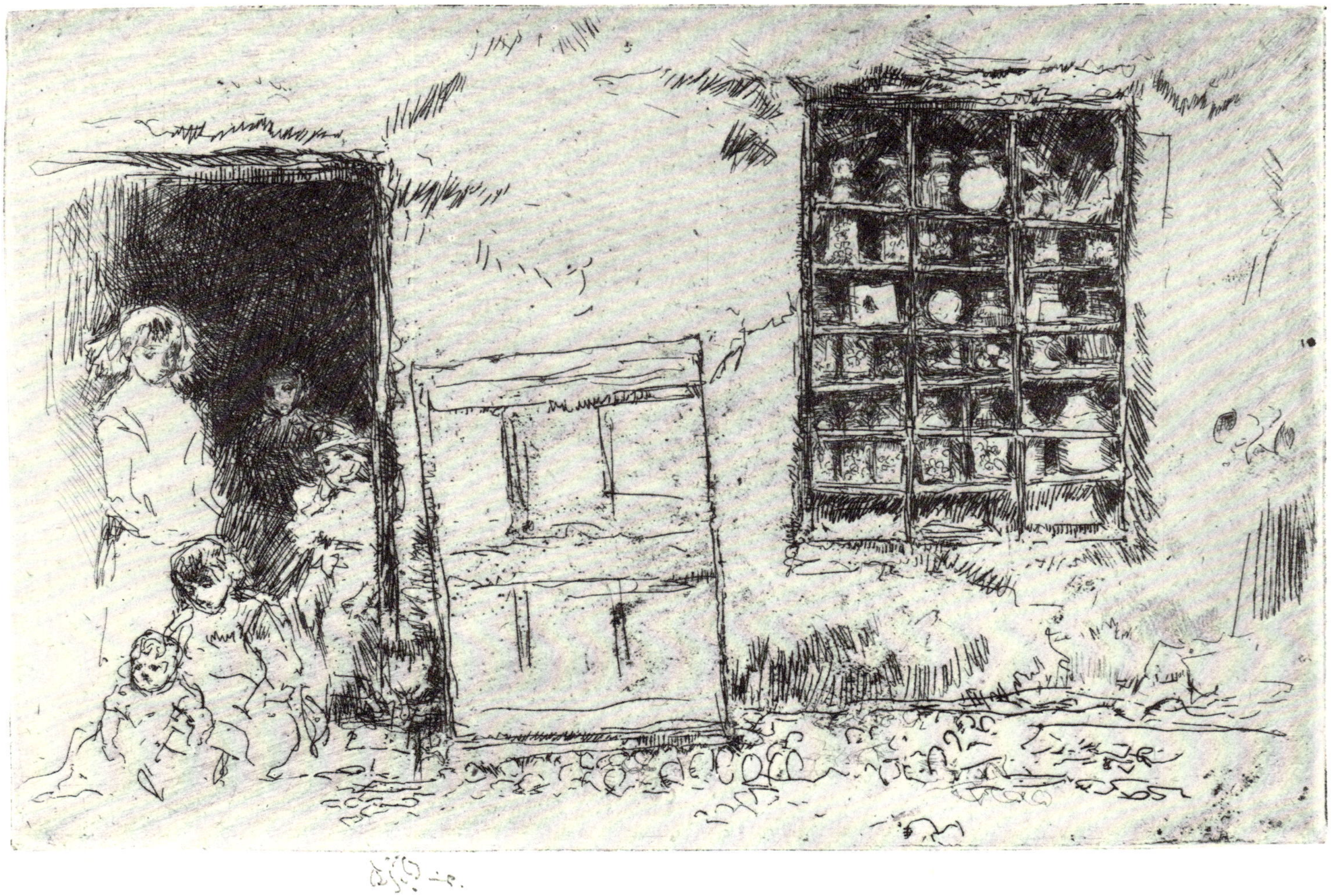

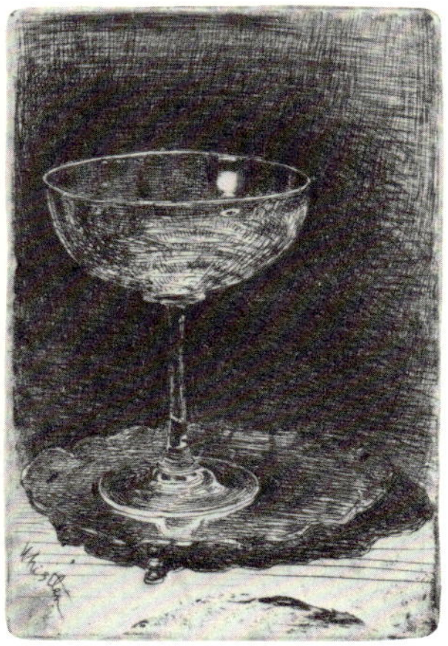

70a.
***The Wine-Glass,** K. 27*
3 1/4 x 2 1/8 in. (8.3 x 5.4 cm.)
National Gallery of Art,
Rosenwald Collection

70. ***The Village Sweet-Shop,*** *1887*

K. 251 only

Etching and drypoint

3 3/16 x 4 7/8 in. (8.1 x 12.3 cm.)

Brown ink on medium-weight laid paper

Signed lower left on tab with butterfly and ***imp****; signed in plate center right with butterfly*

Provenance: J. H. Wrenn (Lugt 1475); R. M. Light & Co., Inc. (Sotheby's, 13–14 November 1981, lot 494)

The cancelled copper plate for *The Village Sweet-Shop* is in the Hunterian Art Gallery, University of Glasgow. A list of the etching plates in the collection, prepared by Whistler's executrix, Rosalind Birnie Philip, identifies the location of the shop as Sandwich.

This is a charming scene, populated by a group of children, one of whom, not surprisingly, is hovering in the shadows. *The Village Sweet-Shop* has the distinction of including one of Whistler's few still life subjects–he only did one print (quite early in his career) which specifically is a still life (fig. 70a)–but how else would one describe those window frames enclosing shelves chock-full of marvelous treats? In few of the etchings of shop fronts does Whistler so elaborately describe the actual objects for sale. Here, however, he makes extravagant use of the etching needle to define tiny candies and other sweets.

LITERATURE: Mansfield, p. 169, no. 247; Naylor, p. xxxii, no. 109; Wedmore, p. 80, no. 205.

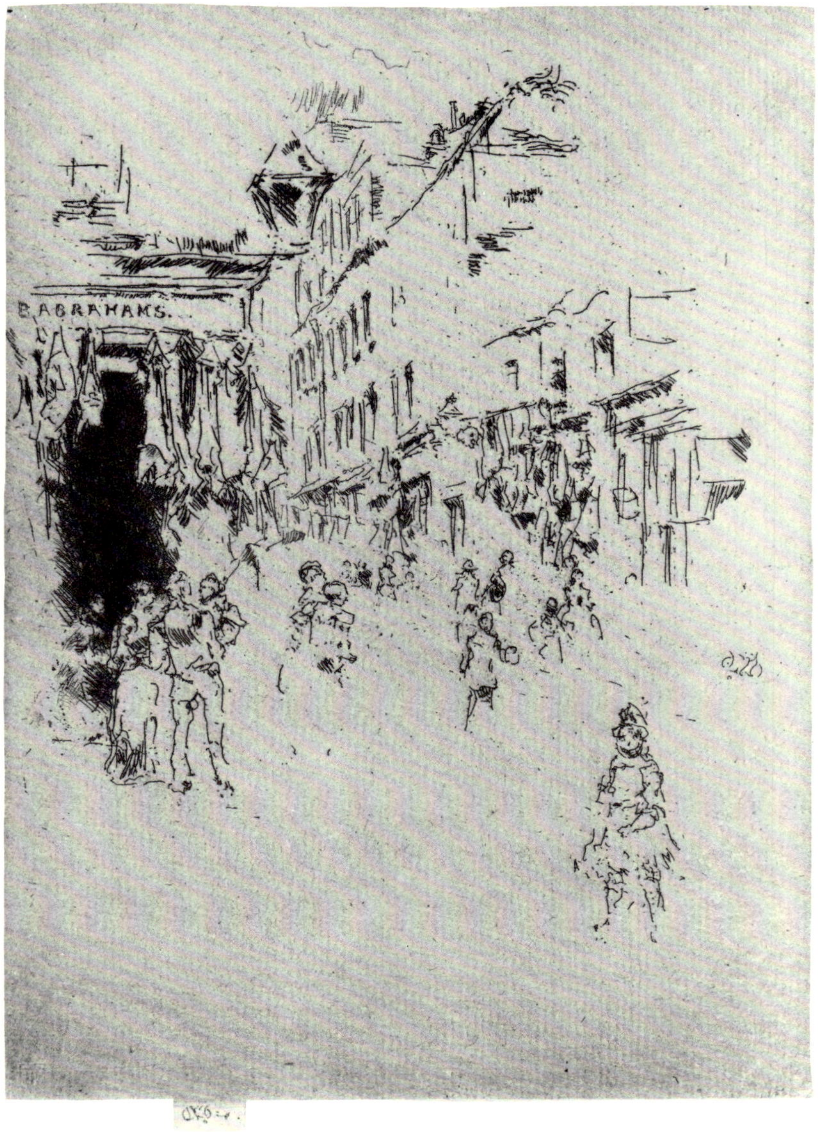

71a.
Little Court, Cloth Fair
Lithograph
7 5/8 x 3 3/4 in. (19.3 x 9.5 cm.)
Freer Gallery of Art

71. *Cutler Street, Houndsditch, 1887*

K. 292 2/2

Etching

6 13/16 x 4 7/8 in. (17.3 x 12.5 cm.)

Brown ink on medium-weight, antique laid paper with partial watermark: Pro Patria

Signed lower left on tab with butterfly and ***imp****; signed in plate center right with butterfly*

Provenance: purchased from David Tunick, Inc., 1978

Cutler Street, Houndsditch is one of several subjects Whistler etched in 1887 in the Houndsditch area of the East End, apparently with the intention of publishing a Little London Set. Like a number of etchings of this period, it is printed with an overall thin layer of surface tone that evokes the mood of a dark day rather than a day flooded with sunlight. In addition, most of the new work in this second state reinforces areas of darkness.

After a break of several years, Whistler began to make lithographs again in 1887, and in studying the etchings of the next decade, it is useful to be aware of his work in lithography as well. While not directly related, *Little Court, Cloth Fair* (fig. 71a) is similar in feeling to the present subject.

The ink color and paper type of this impression are typical of the few seen elsewhere; all of the Houndsditch etchings appear to be rather rare. The copper plate is in the Hunterian Art Gallery, University of Glasgow.

LITERATURE: MacDonald, p. 23, no. 34; Mansfield, p. 185, no. 287.

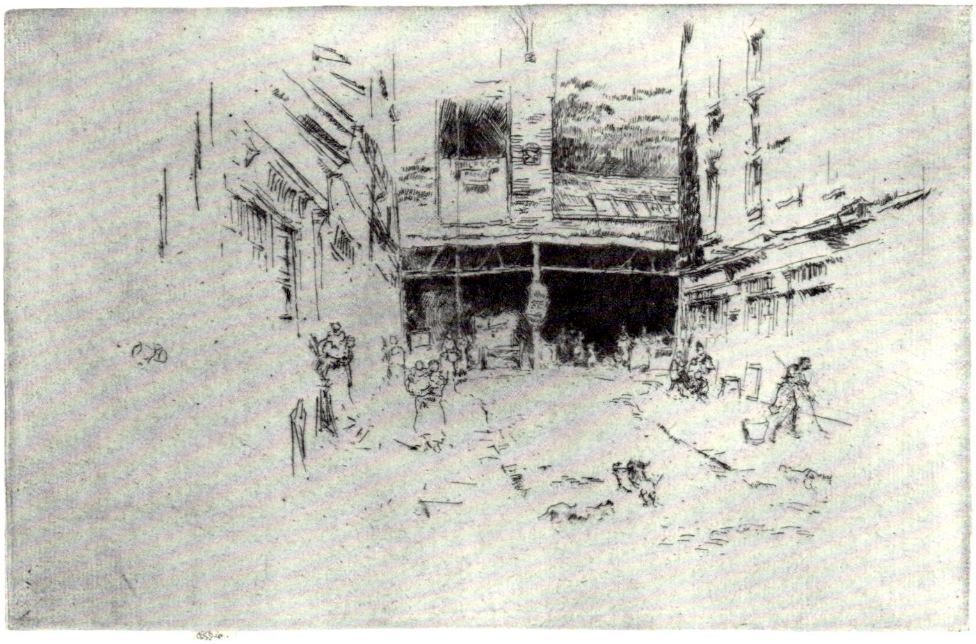

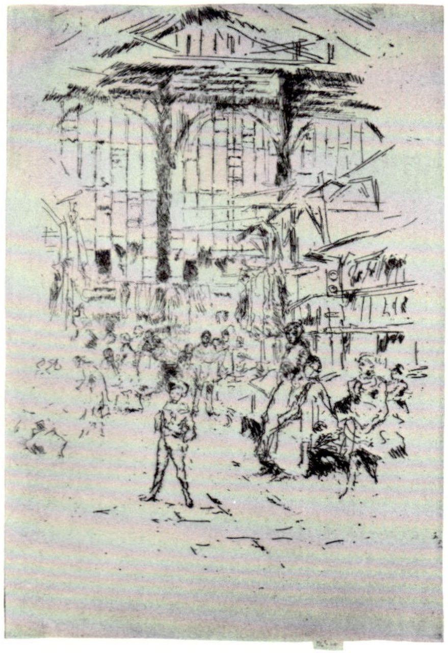

72a.
Clothes-Exchange, No. 2, *K. 288*
9 x 5 7/8 in. (22.9 x 14.9 cm.)
Freer Gallery of Art

72. ***Clothes-Exchange, No. 1,*** *1887*

K. 287 2/2

Etching

6 1/4 x 9 7/16 in. (15.9 x 24 cm.)

Brown ink on lightweight laid paper with watermark: Pro Patria

Signed lower left on tab with butterfly and ***imp****; signed in plate center left with butterfly*

Provenance: purchased from David Tunick, Inc., 1979

Another of the East End subjects, *Clothes-Exchange, No. 1* is the first of two versions of this particular scene. The second (fig. 72a) is an active interior view. The exhibited piece is recorded in two states, the major differences being in the quantity of shading on the rear wall and in the interior space.

This is a fine impression of the second state. It offers an exceedingly fresh example of the drypoint that defines the freely blocked-in dogs playfully activating the foreground. Note too the now-familiar woman holding a child on the path at the left.

This print provides a readily visible example of at least two distinct line variations resulting from successive immersions in acid: they can be seen by examining the dark area at the rear under the shed, especially the right half. The subject is generally seen printed in brown ink with the surface retaining a light and consistent film of ink throughout.

The copper plate is in the Hunterian Art Gallery, University of Glasgow.

LITERATURE: MacDonald, p. 24, no. 35; Mansfield, p. 183, no. 282.

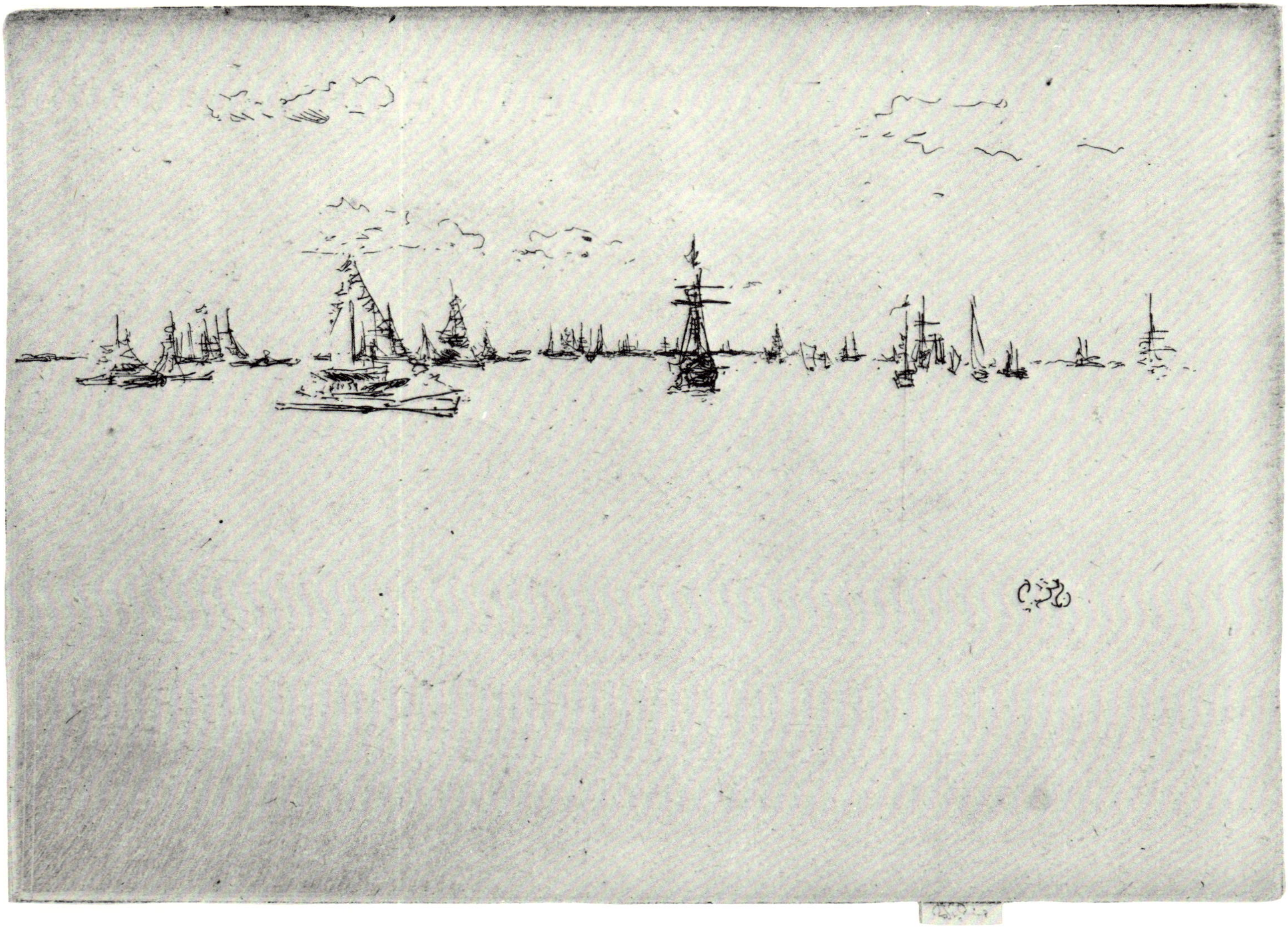

73. **The Turret-Ship,** *1887*

K. 321 only

Etching

5 x 6 15/16 in. (12.7 x 17.5 cm.)

Black ink on lightweight, antique laid paper with partial watermark

Signed lower right on tab with butterfly and ***imp****; signed in plate lower right with butterfly*

Provenance: anonymous collector's stamp; purchased from P. & D. Colnaghi & Co., 1981

In format *The Turret-Ship* can almost be seen as a later version of *Little Venice* (cat. no. 65): the ships function in place of the picturesque city's architecture. The etching is one of a dozen plates that Whistler executed on a single day, July 27, 1887. As a group, they depict the naval review in honor of Queen Victoria's Jubilee, the fiftieth anniversary of her reign.

Whistler wrote to the queen that "to have looked upon that august and stately scene will be cherished as an inspiring privilege. . . ." In appreciation, he presented a set of his Jubilee etchings to her, housed in a splendid gold leather portfolio, decorated with a crown and roses. Tooled in gold was the inscription, "To the Queen's Most Excellent Majesty"; his butterfly signature was tooled on the back. The set was later sold by Edward VII and is now in the Hunterian Art Gallery, University of Glasgow, as are the twelve copper plates for the series.

All of the Jubilee plates are recorded in only one state, but many had additions made in drypoint. As those additions wore (it would appear in some instances almost immediately), new lines, not necessarily the same, were added. For example, an impression of *The Turret-Ship* in the Freer Gallery of Art, printed in brown, has a wave in drypoint about an inch below the darkest ship to the right of center. Whether the impression exhibited here is before that wave was added or after it wore away is difficult to determine.

LITERATURE: GUL Whistler, V65–67; Mansfield, p. 194, no. 316; Naylor, p. xxxiii, no. 123.

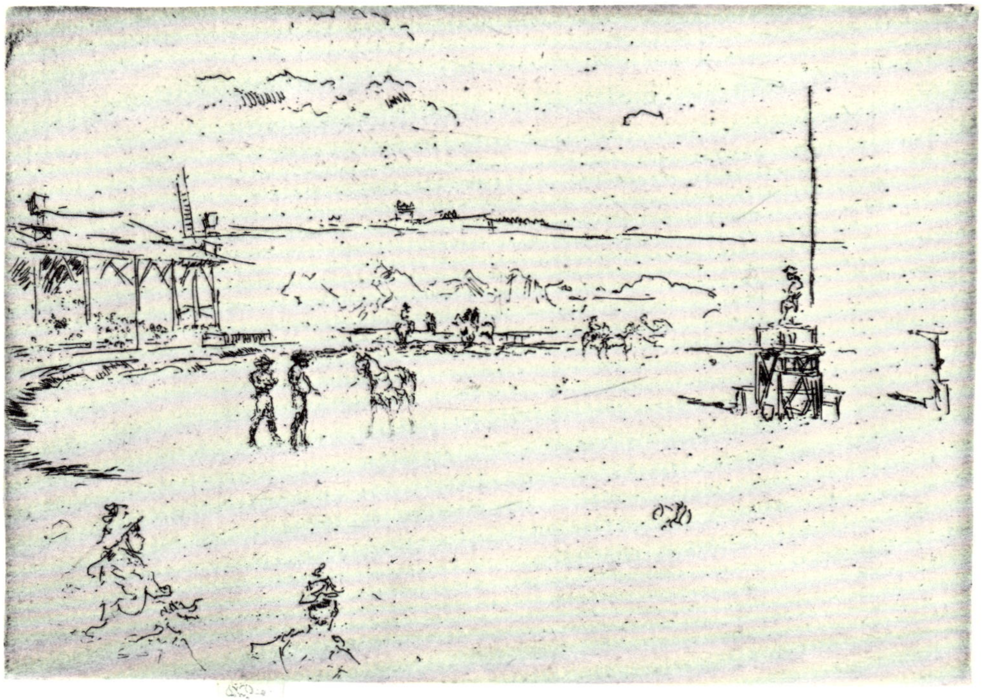

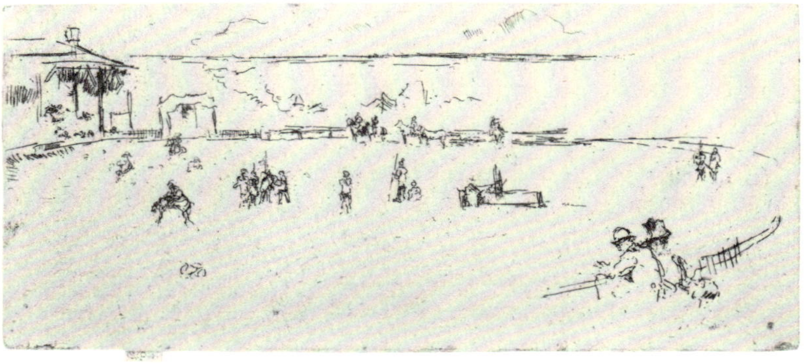

74a.
The Bucking Horse, *K. 315*
3 1/4 x 7 1/4 in. (8.3 x 18.4 cm.)
Julius L. and Anita Zelman

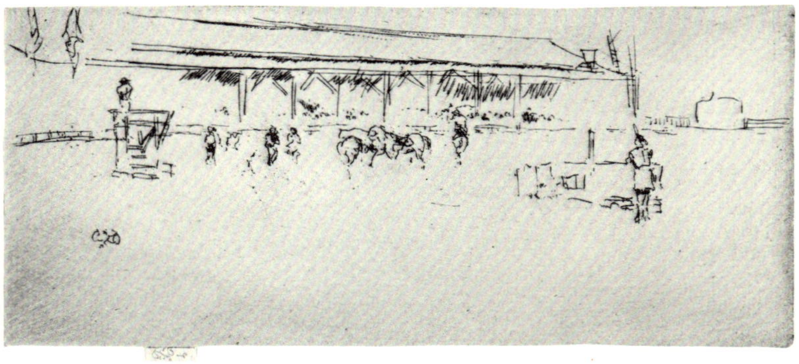

74b.
Wild West, *K. 314*
3 1/8 x 7 1/4 (7.9 x 18.4 cm.)
Julius L. and Anita Zelman

74. ***Wild West, Buffalo Bill,*** *1887*

K. 313 only

Etching and drypoint

4 15/16 x 6 15/16 in. (12.5 x 17.5 cm.)

Black ink on lightweight, antique laid paper with partial watermark

Signed lower left on tab with butterfly and ***imp****; signed in plate lower right with butterfly; inscribed verso lower right* ***1st proof***

Provenance: anonymous collector's stamp; purchased from R. M. Light & Co., Inc., 1980

"Buffalo Bill" Cody and his Wild West show performed in London at Earl's Court in 1887. Whistler celebrated the event by making *Wild West, Buffalo Bill* as well as two other tiny prints (figs. 74a and 74b), all in the course of one performance.

Typical of the small etchings of 1887, all three of the *Wild West* etchings are exceedingly sparse, capturing with remarkably few strokes the activity of the rodeo and the sense of an enthusiastic audience. They allow one to see Whistler's flexibility in adapting his style to a wide range of subjects and pictorial demands.

The copper plates for all three Wild West subjects are in the Hunterian Art Gallery, University of Glasgow.

LITERATURE: Mansfield, p. 192, no. 308–10; Naylor, p. xxxiii, nos. 130–32.

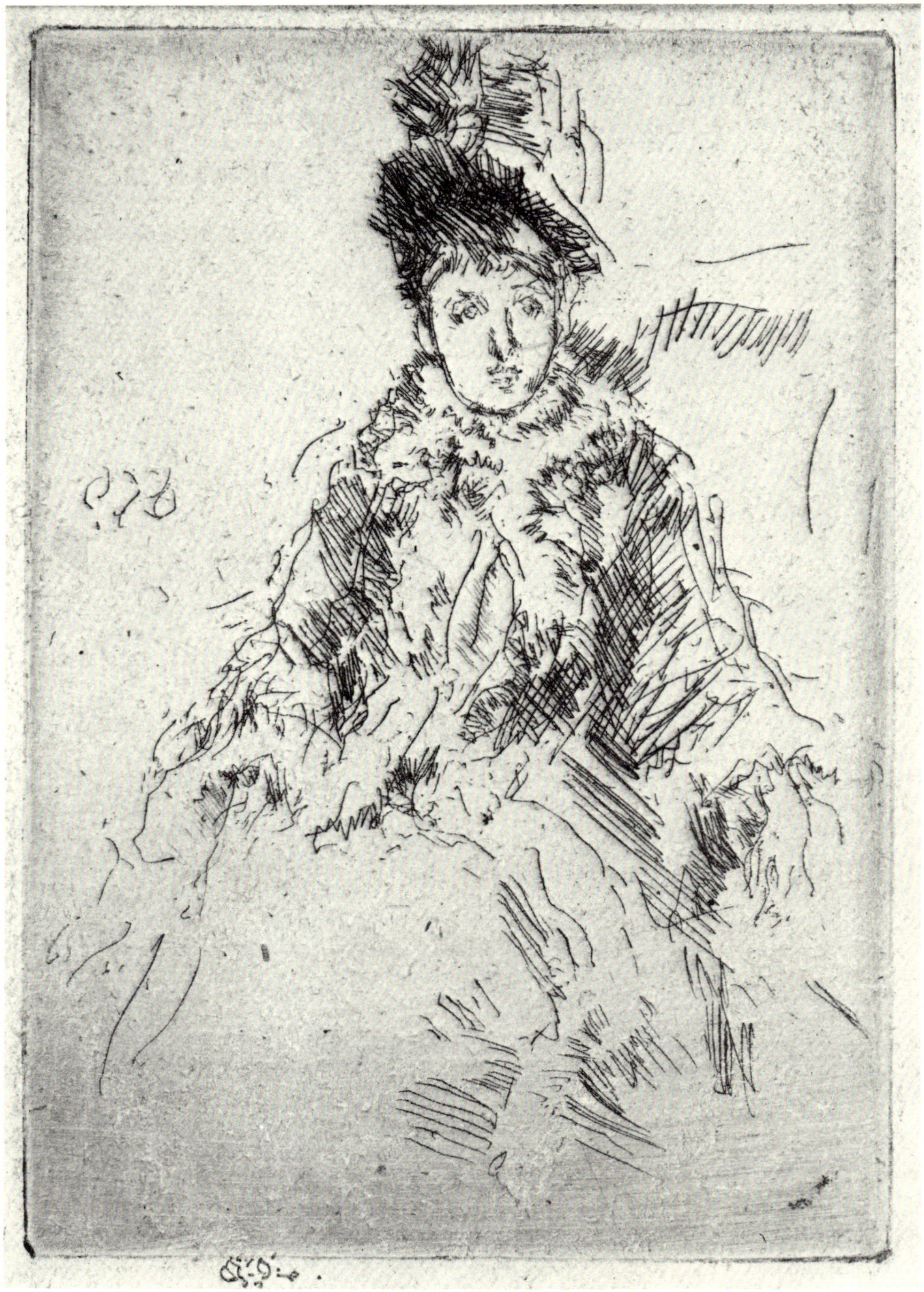

75. ***Miss Lenoir,*** *c. 1887*

K. 334 only

Etching and drypoint

3 7/8 x 2 5/8 in. (9.9 x 6.7 cm.)

Brown ink on lightweight laid paper with partial watermark: Arms of Amsterdam

Signed lower left with butterfly and ***imp****;*
signed in plate center left with butterfly

Provenance: Charles Deering (Lugt 516); Art Institute of Chicago (not in Lugt); purchased from R. M. Light & Co., Inc., 1971

Miss Helen Lenoir was Mrs. D'Oyly Carte, and it was she who was responsible for making arrangements for the presentation of Whistler's "Ten O'Clock" lecture in London in 1885.

In the early 1870s, Whistler's portraits were worked in drypoint, the directness of the medium seemingly an essential element in their spontaneous grasp of the sitters' personalities. Closest to *Miss Lenoir* among them, both in scale and type, is a drypoint, *The Muff* (cat. no. 35). In comparing the two, one sees here, first, that Whistler has become equally free-wielding with the etching medium and, second, that his general approach to form in this later piece is much more fluid and abbreviated.

In addition to examples like this one, made during Whistler's lifetime, impressions of *Miss Lenoir* printed by Frederick Goulding in 1906 (and so annotated) are known. The copper plate was then cancelled and is in the Hunterian Art Gallery, University of Glasgow.

LITERATURE: Mansfield, p. 198, no. 330.

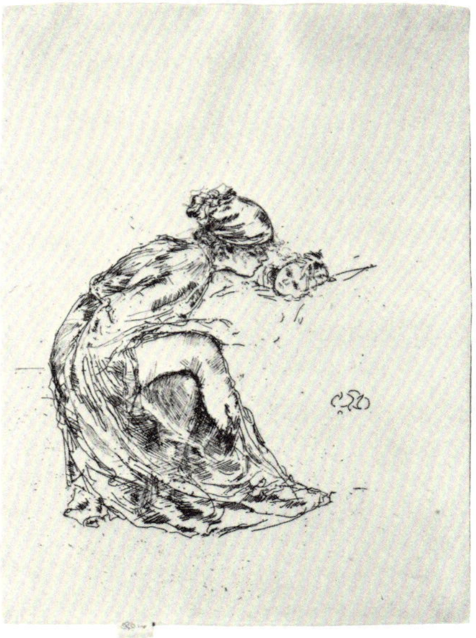

76a.
Cameo, No. 1, *K. 347*
6 7/8 x 5 in. (17.5 x 12.7 cm.)
Freer Gallery of Art

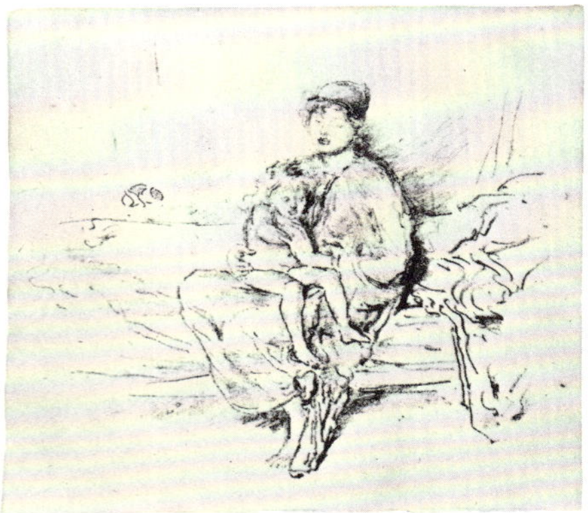

76b.
Mother and Child, No. 2
Lithograph
6 3/4 x 8 in. (17.1 x 20.3 cm.)
Freer Gallery of Art

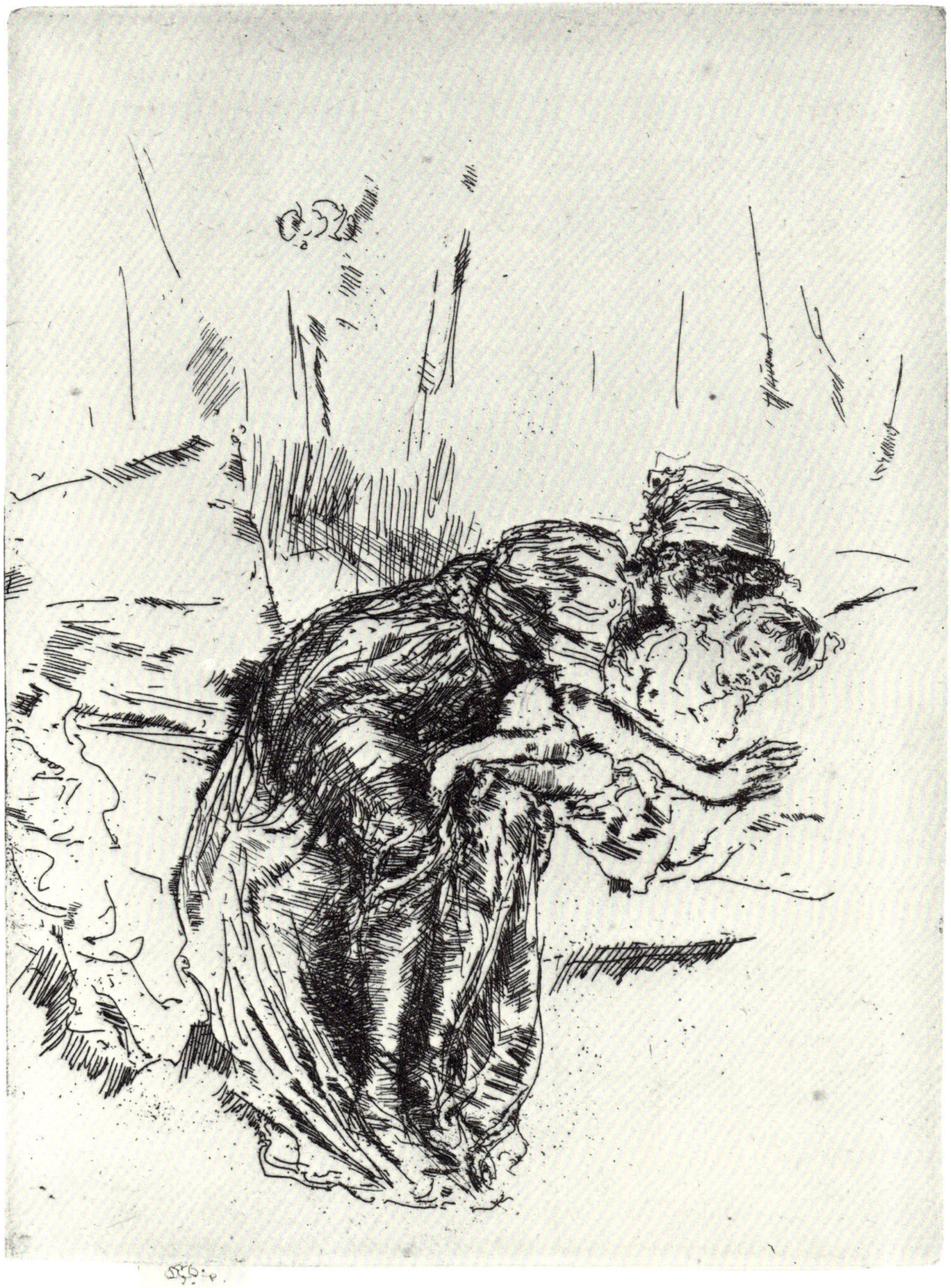

76. ***Cameo, No. 2,*** *c. 1892*

K. 348 only

Etching and drypoint

6 15/16 x 5 in. (17.6 x 12.8 cm.)

Brown ink on medium-weight laid paper with partial watermark: Arms of Amsterdam

Signed lower left on tab with butterfly and ***imp****; signed in plate upper left with butterfly; inscribed verso lower right* ***2nd proof*** *and signed with butterfly*

Provenance: Howard Mansfield (Lugt 1342); Harris G. Whittemore (Lugt 1384a); Emma Regina Martin (initials verso); anonymous collector's stamp; purchased from R. M. Light & Co., Inc., 1981

Although the woman-and-child theme is repeatedly encountered as an aspect of many of Whistler's etchings, as a total motif we know only two examples: the present one and a closely related *Cameo, No. 1* (fig. 76a). There are, however, a number of drawings and lithographs that are similar, such as *Mother and Child* (fig. 76b). The models for all of these related pieces–the etchings, drawings, and lithographs–are thought to be the three Pettigrew sisters–Hetty, Lily, and Rose–and the child of one of them.

The lithos, dated by Way to 1895, probably were drawn on transfer paper about the time of the etchings but not placed on the stone until some years later.

As a group, the prints and drawings show Whistler's ability to capture the essential warmth and tenderness necessary to his subject without entering the realm of sentimentality.

The copper plate for *Cameo, No. 2* is in the Hunterian Art Gallery, University of Glasgow. Also in Glasgow is an impression of the print that is heavily reworked throughout with crayon (reproduced, MacDonald, pl. 2). The additions seem never to have been made to the plate, however, as impressions are known in only one state.

LITERATURE: GUL Whistler, NB1, p. 114; MacDonald, p. 28, no. 52; Mansfield, p. 199, no. 334; Naylor, p. xxxiv, no. 134.

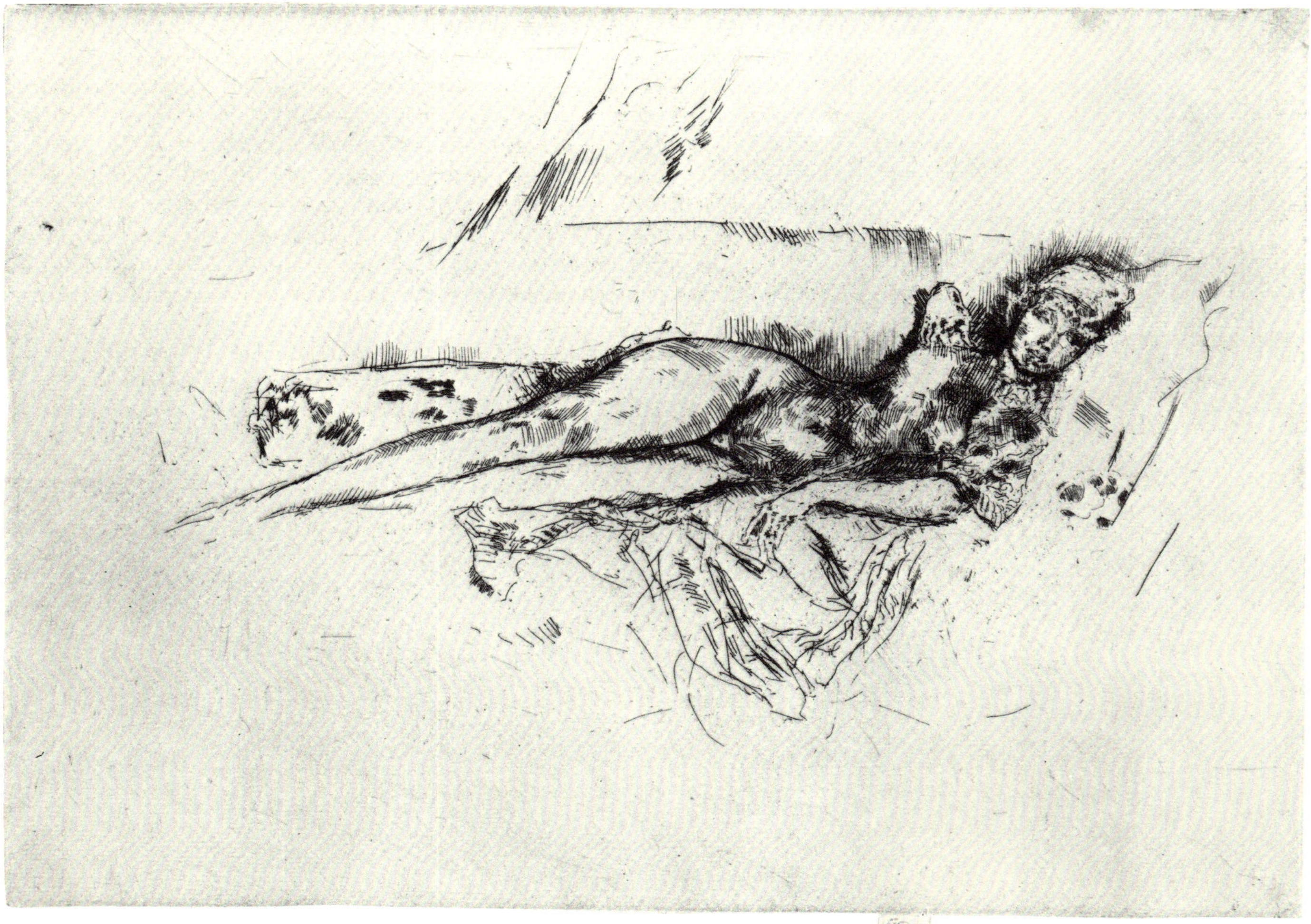

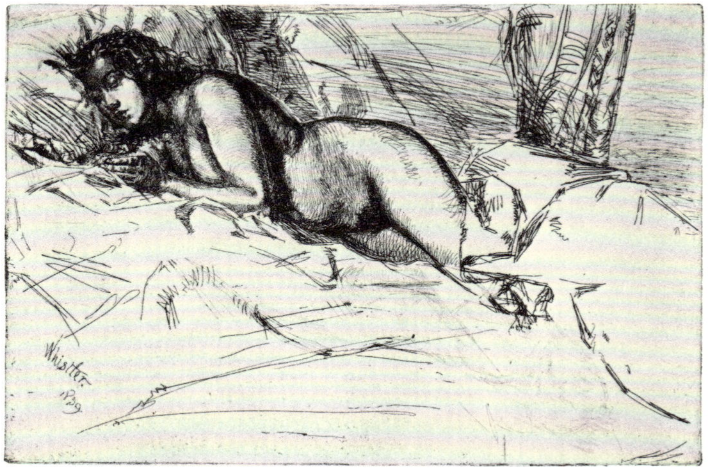

77a.
Venus, *K. 59*
6 x 9 in. (15.2 x 23.9 cm.)
Julius L. and Anita Zelman

77. ***Nude Figure Reclining,***

late 1890s

K. 343 only

Etching

7 1/2 x 10 7/16 in. (19.1 x 26.5 cm.)

Black ink on lightweight laid paper

Signed lower right on tab with butterfly and ***imp****; signed in plate center right with butterfly*

Provenance: purchased from Linda M. Papaharis (Christie's, New York, 10–11 May 1982, lot 118)

Although Whistler made many pastel drawings and lithographs of nudes and semidraped figures, and a reclining nude, *Venus* (fig. 77a), was among his earliest etchings, very few other nude figures appear in the medium between that and this late piece, *Nude Figure Reclining.*

Margaret MacDonald has dated the print to the late 1890s. Stylistically, it is quite distinctive: the shading is distributed in areas that are somewhat blocklike, similar to a few late pastel drawings.

In the Hunterian Art Gallery, University of Glasgow, there are several impressions of a first state of *Nude Figure Reclining* (unknown to Kennedy) prior to some of the shading at the model's waist (reproduced, Getscher, p. 44). Also in Glasgow is the copper plate. The print is rather scarce, but impressions are known on both Oriental and Western papers.

LITERATURE: Getscher and Staley, p. 45, no. 18; MacDonald, p. 29, no. 56; Mansfield, p. 201, no. 341.

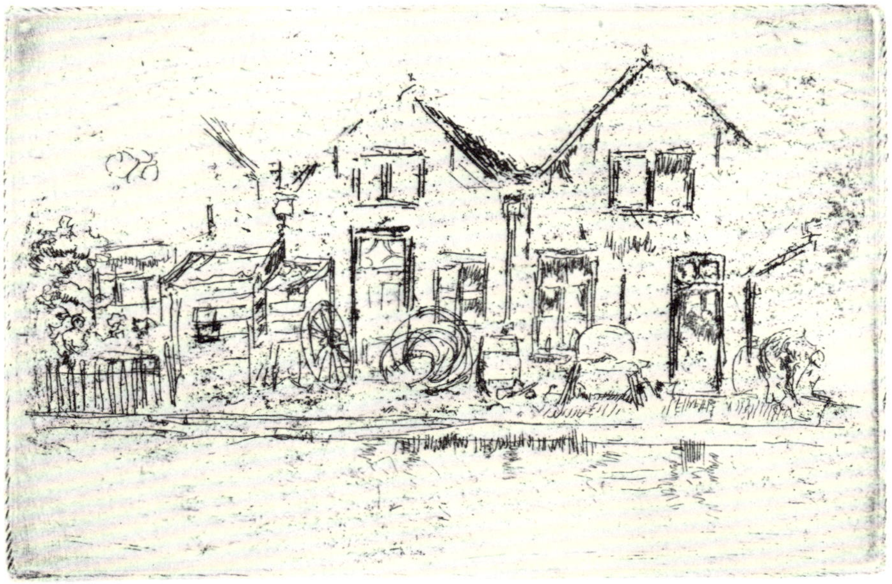

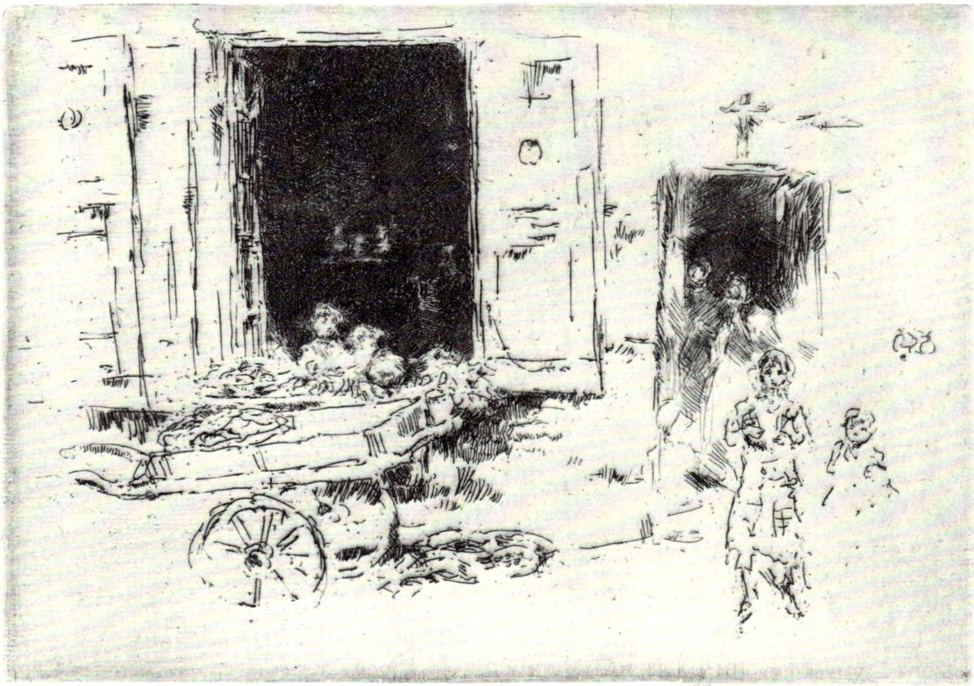

78. ***The Little Wheelwright's,*** *1884*

K. 245 only

Etching

2 5/8 x 3 7/8 in. (6.6 x 9.9 cm.)

Black ink on lightweight laid paper

Signed in plate upper left with butterfly

Provenance: Emma Regina Martin (initials verso); anonymous collector's stamp; purchased from R. M. Light & Co., Inc., 1980

The Little Wheelwright's was attributed by Mansfield to Whistler's 1884 trip to Dordrecht, during which he made several etchings and watercolors. Among the artist's tiniest etchings, it nonetheless vividly depicts many elements found in his larger, more complicated pieces: a horizontal, continuous frieze of houses; reflections in water; a woman behind a fence (at the left); decorative architectural detail (the window above the door of the central house); and an interior view through an open door (at the right). The dots throughout the surface result from foul biting.

The copper plate from the Mortimer Menpes collection may have been sold at Sotheby's in 1960, but we have been unable to track it further. This and the fact that the sheet has wide margins and is unsigned except for the butterfly (typical of impressions we have seen) suggest that this impression is posthumous.

LITERATURE: *An Exhibition of Etchings, Drypoints & Lithographs by James McNeill Whistler* (London: P. & D. Colnaghi & Co., 1971), p. 33, no. 108; Howard Mansfield, "Whistler in Belgium and Holland," *Print Collector's Quarterly* 6 (1916): 376, 378; Mansfield, p. 167, no. 242; Wedmore, p. 71, no. 162.

79. ***The Barrow, Brussels,*** *1887*

K. 357 3/3

Etching and drypoint

5 x 6 7/8 in. (12.6 x 17.5 cm.)

Brown ink on lightweight laid paper with partial watermark: crown (?)

Signed lower right on tab with butterfly and ***imp****; signed in plate center right with butterfly*

Provenance: Otto Gerstenberg (Lugt 2785); purchased from R. E. Lewis, Inc. (Sotheby's, 10 November 1978, lot 394)

The Barrow, Brussels convincingly shows how Whistler found Whistlerian views wherever he went: his personal vision was immediately activated in his response to new places. Children everywhere captivated him, as did murky interior views. Mansfield has placed this particular scene in the Quartier des Marolles. During Whistler's 1887 journey to Belgium with his brother William and William's wife, the artist also depicted scenes in Ostend and Bruges.

Impressions of *The Barrow, Brussels* are known in black ink as well as brown on both Western and Oriental papers. The copper plate is in the Hunterian Art Gallery, University of Glasgow.

LITERATURE: Howard Mansfield, "Whistler in Belgium and Holland," *Print Collector's Quarterly* 6 (1916): 382; Mansfield, p. 205, no. 356.

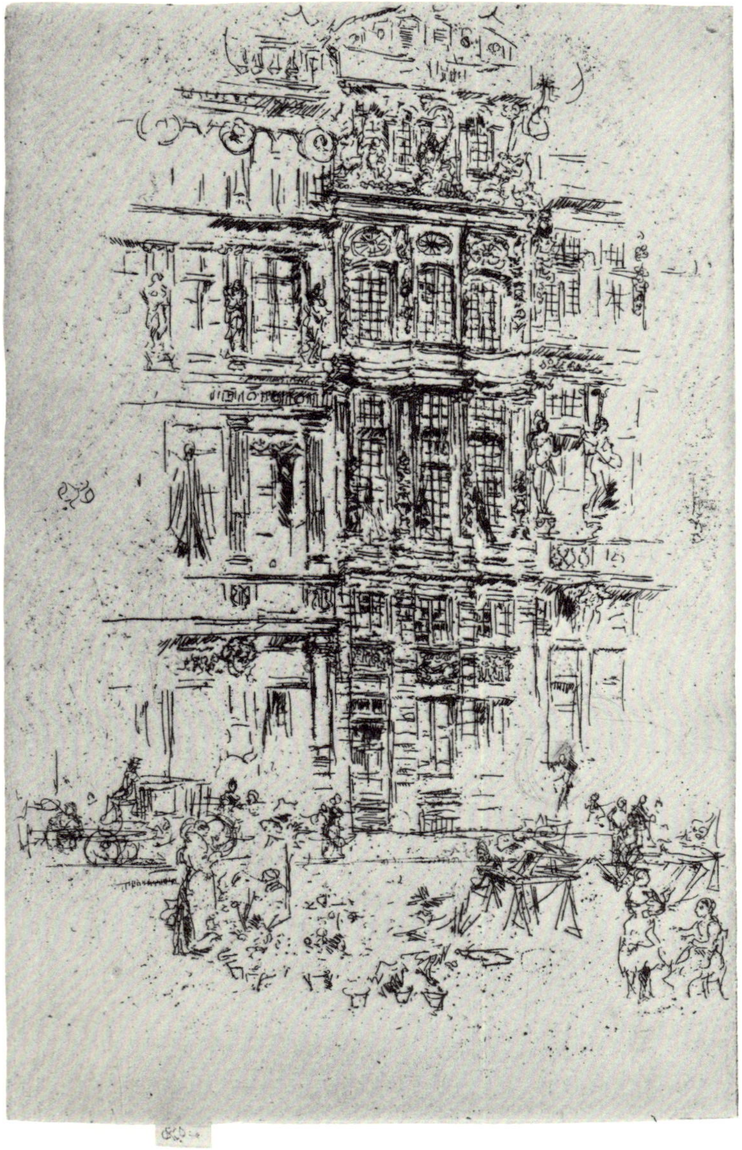

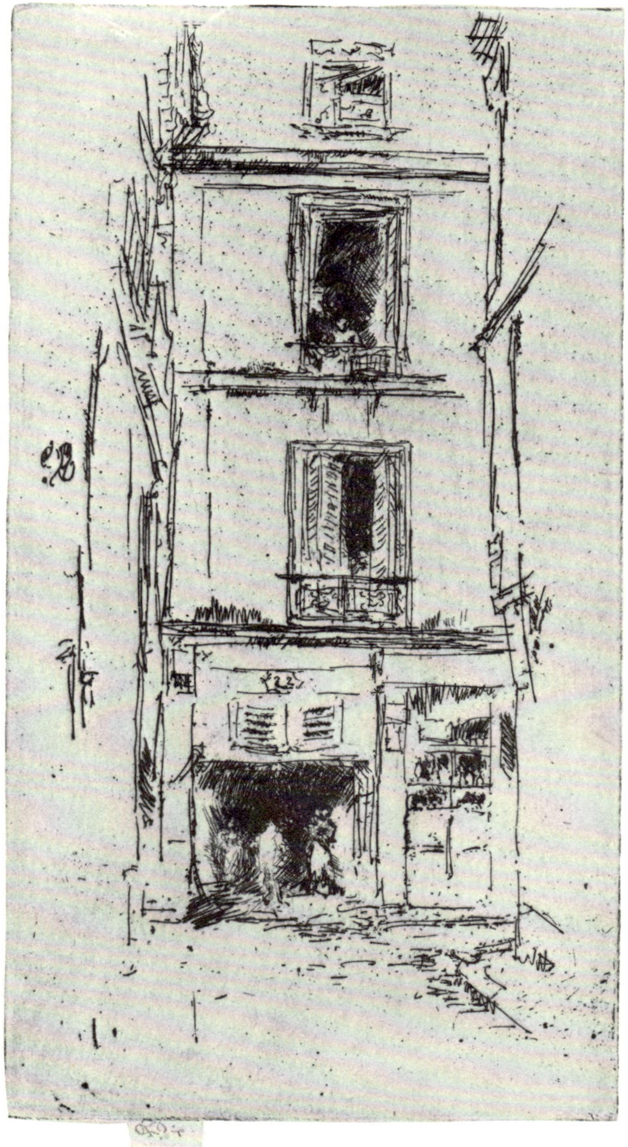

80. **Palaces, Brussels,** 1887

K. 361 1/2

Etching and drypoint

8 9/16 x 5 7/16 in. (21.7 x 13.8 cm.)

Brown ink on lightweight laid paper

Signed lower left on tab with butterfly and ***imp****; signed in plate center left with butterfly; inscribed verso* 

Provenance: Otto Gerstenberg (Lugt 2785); purchased from Ira D. Gale, 1972

Whistler's largest etching, *The Palaces* (cat. no. 54) functions as a centerpiece for the First Venice Set. Likewise, *Palaces, Brussels* is the most impressive of the Brussels subjects. They too may have been conceived in series for publication like the Venice etchings. None was formally published, however, and all of them are relatively rare. In this most elaborate of the group, the architecture is virtually a celebration of majestic ornamentation, while the figures on the foreground plaza, in contrast, are as homespun as those in the rather dilapidated courtyard depicted in *Turkeys* (cat. 47).

Palaces, Brussels provided an interesting visual intermediary between the earlier Venice etchings and the Amsterdam etchings to follow. Not exhaustively drawn, the Venice scenes often rely on surface tone for completion, while in the Amsterdam prints the elaborate line work far exceeds the central facade seen here. Whistler's tendency to concentrate on particular aspects of an image is at its most eloquent in pieces like this: moving from the dense central building, the scene practically dissolves at its edges. The copper plate is in the Hunterian Art Gallery, University of Glasgow.

LITERATURE: Fryberger, p. 61, no. 62; Mansfield, p. 205, no. 355; Naylor, p. xxxiv, no. 135.

81. **Rue des Bons Enfants, Tours,** 1888

K. 372 3/3

Etching

5 13/16 x 3 1/8 in. (14.7 x 7.9 cm.)

Dark brown ink on medium-weight laid paper

Signed lower left on tab with butterfly and ***imp****; signed in plate center left with butterfly*

Provenance: Charles Deering (Lugt 516); Art Institute of Chicago (not in Lugt); anonymous collector's stamp; purchased from R. M. Light & Co., Inc., 1980

Rue des Bons Enfants is one of some half-dozen etchings Whistler made at Tours during his honeymoon trip through France. Typical of these pieces and others sketched while traveling (Whistler later referred to them as the Renaissance Set), it is relatively tiny. Most of the etchings of the late 1880s were completed without going through more than one state; but when alterations were necessary, they generally took the form, as here, of darkening the dark areas rather than of substantially changing the image in any way.

Evident is Whistler's continuing interest in facades and in views through windows, doorways, and passages. But he is no longer as finicky about subtleties and nuances as he was in Venice. Spontaneity is much more to the point. The print is extremely rare. The copper plate is in the Hunterian Art Gallery, University of Glasgow.

LITERATURE: GUL Whistler, F164; Mansfield, p. 212, no. 372.

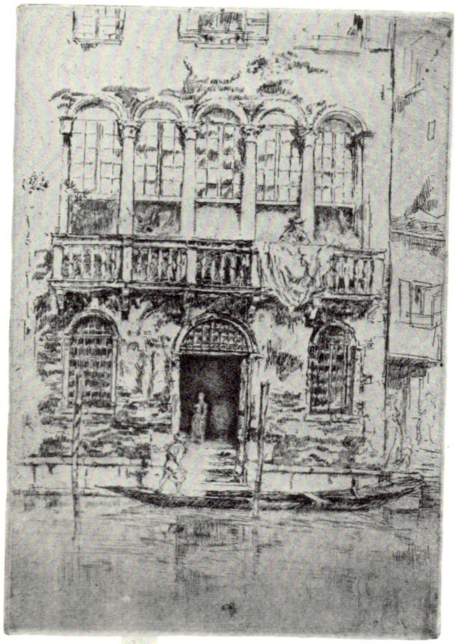

82a.
The Balcony, *K. 207*
11 5/8 x 7 7/8 in. (29.5 x 20 cm.)
Julius L. and Anita Zelman

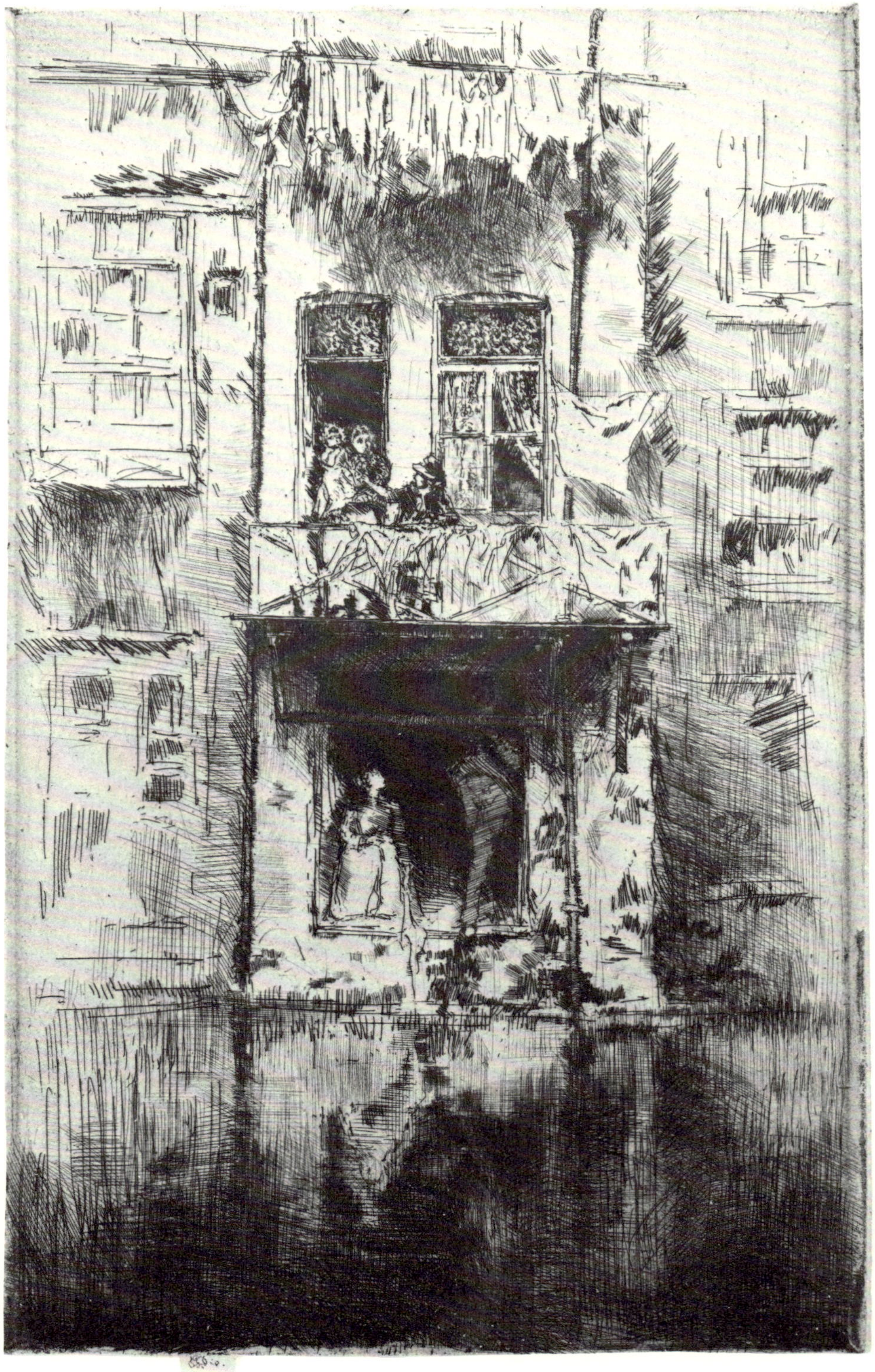

82. **Balcony, Amsterdam,** 1889

K. 405 3/3

Etching and drypoint

10 11/16 x 6 11/16 in. (27.2 x 16.9 cm.)

Brown ink on medium-weight, antique laid paper with watermark: GR surmounted by CB surmounted by crown

Signed lower left on tab with butterfly and ***imp****; signed in plate lower right with butterfly; inscribed verso with two tiny circles*

Provenance: Emma Regina Martin (initials verso); purchased from Kennedy Galleries, Inc., 1977

In *Balcony, Amsterdam* Whistler juxtaposed broad, open areas of line work–the water, the buildings flanking the house with the balcony–and rather intricate drawing of the sort most fully realized in *The Embroidered Curtain* (cat. no. 90). The image is strangely diffuse despite its taut organization, defined by parallel and repeated elements such as the dark shadow below the laundry at the top of the plate, echoed by the shadow of the balcony overhang, echoed finally by the rich darkness in the water. This last is heightened by a light film of surface tone. One need only place *Balcony, Amsterdam* next to the balcony in the Venice series (fig. 82a) to see the extent to which, over a decade, Whistler had extended his range of line work.

Although the Amsterdam etchings were not formally published, Whistler printed several impressions of many of them, including at least a dozen of this one. *Balcony, Amsterdam* is also known in a few posthumous impressions printed by Nathaniel Sparks (and so annotated) as authorized by Rosalind Birnie Philip. The plate was then cancelled and is now in the Hunterian Art Gallery, University of Glasgow.

LITERATURE: MacDonald, p. 50, no. 109; Mansfield, p. 225, no. 404; Naylor, p. xxxiv, no. 140.

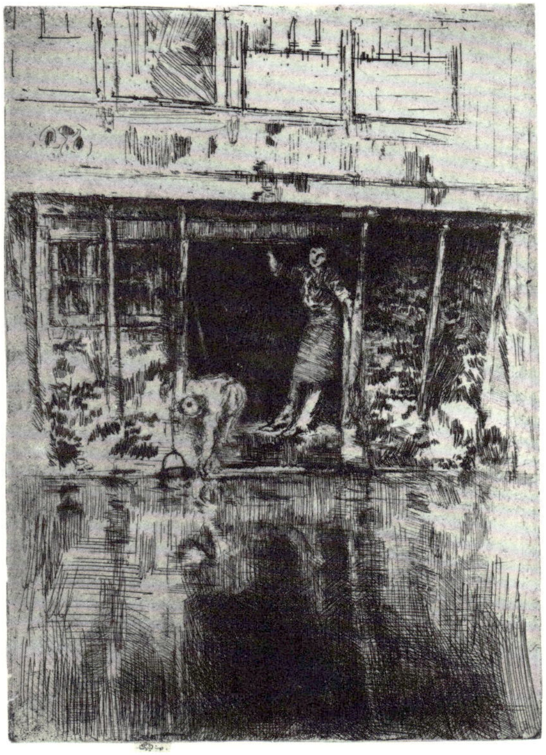

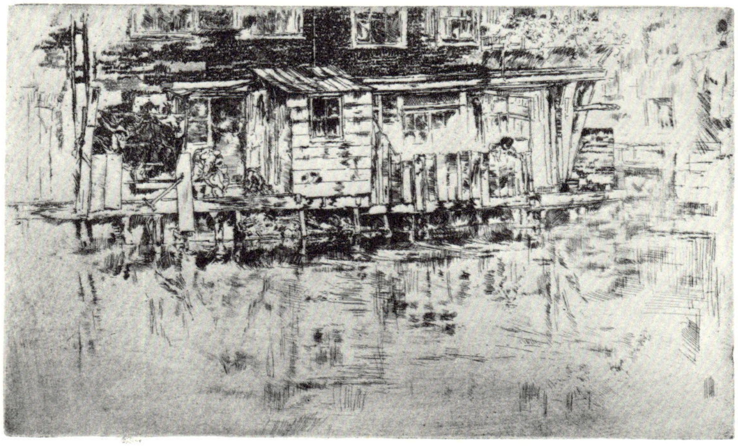

83. ***Pierrot*, 1889**

K. 407 4/5

Etching and drypoint

9 x 6 5/16 in. (22.9 x 16.1 cm.)

Brown ink on lightweight, antique laid paper

Signed lower left on tab with butterfly and ***imp****; signed in plate upper left with butterfly*

Provenance: Otto Gerstenberg (Lugt 2785); purchased from Ira D. Gale, 1972

Pierrot, according to Mansfield, "probably a study of dyers standing in a doorway of a dilapidated building," was Whistler's favorite among the Amsterdam plates. Like the Venice *Dyer* (cat. no. 44), it is characterized by its focus on the single monumental central figure with a clearly defined, expressive face. (Here, however, there is another figure of secondary importance.) In addition, in both of these etchings, the area surrounding the central figure is fairly open.

In *Pierrot* densities are developed by overlapping line networks. The darkest areas, most emphatically in the water at center, are etched versions of what would have been plate tone had this dated from the Venice period. A completely new kind of spatial ambiguity comes into play in areas of the image, however. To the right of Pierrot, for instance, this is defined by patches of short, parallel strokes of a sort that were to be further explored during the 1890s (cat. no. 77).

Several states beyond the five described by Kennedy exist. Impressions are printed in brown on a variety of Western and, somewhat more frequently, Oriental papers. The copper plate is in the Hunterian Art Gallery, University of Glasgow.

LITERATURE: Fryberger, p. 65, no. 68; GUL Whistler, M266; MacDonald, p. 51, no. 112; Mansfield, p. 226, no. 406; Naylor, p. xxxiv, no. 142; Wiehl, p. 7.

84. ***Long House–Dyer's–Amsterdam*, 1889**

K. 406 1/3

Etching and drypoint

10 5/8 x 6 1/2 in. (27 x 16.5 cm.)

Brown ink on medium-weight, antique laid paper with watermark: LVG (?)

Signed lower left on tab with butterfly and ***imp****; signed in plate at center with butterfly; inscribed verso* **1st state** *and signed with butterfly*

Provenance: George W. Vanderbilt (initials verso); anonymous collector's stamp; purchased from R. M. Light & Co., Inc., 1981

This impression of *Long House–Dyer's–Amsterdam* is the one reproduced in Kennedy for the very rare first state. It lacks a woman (added later) holding a child behind the fence in the vertical, rectangular white area to the left of the figure at the right. It also lacks considerable work throughout the plate that defines and refines the image. In particular, the reflections in the water are much more fully observed in the final version.

Long House–Dyer's–Amsterdam is a lovely example of Whistler's ultimate coordination of specific description as manifested in the Thames Set and the allusion that marked the most successful and unusual of the Venice etchings. The copper plate is in the Hunterian Art Gallery, University of Glasgow.

LITERATURE: Mansfield, p. 28, no. 408; Naylor, p. xxxiv, no. 141.

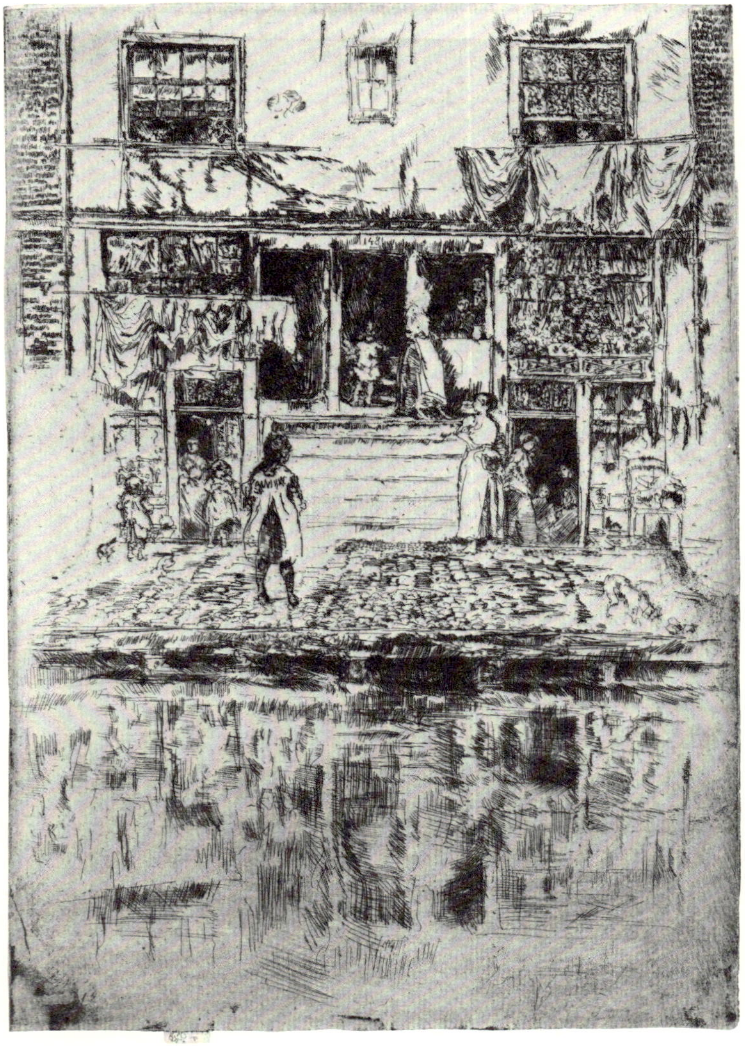

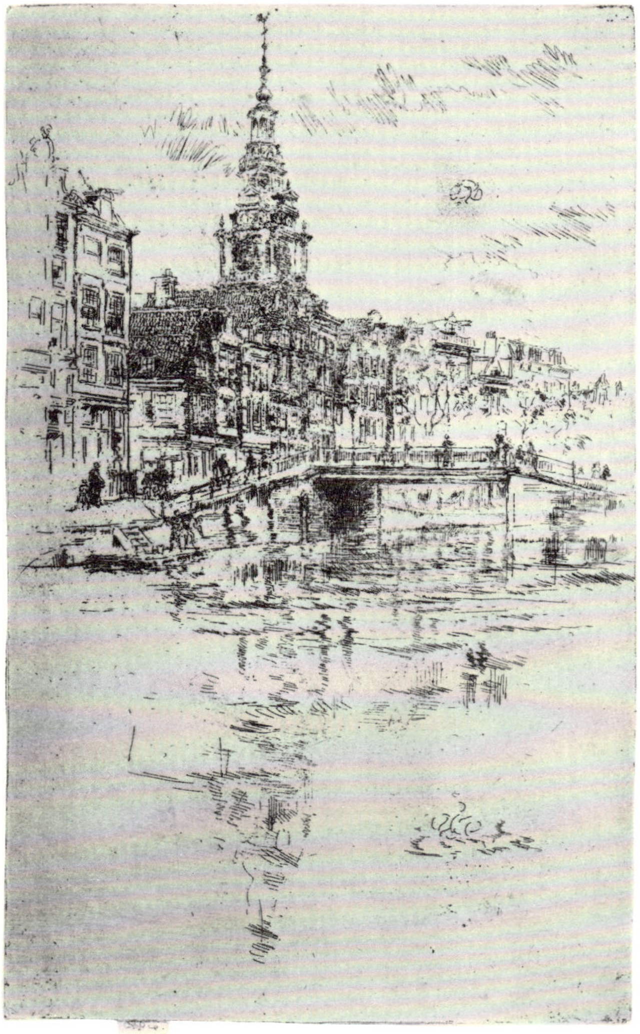

85. **Steps, Amsterdam,** 1889

K. 403 1/4

Etching and drypoint

9 7/16 x 6 1/2 in. (24 x 16.5 cm.)

Brown ink on lightweight, antique laid paper

Signed lower left on tab with butterfly and ***imp****; signed in plate upper center with butterfly; inscribed verso lower left* ***Wunderlich*** *and signed with butterfly; inscribed verso lower right* ***2nd proof pulled*** *and signed with butterfly*

Provenance: Hermann Wunderlich (presentation verso); George W. Vanderbilt (?) anonymous collector's stamp; purchased from R. M. Light & Co., Inc., 1981

Of the Amsterdam etchings, *Steps, Amsterdam* most cogently shows Whistler's affectionate response to children. Each of them is rendered with an immediate grasp of essential gesture: the little girl with her back to us is totally at ease as she waits for the child at the top of the steps to descend. The site is the Rozen Gracht, and this first-state impression, before the shadows become more fully worked, is a splendid example of Whistler's instant survey of the scene.

Impressions are known on both Western and Oriental papers. This impression is inscribed to Hermann Wunderlich, the founder of what is now Kennedy Galleries, Inc. Wunderlich was one of Whistler's dealers and strong supporters in the United States. The copper plate for *Steps, Amsterdam* is in the Hunterian Art Gallery, University of Glasgow.

LITERATURE: MacDonald, p. 50, no. 110; Mansfield, p. 223, no. 402; Naylor, p. xxxiv, no. 138; Wiehl, p. 23, no. 20.

86. **Church, Amsterdam,** 1889

K. 411 only

Etching

8 1/2 x 5 1/8 in. (21.6 x 12.9 cm.)

Brown ink on lightweight, antique laid paper

Signed lower left on tab with butterfly and ***imp****; signed in plate upper right with butterfly, which is reflected lower right*

Provenance: Emma Regina Martin (initials verso); anonymous collector's stamp; purchased from R. M. Light & Co., Inc., 1982

Church, Amsterdam is one of the rarest of the Amsterdam etchings. In its elaborate attention to architectural detail, particularly concentrated in a vertical central space, it is reminiscent of *Palaces, Brussels* (cat. no. 80).

Spatially it lacks the intimacy so evident in the Brussels image and, indeed, is the least intimate of the dozen Amsterdam plates. Exceedingly delicate, it is unusual in its drawing style for the period: entirely composed of the briefest of short strokes, almost never overlapping. Further, it is marked throughout with dots, probably evidence of foul bite.

Known only in one state, there is some question whether Whistler considered it complete or whether he abandoned it. The copper plate is in the Hunterian Art Gallery, University of Glasgow.

LITERATURE: Mansfield, p. 229, no. 410.

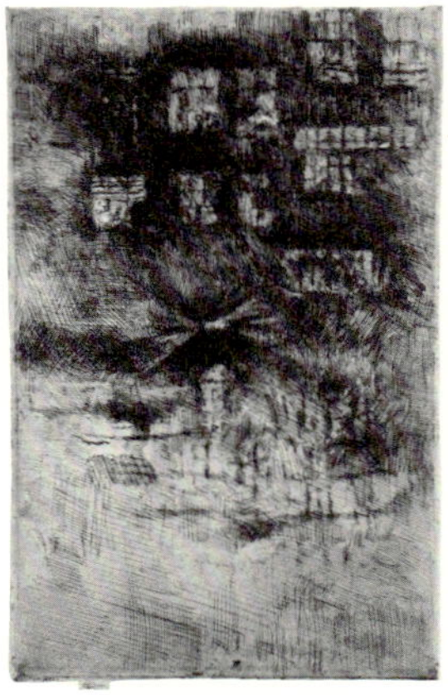

87a.
Nocturne: Dance-House, *K. 408*
Unrecorded state prior to 1/2
10 5/8 x 6 1/2 in. (27 x 16.5 cm.)
Hunterian Art Gallery, University of Glasgow, Birnie Philip Bequest

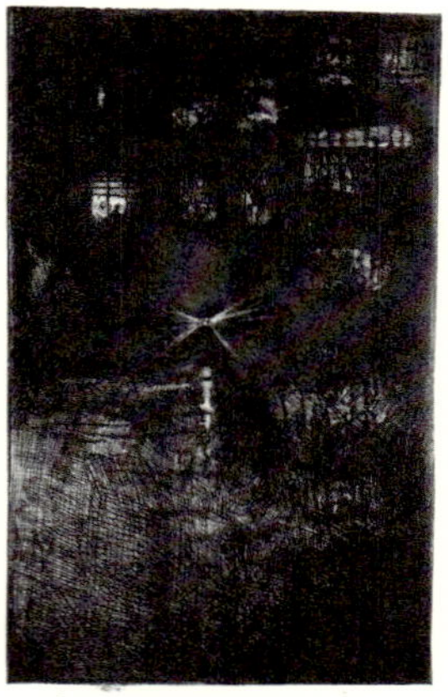

87b.
Nocturne: Dance-House, *K. 408 2/2*
10 5/8 x 6 1/2 in. (27 x 16.5 cm.)
National Gallery of Art, Rosenwald Collection

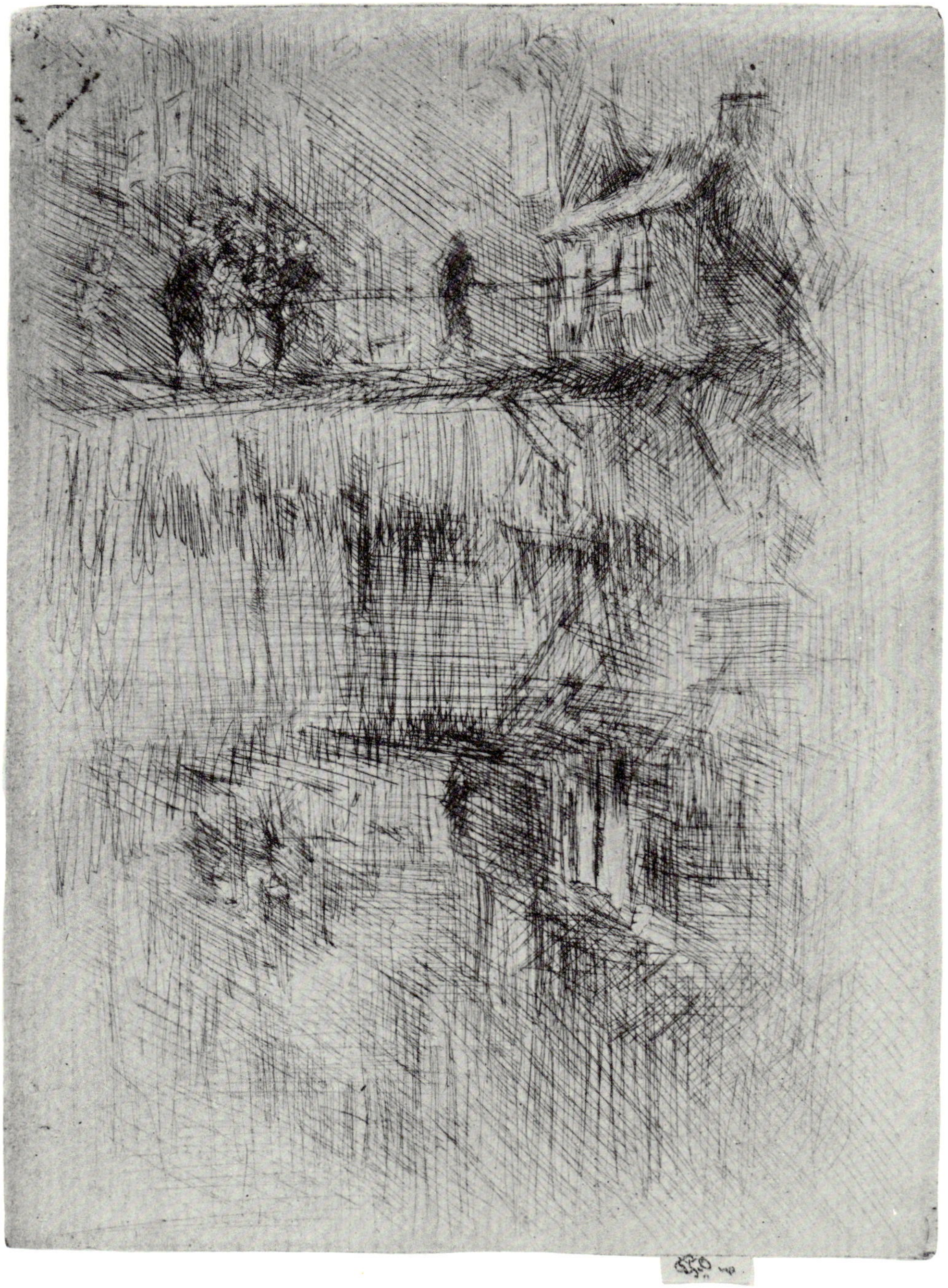

87. ***Little Nocturne, Amsterdam, 1889***

K. 414 only

Etching

5 5/16 x 3 13/16 in. (13.3 x 9.8 cm.)

Brown ink on medium-weight laid paper with partial watermark: shield surmounted by crown

Signed lower right on tab with butterfly and ***imp****; inscribed verso lower right* ***1st proof*** *and signed with butterfly*

Provenance: Howard Mansfield (Lugt 1342); Harris G. Whittemore (Lugt 1384a); anonymous collector's stamp; purchased from R. M. Light & Co., Inc., 1981

Whistler's two Amsterdam Nocturnes, *Little Nocturne* and *Nocturne: Dance-House* (figs. 87a and 87b) are among his most extraordinary works. In quite different ways–the *Dance-House* being far more dramatic–they are the culmination of Whistler's presentations of the penetrating mystery of night's darkness. *Little Nocturne* does this without, in fact, being a very dark image. In it, Whistler appears to be pushing to extreme limits his use of fairly open patches of lines and line networks, overlapping them to establish a variety of densities. As Mansfield put it, "Numberless fine lines produce an evening effect." The figures on the bridge are especially muted and enveloped in a foglike atmosphere, adding to the general sense of diffusion.

This is one of Whistler's most daring and interesting etchings. He completely set aside his skills at producing an image dependent upon the graceful mark, which had come to characterize his work. Instead, while working equally directly, he seems to have pointedly circumvented his superb facility and flair at description in favor of atmospheric abstraction.

Little Nocturne, Amsterdam is extremely rare. Only two impressions were known to Kennedy and Mansfield (who owned the one exhibited here), but two more are in the Hunterian Art Gallery, University of Glasgow, as is the copper plate.

LITERATURE: MacDonald, p. 52, no. 115; Mansfield, p. 232, no. 413.

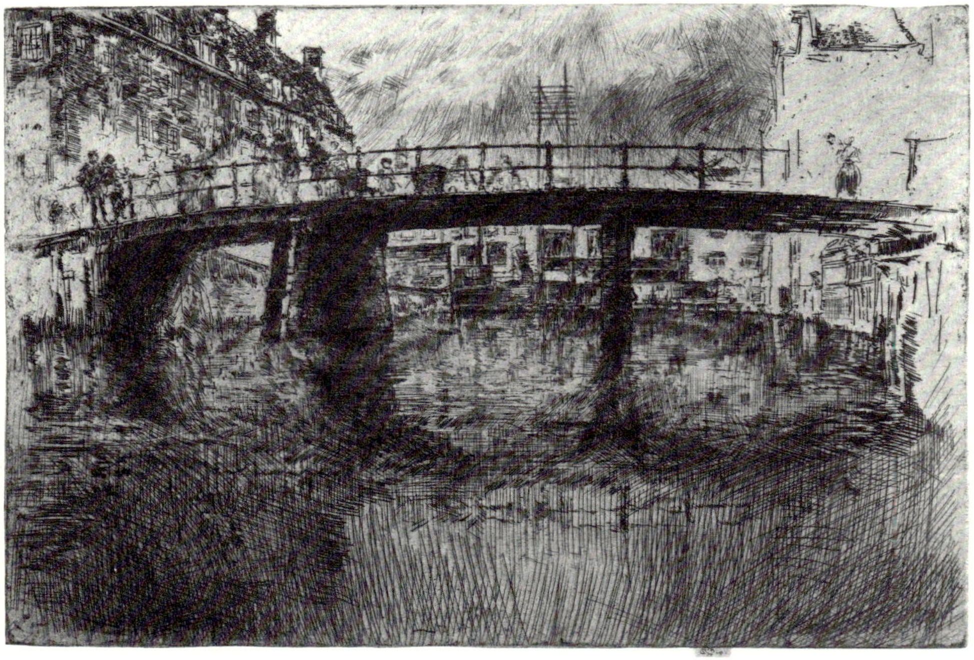

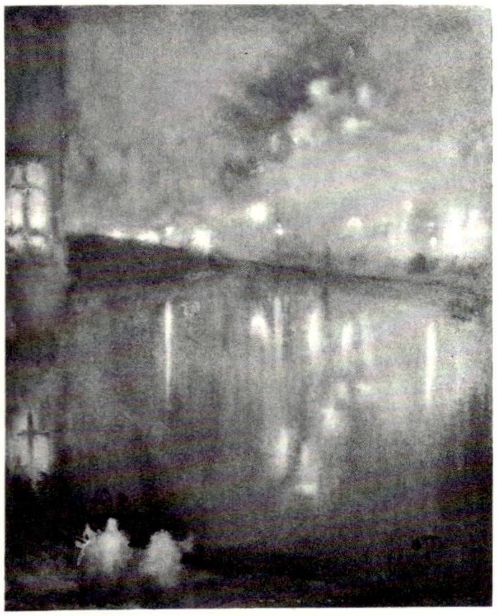

88a.
Nocturne: Grey and Gold, Canal, Holland
Watercolor
11 9/16 x 9 1/8 in. (29.4 x 23.2 cm.)
Freer Gallery of Art

88. ***Bridge, Amsterdam,*** *1889*

K. 409 3/3

Etching

6 1/2 x 9 7/16 in. (16.4 x 24 cm.)

Brown ink on lightweight Oriental paper

Signed lower right on tab with butterfly and ***imp****; inscribed verso lower right* ***for Wunderlich*** *and signed with butterfly*

Provenance: Emma Regina Martin (initials verso); anonymous collector's stamp; purchased from Thos. Agnew & Sons, Ltd., 1981

Whistler obviously wanted to be certain that we noted the figure on the bridge at the right, so he simply omitted the rails that in any way would have obscured her. The same is true for the figures at the far left, who are emphasized by the white area of the building, left unworked in order to frame the group dramatically.

The activity in the sky and water suggests an approaching storm; apart from the two Nocturnes (cat. no. 87 and fig. nos. 87a and 87b), *Bridge, Amsterdam* is the most atmospheric of the Amsterdam etchings. This particular quality also characterizes many of the exquisite watercolors Whistler painted in the city (e.g., fig. 88a).

The copper plate for *Bridge, Amsterdam* is in the Hunterian Art Gallery, University of Glasgow.

LITERATURE: MacDonald, p. 52, no. 116; Mansfield, p. 229, no. 409; Naylor, p. xxxv, no. 144.

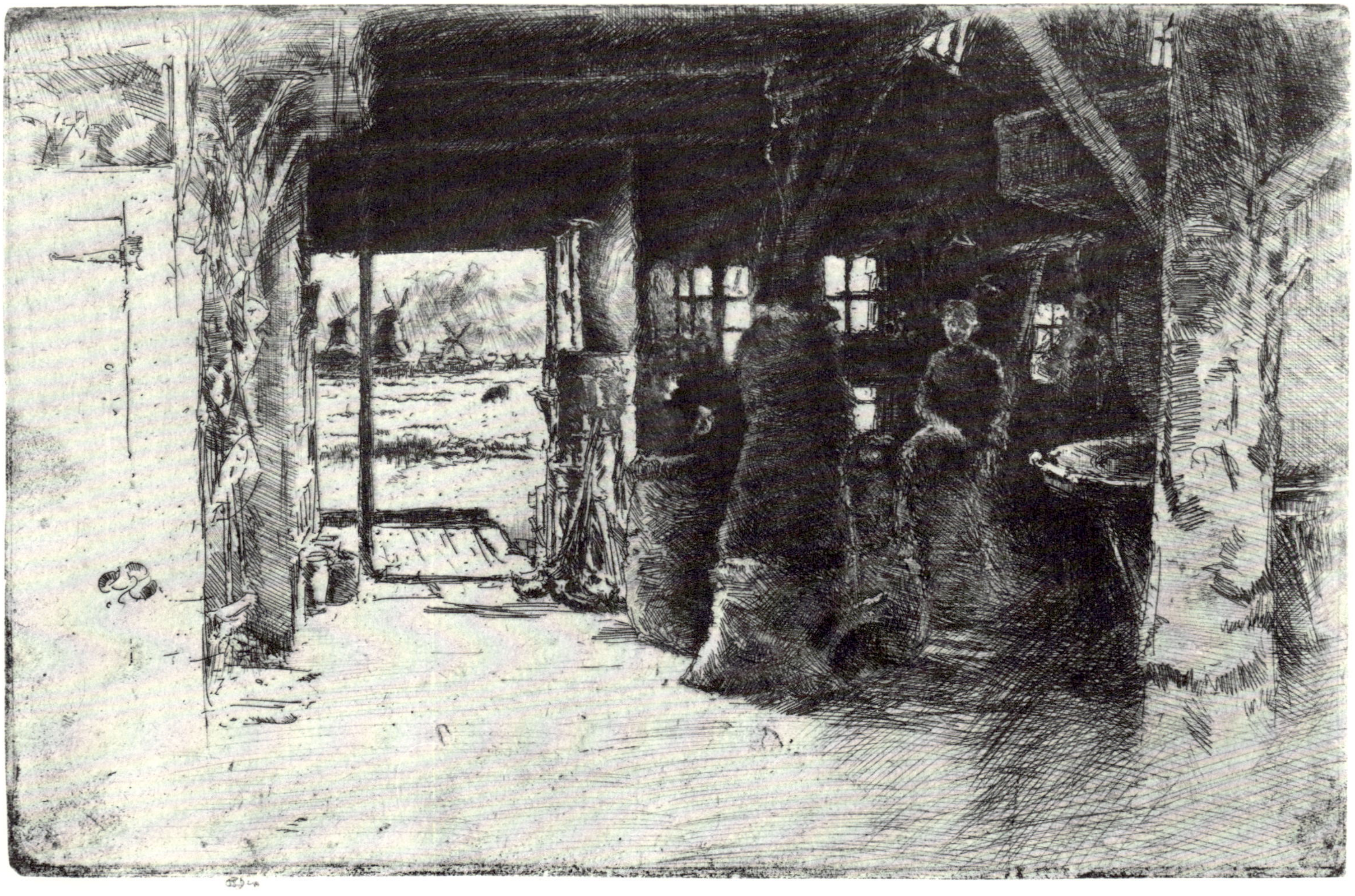

89. **The Mill,** *1889*

K. 413 5/5

Etching and drypoint

6 5/16 x 9 7/8 in. (16.1 x 24 cm.)

Brown ink on lightweight laid paper with lumps of pulp throughout

Signed lower left on tab with butterfly and ***imp****; signed in plate lower left with butterfly*

Provenance: Emma Regina Martin (initials verso); anonymous collector's stamp; purchased from R. M. Light & Co., 1982

In *The Dyer* (cat. no. 44), we saw an earlier example of Whistler's looking into a darkened interior and, through it, to the landscape beyond. Here, in *The Mill,* we see this construction more fully explored. Lacking the spatial barrier of an exterior wall, the main compositional tensions are set up between the dark, rather realistically drawn corner of the mill and the bright landscape, its sunlight flooding through the open door.

Mansfield, in acclaiming Whistler for meeting Rembrandt on his own ground, praised the etching's "flat landscape with its calm canals and busy windmills . . . expressed with a delicacy and charm which the older master never surpassed, while the interior of the flourmill, with its strongly braced timbers, wide door and big windows, its heaped bags, and two quiet figures, all enveloped in a dusty atmosphere, conjures a sense of what both is and long has been–a record and epitome."

Precise tonal modulations are developed throughout the darkened area to describe very tautly, for example, the figure seated at the right and the overhanging balcony above him. In contrast, the lighter spaces, the landscape, and the left side and foreground of the interior are characterized by very loose and open description of form. Furthermore, the broad, spatially fluid networks of line, especially at the lower right, allude to the kind of abstracted structuring that is most far-reaching in *Little Nocturne* (cat. no. 87).

Little known because of its rarity, *The Mill* is a very complex piece, one that rewards careful and repeated study. The copper plate is in the Hunterian Art Gallery, University of Glasgow.

LITERATURE: Fryberger, p. 70, no. 71; Howard Mansfield, "Whistler in Belgium and Holland," *Print Collector's Quarterly* 6 (1916): 386; Mansfield, p. 232, no. 415; Naylor, p. xxxv, no. 146.

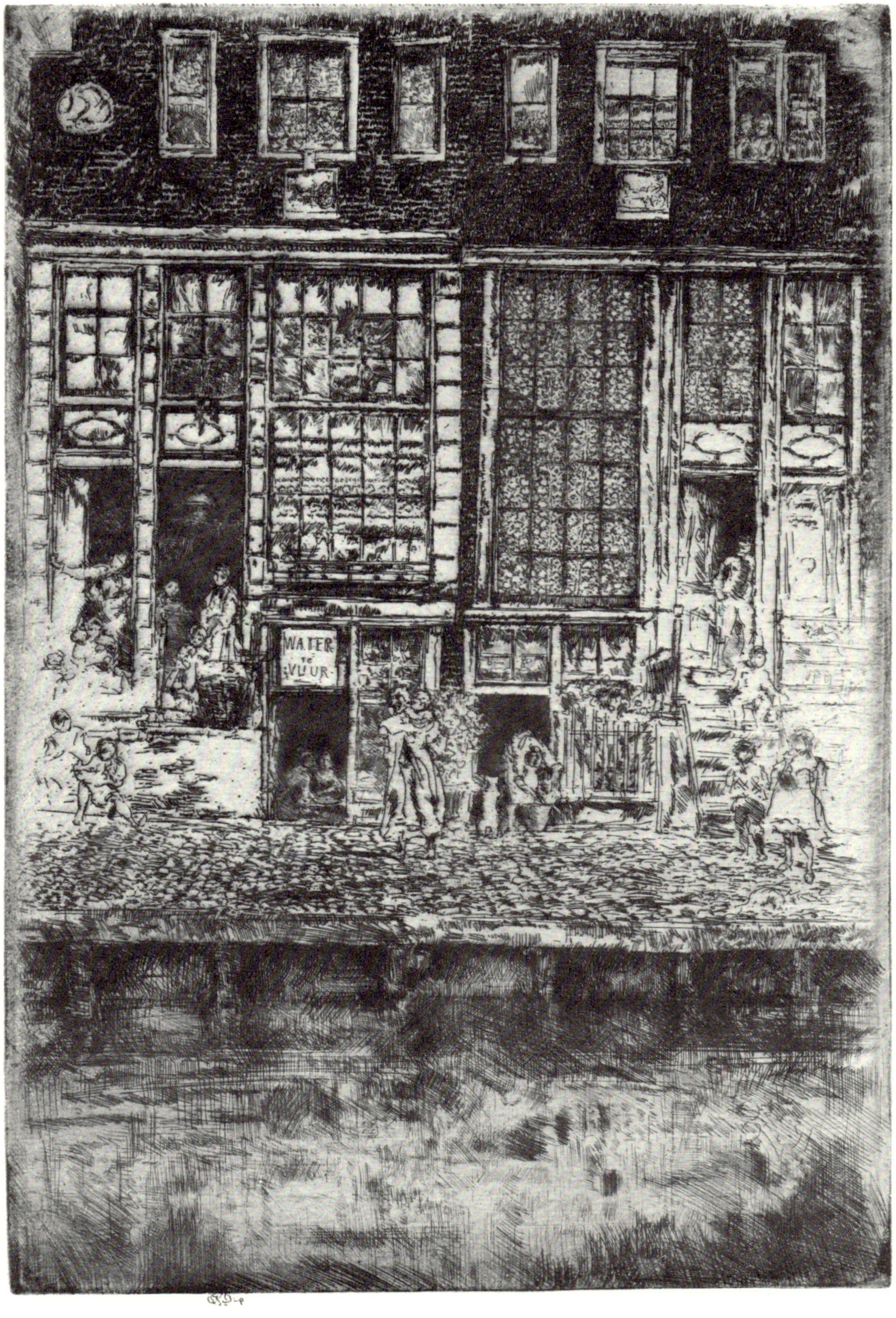
WATER
VUUR

90. ***The Embroidered Curtain,*** *1889*

K. 410 3-4/7

Etching and drypoint

9 3/8 x 6 1/4 in. (23.8 x 15.8 cm.)

Brown ink on lightweight, antique laid paper with watermark: horn in shield surmounted by crown

Signed lower left on tab with butterfly and ***imp****; signed in plate upper left with butterfly; inscribed verso lower right* ***Trial Proof*** *and* ***Wunderlich*** *and signed with butterfly*

Provenance: Hermann Wunderlich (presentation verso); J. Caldwell (?); J. H. Seaman (?); Emma Regina Martin (initials verso); purchased from R. E. Lewis, Inc., 1972

The Embroidered Curtain, or *The Lace Curtain* (both titles were used by Whistler), is probably the best known of the Amsterdam etchings. Fully composed and showing no evidence of the artist's tendency toward a vignetted image, it is also the most intricately worked of the group and, in its use of surface manipulation, possibly the most fully developed of all of Whistler's etchings. Returning to the specificity and textural delineation of the more elaborate Thames Set pieces, such as *The Lime-Burner* (cat. no. 17), the essential composition derives from the shop facades that preoccupied Whistler during the decade of the 1880s.

The Embroidered Curtain is best seen in the earlier states, such as this one, the later ones displaying a coarsening of line from repeated exposure to the acid. The copper plate is in the Hunterian Art Gallery, University of Glasgow.

LITERATURE: Fryberger, p. 70, no. 70; Getscher and Staley, p. 84, no. 50; MacDonald, p. 49, no. 108; Howard Mansfield, "Whistler in Belgium and Holland," *Print Collector's Quarterly* 6 (1916): 384; Mansfield, p. 230, no. 411; Naylor, p. xxxv, no. 145.

by Eric Denker

Catalogues Raisonnés of the Etchings

Kennedy, Edward G. *The Etched Work of Whistler, Illustrated by Reproductions in Collotype of the Different States of the Plates.* New York: Grolier Club, 1910. Reprints. New York: Da Capo Press, 1974; San Francisco: Alan Wofsy Fine Arts, 1979. The standard illustrated catalogue of the etchings, and the starting point for all scholarship on the subject. A revision is in preparation by Katherine A. Lochnan, Margaret F. MacDonald, and Ruth E. Fine.

Mansfield, Howard. *A Descriptive Catalogue of the Etchings and Drypoints of James Abbott McNeill Whistler.* Chicago: Caxton Club, 1909. A comprehensive catalogue of the etchings, containing descriptions of the various states of each plate and a wealth of information on exhibitions and collections. Not illustrated.

Thomas, Ralph. *A Catalogue of the Etchings and Drypoints of James Abbott MacNeil [sic] Whistler.* London: privately printed by John Russell Smith, 1874. The initial, rudimentary catalogue of Whistler's etchings, listing eighty-six prints. In an edition of only fifty, it is extremely rare.

Wedmore, Frederick. *Whistler's Etchings, A Study and a Catalogue.* London: A. W. Thibaudeau, 1886. 2d rev. ed. London: Colnaghi and Co., 1899. A summary essay on the artist's merits is followed by a descriptive catalogue of 214 etchings. The revised edition lists 268 prints.

Exhibition Catalogues

Donnelly, Kate, and Thorp, Nigel R. *Whistlers and Further Family.* Glasgow: Glasgow University Library, 1980. An exceedingly useful catalogue, comprising a variety of materials relating to family and associates of James McNeill Whistler drawn from the university's collections.

Fryberger, Betsy G. *Whistler: Themes and Variations.* Stanford, Calif.: Stanford University Museum of Art, 1978. The catalogue for an exhibition organized around such themes as "Whistler and Degas," "The Amsterdam Etchings," and others. Several prints from the Zelman Collection were included.

Getscher, Robert H., and Staley, Allen. *The Stamp of Whistler.* Oberlin, Ohio: Allen Memorial Art Museum, Oberlin College, 1977. A comprehensive examination of Whistler's graphic work and his influence on pupils and followers.

Hobbs, Susan, and Spink, Nesta R. *The Lithographs of J. M. Whistler from the Collection of Steven Louis Block.* Washington, D.C.: Smithsonian Institution Traveling Exhibition Service, 1982. An evaluation of Whistler's development as a lithographer, with good technical data accompanying the brief catalogue entries. There is also a related unpublished supplement by Spink, "Supplementary Technical Notes."

MacDonald, Margaret F. *Whistler, the Graphic Work: Amsterdam, Liverpool, London, Venice.* London: Thos. Agnew & Sons, 1976. A small, interesting catalogue analyzing Whistler's prints and drawings relating to these four port cities.

Staley, Allen, and Reff, Theodore. *From Realism to Symbolism: Whistler and His World.* New York: Wildenstein, 1971. A catalogue focusing attention on Whistler's place within the major artistic crosscurrents of his time.

Sweet, Frederick A. *James McNeill Whistler.* Chicago: Art Institute of Chicago, 1968. A useful introduction to Whistler's life, followed by entries on the 225 objects in this extensive exhibition. Many major works were absent from the show, but many lesser-known pieces were included.

Wiehl, M. Lee. *A Cultivated Taste: Whistler and American Print Collectors.* Middletown, Conn.: Davison Art Center, Wesleyan University, 1983. An interesting evaluation of American collectors, their relationships with Whistler during his lifetime, and later their interest in his prints.

Young, Andrew MacLaren. *James McNeill Whistler.* London: Arts Council Gallery, 1960. An excellent catalogue containing lengthy entries, a concise list of exhibitions, an extended chronology, and a valuably annotated bibliography.

Books and Articles

Bacher, Otto H. *With Whistler in Venice.* 2d ed. New York: Century, 1908. (First edition suppressed for publishing facsimiles of Whistler's letters.) An entertaining account of Whistler's Venetian period by a friend and pupil, containing good technical information on Whistler's working habits.

Brownell, William C. "Whistler in Painting and Etching." *Scribner's Magazine* 18 (1879): 481–95. The initial consideration in America of Whistler's artistic accomplishments.

Dowdeswell, Walter. "Whistler." *Art Journal* 39 (April 1887): 97–103. The first serious treatment in England of the art and life of Whistler. Contains numerous quotations from the artist.

Duret, Theodore. *Whistler.* Translated by Frank Rutter. Philadelphia: J. B. Lippincott, 1917. A sympathetic appreciation of Whistler's life and art provided by a critic who was simultaneously a friend, a patron, and a historian.

Getscher, Robert H. *Whistler and Venice.* Ann Arbor, Mich.: University Microfilms, 1970. An important dissertation (Case Western Reserve University) focusing on an extremely fertile period of the artist's career.

Hamerton, Philip G. *Etching and Etchers.* London: Macmillan, 1876. Reprint. New York: British Book Center; West Yorkshire: EP Publishing, 1975. A history of the art of etching from Durer to Seymour Haden. Within a lengthy section devoted to nineteenth-century etching, Whistler is measured against the standards of his time.

Menpes, Mortimer. *Whistler as I Knew Him.* New York: Macmillan; London: Adam & Charles Black, 1904. An anecdotal account of Whistler and his circle in the 1880s as recalled by a friend and pupil.

Naylor, Maria. *Selected Etchings of James A. McN. Whistler.* New York: Dover Publications, 1975. The most readily available source for illustrations of the more popular etchings.

Pennell, Elizabeth R., and Pennell, Joseph. *The Life of James McNeill Whistler.* 2 vols. London: William Heinemann; Philadelphia: J. B. Lippincott, 1908. The essential biography of Whistler, which had the benefit of the artist's own collaboration. The immense quantity of information outweighs the inherent hyperbole and misinformation recorded by the Pennells. The 5th edition (Heinemann, and Lippincott, 1911) was issued as a single volume.

———. *The Whistler Journal.* Philadelphia: J. B. Lippincott, 1921. Containing much anecdotal information omitted from the earlier, more formal biography.

Pennell, Joseph. *Etchers and Etching.* New York: Macmillan, 1919. A distinctly personal and mannered work on the important etchers in history, Whistler's accomplishments being greatly magnified at the expense of Rembrandt's and others'.

Seitz, Donald C. *Writings by and about James McNeill Whistler.* Edinburgh: Otto Schulze, 1910. The first comprehensive bibliography of Whistler sources. A new bibliography is being compiled by Robert H. Getscher and Paul G. Marks. *James McNeill Whistler and John Singer Sargent: Two Annotated Bibliographies.* New York: Garland Publishing, forthcoming.

Sutton, Denys. *James McNeill Whistler: Paintings, Etchings, Pastels and Watercolours.* London: Phaidon Press, 1966. A well-illustrated volume that includes color plates of many important works.

———. *Nocturne: The Art of James McNeill Whistler.* London: Country Life, 1963. The first modern monograph to focus on Whistler's development as an artist and his position in the art world of the nineteenth century.

Taylor, Hilary. *James McNeill Whistler.* London: Studio Vista, 1978. A useful and well-written overview of Whistler's artistic development.

Way, Thomas R. *Memories of James McNeill Whistler, the Artist.* New York: John Lane; London: John Lane, Bodley Head, 1912. An account of Whistler's life and work from 1878. Way printed many of Whistler's lithographs; his intimate knowledge of the artist's ideas and working methods is very useful.

Way, Thomas R., and Dennis, George R. *The Art of James McNeill Whistler: an Appreciation.* London: George Bell and Sons, 1903. A laudatory study of Whistler's art that analyzes each of the diverse media he used. The first of many posthumous surveys.

Whistler, James M. *The Gentle Art of Making Enemies.* London: William Heinemann, 1890. Reprint. New York: Dover Publications, 1967. Whistler's most important lectures and letters are included in this volume prepared by the artist.

Young, Andrew MacLaren; MacDonald, Margaret F.; Spencer, Robin; and Miles, Hamish. *The Paintings of James McNeill Whistler.* 2 vols. New Haven and London: Yale University Press, 1980. The first fully illustrated catalogue of the artist's paintings. Extensive and complete catalogue entries augmented by a thorough bibliography, chronology, and exhibition listing.

Note: Italic numbers indicate illustrations

Index of Works